Democratic Theory:
Essays in Retrieval

Democratic Theory: Essays in Retrieval

C. B. MACPHERSON

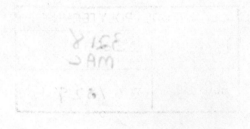

CLARENDON PRESS · OXFORD
1973

Oxford University Press, Ely House, London W.1
GLASGOW NEW YORK TORONTO MELBOURNE WELLINGTON
CAPETOWN IBADAN NAIROBI DARESSALAAM LUSAKA ADDISABABA
DELHI BOMBAY CALCUTTA MADRAS KARACHI LAHORE DACCA
KUALALUMPUR SINGAPORE HONGKONG TOKYO

PRINTED IN GREAT BRITAIN
BY WILLIAM CLOWES & SONS, LIMITED
LONDON, BECCLES AND COLCHESTER

To my Toronto graduate seminar, without whose sharp criticisms these essays would have been more imperfect than they are.

Preface

THIS volume explores, in five new essays, some implications of the ideas about democracy I have offered in two previous books[1] and a scattering of published essays. Two of the published essays, which link the argument of those books with the first four of the new essays, are placed here as Essays I and II. Readers are asked to forgive some redundancy between Essays I and II: they make different points, but some of the arguments had to be the same.

The new essays III to VI build on the earlier work. Essay III modifies, extends, and I hope clarifies, the concept of a man's power, and that of the 'transfer of powers', presented in Essay I (and earlier), and argues that a liberal-democratic theory can be based on an adequate concept of human powers and capacities without insuperable difficulties. Essays IV and V argue that what may be called the neo-classical liberalisms of Chapman, Rawls, and Berlin, fall short of providing an adequate basis for a twentieth-century liberal-democratic theory largely because, in different ways, they fail to see or understate the transfer of powers. Essay VI focuses on the liberal theory of property, and argues that it should be, and can be, revised fundamentally to accommodate new democratic demands.

The first six essays, as a sequence, are intended to establish the need and possibility of a theory of democracy which will get clear of the disabling central defect of current liberal-democratic theory, while holding on to, or recovering, the humanistic values which liberal democracy has always claimed. I am aware that these essays do not amount to a new theory of democracy sufficient to the need I have propounded, but I publish them now as at least a contribution to identifying the problem.

Part Two collects five papers which lead up to or supplement the essays in Part One. They were published in various places, mostly between 1961 and 1968, and are not now all readily available. They are placed here in reverse chronological order of publication.

Part Three consists of three papers on the seventeenth-century roots of the twentieth-century liberal-democratic dilemma. The first of them (Essay XII) is new: it puts in perspective a controversy with Peter Laslett which has until now been conducted on both sides mainly in footnotes and *obiter dicta*. The others (Essays XIII and XIV)

[1] *The Political Theory of Possessive Individualism: Hobbes to Locke* (1962); *The Real World of Democracy* (1965).

bring within these covers two earlier papers which supplement the analysis of *Possessive Individualism*.

I should like to record my thanks to my own university, both for encouraging me continuously to arrange my undergraduate and graduate teaching in such a way that much of my teaching time could be given to working up the ideas here presented, and for a leave of absence at a critical period in their formulation. And I am grateful to the Master and Fellows of Churchill College, Cambridge, who, happily complementing that leave, made me one of themselves.

C. B. MACPHERSON

University of Toronto
18 November 1971

Acknowledgements

My thanks are due to the editors and publishers of the following journals and books in which the essays listed were first published: Basil Blackwell, Oxford (for Essay I, first published in *Philosophy, Politics and Society, Third Series*, edited by Peter Laslett and W. G. Runciman, 1967); Atherton Press, New York (for Essay II, in *Political Theory and Social Change*, edited by David Spitz, 1967; and for Essay VIII, in *Revolution, Nomos* 8, edited by Carl Friedrich, 1966); *The Canadian Journal of Political Science* (for Essay VII, 1968); *The Canadian Journal of Economics and Political Science* (for Essays IX, 1964; X, 1961; XIV, 1945); *The Cambridge Journal* (for Essay XI, 1954); Macmillan & Co. Ltd., London (for Essay XIII, in *Political Theory and the Rights of Man*, edited by D. D. Raphael, 1967).

Contents

PART TWO
RELATED PAPERS ON THE TWENTIETH-CENTURY PREDICAMENT

PART THREE
SEVENTEENTH-CENTURY ROOTS OF THE TWENTIETH-CENTURY PREDICAMENT

PART ONE

Democracy and Property: The Twentieth Century and After

ESSAY I

The Maximization of Democracy

THIS paper sketches an analysis of the justifying theory of Western democracy which I hope may be useful in identifying fundamental defects and in suggesting the kind of rebuilding that is possible and needed. I shall argue that the justifying theory of our Western democracies rests on two maximizing claims—a claim to maximize individual utilities and a claim to maximize individual powers; that neither of these claims can be made good, partly because of inherent defects, partly because of changed circumstances: and that the changed circumstances both permit and require a change in some of the theory's assumptions.

Changed circumstances have created new difficulties for democratic theory because of the very breadth of its claims. One of the central values of our democratic theory has been the surpassing importance of freedom of choice. We have claimed a sort of political consumers' sovereignty which ensures that the society will respond to changes in consumer preference, just as the market economy on which our Western democracies are based responds to changes in effective demand. But what is not often noticed in this connection is that, in what might be called the world-wide political market, consumers' preferences are rapidly changing. We in the West have still the same predominant preference for a 'free society', but the other two-thirds of the world—the communist nations and the newly independent, underdeveloped countries which are neither communist nor liberal-democratic—have now become global effective demanders, and are demanding something different. If we believe in consumers' sovereignty we must be prepared to let the new effective demand take its course and to admit that it has moral claims. To grant this is not to demonstrate that we should abandon our cherished theory: it is at most an argument for coexistence of theories.

But our situation is both worse and better than this suggests. Worse, in that the appearance of serious competitors to liberal-democratic society has stiffened the requirements of a justifying theory. Better, in that certain twentieth-century developments have opened a possibility of avoiding the main fault in the justifying theory we inherited from the nineteenth century. Whether twentieth-century developments also make possible a sufficiently fundamental change in our institutions this paper does not attempt to explore.

1

The main elements of the justifying theory of our Western or liberal democracies—I use the terms interchangeably, for reasons that will be apparent[1]—can, I suggest, be stated as two maximizing claims: the claim to maximize individual utilities, and the claim to maximize individual powers. The first claim is familiar to students of political theory in its nineteenth-century Utilitarian form. The second, less immediately familiar, is I suggest a useful and revealing way of formulating the extra-Utilitarian claims that were built into the liberal theory as soon as it became liberal-democratic, say from John Stuart Mill on. Both claims are made in the name of individual personality. The argument in both cases is that the liberal society provides for the greatest measure of realization of human personality, though in the two cases the essential character of that personality is seen differently, and the different views have different historical roots. Before examining the two claims it may be useful to place them, provisionally at least, in the Western intellectual tradition.

The first claim is that the liberal-democratic society, by instituting a wider freedom of individual choice than does any non-liberal society, maximizes individual satisfactions or utilities. The claim is not only that it maximizes the aggregate of satisfactions, but that it does so equitably; that it maximizes the satisfactions to which, on some concept of equity, each individual is entitled. This claim implies a particular concept of man's essence. To treat the maximization of utilities as the ultimate justification of a society, is to view man as essentially a consumer of utilities. It is only when man is seen as essentially a bundle of appetites demanding satisfaction that the good society is the one which maximizes satisfactions. This view of man, dominant in Benthamism, goes back beyond the classical political economists. It is firmly embedded in the liberal tradition and has remained a considerable part of the case for the liberal-democratic society today.

The second claim is that the liberal-democratic society maximizes men's human powers, that is, their potential for using and developing their uniquely human capacities. This claim is based on a view of man's essence not as a consumer of utilities but as a doer, a creator, an enjoyer of his human attributes. These attributes may be variously listed and assessed: they may be taken to include the capacity for rational understanding, for moral judgement and action, for aesthetic creation or contemplation, for the emotional activities of friendship and love, and, sometimes, for religious experience. Whatever the uniquely human attributes are taken to be, in this view of man their

[1] On the distinction between liberal democracy and other types, see my *The Real World of Democracy* (Toronto, 1965; Oxford, 1966).

exertion and development are seen as ends in themselves, a satisfaction in themselves, not simply a means to consumer satisfactions. It is better to travel than to arrive. Man is not a bundle of appetites seeking satisfaction but a bundle of conscious energies seeking to be exerted.

This is almost an opposite view of the essence of man from that of the Utilitarians. It came, indeed, as a reaction against the crude Benthamite view of man as consumer. Benthamism provoked in the nineteenth century a variety of reactions, conservative, radical, and middle of the road, ranging from Carlyle and Nietzsche, through John Stuart Mill, to Ruskin and Marx. All these thinkers brought back, in one way or another, the idea of the essence of man as activity rather than consumption. I say brought back, because it is an old idea in the Western humanist tradition. From Aristotle until the seventeenth century it was more usual to see the essence of man as purposeful activity, as exercise of one's energies in accordance with some rational purpose, than as the consumption of satisfactions. It was only with the emergence of the modern market society, which we may put as early as the seventeenth century in England, that this concept of man was narrowed and turned into almost its opposite. Man was still held to be essentially a purposive, rational creature, but the essence of rational behaviour was increasingly held to lie in unlimited individual appropriation, as a means of satisfying unlimited desire for utilities. Man became an infinite appropriator and an infinite consumer; an infinite appropriator because an infinite desirer. From Locke to James Mill this concept of man became increasingly prevalent. The nineteenth-century reaction against it, radical, moderate, and conservative, was an attempt to reclaim and restate the much older tradition. But the Utilitarian concept was by then too deeply rooted in the market society to be driven out of the liberal tradition, while too clearly inadequate to be allowed any longer to dominate it. The result can be seen in John Stuart Mill and T. H. Green and the whole subsequent liberal-democratic tradition: an uneasy compromise between the two views of man's essence, and, correspondingly, an unsure mixture of the two maximizing claims made for the liberal-democratic society.

It is not surprising that the two concepts of man, and the two maximizing claims, were brought together. For the problem which the first liberal-*democratic* thinkers faced, in the nineteenth century, was to find a way of accommodating the pre-democratic liberal tradition of the previous two centuries to the new moral climate of democracy. The liberal tradition had been built in a market society, whose ethos was competitive maximization of utilities. The liberal thinkers of the seventeenth and eighteenth centuries had assumed, quite correctly, that the society they were talking about was a market society operating by contractual relations between free individuals who offered their powers, natural and acquired, in the market with a view to getting the greatest return they could. A man's powers, in this view, were not of his essence but were merely instrumental: they were, in Hobbes's classic phrase, 'his present means to obtain some future apparent good'. Powers were a way of getting utilities.[2] The society was permeated with utility-maximizing behaviour. Liberal thinkers could not abandon the implicit concept of man as a maximizer of utilities without abandoning all the advantages they found in the liberal society.

Why, then, was it necessary for liberal-democratic thinkers to add the other concept of man and the other maximizing claim? Two reasons are fairly evident. One was the repugnance of men like John Stuart Mill to the crass materialism of the market society, which had by then had time to show what it could do. It clearly had not brought that higher quality of life which the earlier liberals had counted on its bringing. A second reason may be seen in the belief of mid-nineteenth-century liberals that the democratic franchise could not be withheld much longer. Given this conviction, it seemed urgent to moralize the society before the mass took control. It was thus necessary to present an image of liberal-democratic society which could be justified by something more morally appealing (to the liberal thinker and, hopefully, to the new democratic mass) than the old utilitarianism. This could be done, consonantly with the liberal commitment to individual freedom, by offering as the rationale of liberal-democratic society its provision of freedom to make the most of oneself. Thus individual freedom to maximize one's powers could be added to the freedom to maximize utilities. A newly moralized, liberal-democratic society could claim, as a market society, to maximize individuals' chosen utilities, and, as a free society, to maximize their powers. Neither claim has stood up very well.

2

The claim that the liberal-democratic society maximizes individual utilities (and does so equitably) may be reduced to an economic claim. It is in substance a claim that the market economy of individual enterprise and individual rights of unlimited appropriation, i.e. the capitalist market economy, with the requisite social and political institutions, maximizes individual utilities and does so equitably. To reduce the utility-maximizing claim to economic terms is not to exclude from liberal-democratic claims the value attached to other liberal institutions. Civil and political liberties are certainly held to have

[2] This is of course a very different view of man's powers from that contained in the liberal-democratic (and the pre-seventeenth-century) notion of maximization of human powers. For the importance of the distinction, see below, section 3.

a value apart from their instrumental economic value. But they are less often thought of as *utilities* than as prerequisite conditions for the exertion and development of individual *powers*. We may therefore exclude them here and consider them under the other maximizing heading.

The claim that the capitalist market economy maximizes individual utilities has already been pretty well destroyed by twentieth-century economists, although few political theorists seem to realize this. For one thing, the claim to maximize the aggregate of individual utilities involves an insuperable logical difficulty. The satisfactions that different individuals get from particular things cannot be compared on a single measuring scale. Therefore they cannot be added together. Therefore it cannot be shown that the set of utilities which the market actually produces is greater than some other set that might have been produced by some other system. Therefore it cannot be shown that the market maximizes aggregate utility.

The claim that the market maximizes utilities equitably runs into even greater difficulties. Equity here refers to the distribution of the aggregate among the individual members of the society. Equity has, in the liberal tradition, generally been held to require distribution in proportion to the contributions made by each to the aggregate product. How is it claimed that the market does this? Economists can demonstrate that, assuming some specific distribution of resources or income, the operation of the perfectly free competitive market will give each the maximum satisfaction to which his contribution entitles him. But unless it can be shown that the given distribution of resources or income is just, the claim of equitable maximization is not sustained. The most that can be shown by the economists' model is that the pure competitive market gives everyone a reward proportional to what he contributes by way of any resources he owns, whether his energy and skill, his capital, or his land, or other resources. But this leaves open the question whether the actual pattern of ownership of all these resources is equitable. If equity is held to require rewards proportional to the individual energy and skill expended—which was John Stuart Mill's 'equitable principle' of property—the market model can be demonstrated to be inequitable. For it distributes rewards proportionally to other owned resources, as well as energy and skill, however the ownership of the other resources was acquired, and no one argues that the ownership of the other resources is in proportion to the energy and skill exerted by their owners.

The market, then, does not maximize utilities equitably according to work. Nor does it maximize equitably according to need, on any egalitarian concept of need. Bentham, indeed, had made the egalitarian assumption that individuals have equal capacities for pleasure, and

such as

hence have equal need, and had argued that in calculating aggregate utility each individual should count as one and no one as more than one. He then demonstrated that, by the law of diminishing utility, utility would be maximized by an absolutely equal distribution of wealth. He then pointed out that equal distribution would be totally incompatible with security of property, including profit, which he saw as the indispensable incentive to productivity. He concluded that the claims of equality must yield to the claims of security, in order to maximize the aggregate production of utilities. What Bentham showed with admirable clarity was that, as soon as you make the market assumption about profit incentives, you must abandon the possibility of weighting each individual equally in calculating the maximum utility. Bentham did not claim that the market maximizes utilities equitably according to his concept of equity; he demonstrated, rather that the market cannot do so.

Other concepts of equity than the two we have just examined—distribution according to work, and distribution according to assumed equal need—are possible, but none that is consistent with the minimum egalitarian assumptions of a democratic theory provides a demonstration that the market maximizes utilities equitably.

Thus the claim to maximize utilities, and the claim to do so equitably, both fail, even on the assumption of perfect competition. There is the further difficulty that the capitalist market economy moves steadily away from perfect competition towards oligopoly, monopoly, and managed prices and production. In the measure that it does so, its claim to maximize utilities fails on yet another ground.

3

The claim that the liberal-democratic society maximizes men's powers is more complex, though the basic conception is clear enough. To collect into this one principle—maximization of individual powers—all the main claims of liberal democracy other than the utility-maximizing one is no doubt a considerable simplification, but it has the merit of drawing attention to fundamental factors which are often overlooked. The power-maximizing principle is offered here as a reformulation of the extra-Utilitarian principles that were built into the liberal theory in the nineteenth century in order to make it democratic, and as a way of linking them with the pre-liberal (or pre-market) Western tradition. Whether that Western tradition is traced back to Plato or Aristotle or to Christian natural law, it is based on the proposition that the end or purpose of man is to use and develop his uniquely human attributes or capacities. His potential use and development of these may be called his human powers. A good life is one which maximizes these powers. A good society is one which maximizes (or permits and facilitates the maximization of) these powers, and thus enables men to make the best of themselves.

It is important to notice that this concept of powers is an ethical one, not a descriptive one. A man's powers, in this view, are his potential for realizing the essential human attributes said to have been implanted in him by Nature or God, not (as with Hobbes) his present means, however acquired, to ensure future gratification of his appetites. The difference is important. It may be stated as a difference in what is included in each concept.

The ethical concept of a man's powers, being a concept of a potential for realizing some human end, necessarily includes in a man's powers not only his natural capacities (his energy and skill) but also his *ability* to exert them. It therefore includes *access* to whatever things outside himself are requisite to that exertion. It must therefore treat as a diminution of a man's powers whatever stands in the way of his realizing his human end, including any limitation of that access.

The descriptive concept of a man's powers, on the other hand, includes his natural capacities *plus* whatever additional power (means to ensure future gratifications) he has acquired by getting command over the energies and skill of other men, or *minus* whatever part of his energies and skill he has lost to some other men. This concept of powers does not stipulate that a man shall have the ability to use his human capacities fully. It does not require that a man shall have free access to that which he needs in order to use his capacities. It therefore does not treat as a diminution of a man's powers anything that stands in the way of his using his human capacities fully, or any limitation of his access to what he needs for that purpose. A man's powers on this view are the powers he has, not the powers he needs to have in order to be fully human. One man's powers, defined as his present means to get what he wants in the future, will include the command he has acquired over other men's energies and skills; another's will include merely what is left of his energy and skill after some of it has been transferred to others. On this concept of powers there is no diminution of a man's powers in denying him access to that which he needs in order to use his capacities, for his powers are measured after any such diminution has taken place.

One of the ways of transferring another man's powers to oneself is by denying him free access to what he needs in order to use his capacities, and making him pay for access with part of his powers. In any society where limitation of access has taken place on a large scale the resulting situation will appear differently depending on which concept of a man's powers is being used. On the ethical concept, there will be a continuous net transfer of part of the powers of some men to others, and a diminution of the human essence of those from whom power is being transferred. On the descriptive concept, there will be no net transfer of powers (since powers are defined as the means each man has acquired or has been left with), and no diminution of human essence (since the only idea of human essence that is at all implied in this concept of powers is that of man as consumer of satisfactions).

It was, I suggest, the ethical concept of a man's powers that was reintroduced into the Western tradition in the nineteenth century, and its reintroduction was what converted the liberal into the liberal-democratic theory. It is clearly apparent in T. H. Green, slightly less clearly in John Stuart Mill (who had, after all, to fight his way out of the Benthamite, i.e. Hobbesian, position). When this ethical concept was reintroduced in the nineteenth century it contained a more specific egalitarian assumption than it had contained in its ancient and medieval forms. It assumed not only that each individual was equally entitled to the opportunity to realize his human essence, but also (as against the Greeks) that men's capacities were substantially equal, and (as against the medieval tradition) that they were entitled to equal opportunity in this world.

Thus, when this ethical concept was reintroduced in the nineteenth century, by those who were seeking to humanize the market society and the pre-democratic liberal theory, it became a claim that the liberal-democratic society maximizes each individual's powers in the sense of maximizing each man's ability to use and develop his essentially human attributes or capacities.

This concept of maximizing men's human powers does not encounter the logical difficulty that besets the notion of maximizing utilities. Here there is no problem of measuring and comparing the utilities or satisfactions derived by different individuals from the receipt and consumption of the same things. True, the enjoyment one man gets from the use and development of his energies is incommensurable with the enjoyment every other man gets from his. But what is being claimed here is simply that the liberal-democratic society does provide the maximum freedom to each to use and develop what natural capacities he has. There is no need to compare incommensurable quantities of utility.

The difficulty in this claim lies deeper. It lies in the facts that the liberal-democratic society is a capitalist market society,[3] and that the latter by its very nature compels a continual net transfer of part of the power of some men to others, thus diminishing rather than maximizing

[3] I argue at the end of this section that the rise of the welfare state has not altered this equation.

the equal individual freedom to use and develop one's natural capacities which is claimed.

It is easy to see how this comes about. The capitalist market society operates necessarily by a continual and ubiquitous exchange of individual powers. Most men sell the use of their energy and skill on the market, in exchange for the product or the use of others' energy and skill. They must do so, for they do not own or control enough capital or other resources to work on, it being the nature of a capitalist society that the capital and other resources are owned by relatively few, who are not responsible (to the whole society or any section of it) for anything except the endeavour to increase their capitals. The more they increase their capitals, the more control they have over the terms on which those without capital may have access to it. Capital and other material resources are the indispensable means of labour: without access to them one cannot use one's skill and energy in the first business of life, which is to get a living, nor, therefore, in the real business of life, which (on the second view of the essence of man) is to enjoy and develop one's powers. One must have something to work on. Those without something of their own to work on, without their own means of labour, must pay for access to others'. A society in which a man cannot use his skill and energy without paying others, for the benefit of those others, for access to something to use them on, cannot be said to maximize each man's powers (on the ethical concept of a man's powers).

The reason why this has not generally been seen should be clear from our analysis of the two concepts of a man's powers. It has not been seen because the two concepts have been confused. Twentieth-century economists (and most political writers) see no net transfer of powers in a perfectly competitive capitalist market society. They do not see it because, as heirs of the Hobbes-to-Bentham concept of man, they define a man's powers, in the way we have seen, to be whatever means a man has to procure satisfactions, that is, as much power as a man has already acquired, by his acquisition of land or capital, or as little as he is left with (his own capacity to labour) when others have acquired the land and capital. When powers are so defined there is no net transfer of powers in the labour-capital relation.

But this definition of powers is, as we have seen, quite inconsistent with the ethical definition of a man's powers, and it is the latter on which the claim of liberal democracy to maximize individual powers must logically be based.[4]

[4] It would take too long here to demonstrate, what I hope to demonstrate in a subsequent study of nineteenth-century theory, that the same confusion between the two concepts of powers is the root of the inadequacy of Mill's and Green's theories.

If then a man's powers must, in the context of the liberal-democratic maximizing claim, be taken to include his ability to use his natural capacities, it follows that the capitalist market society, which operates by a continual net transfer of part of the powers of some men to others, for the benefit and enjoyment of the others, cannot properly claim to maximize each individual's powers.

It may be objected that while the capitalist market model does necessarily contain a continuous net transfer of powers, our present Western liberal democracies do not do so because they have moved some distance away from the capitalist model. One result, it is commonly held, of the operation of the democratic franchise has been the emergence of the welfare state, whose characteristic feature is the massive continuous transfer payments from owners to non-owners, by way of state provision of free or subsidized services. It may thus be argued that the modern welfare state has, or can, offset the transfer of powers from non-owners that must exist in the capitalist model of society.

This argument cannot be sustained. We need not enter into the question whether the transfer payments of the welfare state have in fact altered the previously prevailing distribution of the whole social product between classes. We need only notice that the modern welfare state does still rely on capitalist incentives to get the main productive work of the society done, and that so long as this is so, any welfare state transfers from owners to non-owners cannot offset the original and continuing transfer in the other direction. This is fully appreciated by the strongest defenders of capitalism, who point out, quite rightly, that if welfare transfers were so large as to eat up profits there would be no incentive to capitalist enterprise, and so no capitalist enterprise.[5] We may conclude, therefore, that the existence of the welfare state does not cancel and cannot substantially alter the net transfer of powers from non-owners to owners which we have seen to be inherent in the capitalist model. The claim that the liberal-democratic welfare-state society maximizes human powers is therefore still unsustained.

4

Our analysis of the maximization-of-powers claim so far has disclosed an inherent defect. The powers which liberal-democratic society actually and necessarily maximizes are different from the powers it claims to maximize, and the maximization it achieves is inconsistent with the maximization that is claimed. The powers which

[5] A not unreasonable speculation by some economists that capitalist entrepreneurs might continue to operate even in those circumstances, is acknowledged (and shown to be irrelevant) in Essay IV, section 2, at p. 84.

it claims to maximize are every man's potential of using and developing his human capacities; the powers it does maximize are some men's means of obtaining gratifications by acquiring some of the powers of other men as a continued net transfer. This defect can be seen to be inherent when the liberal-democratic claim is taken in isolation.

We must, however, go on to look at the liberal-democratic claim comparatively, for the problem in the twentieth century is the confrontation of liberal-democratic claims with other claims. And the liberal-democratic claim to maximize human powers is, after all, a comparative claim: it is a claim that the liberal-democratic market society provides, in greater measure than any other society, the possibility of every individual realizing his human essence. This claim could still be sustained, even granting the continued net transfer of powers from non-owners to owners in our society, if it could be shown that a similar transfer is inherent in any possible society. The transfer of powers would then be irrelevant to any comparison between societies, and a case could be made that the liberal-democratic market society gives the individual a better chance than could any other society. The important question, then, is whether such a continued net transfer is inherent in any possible society.

Since the transfer is a payment for access to the means of labour, the question is whether free access would be possible in any society. Two models of society giving free access to the means of labour come to mind at once: neither of them, for different reasons, can settle our problem, but we should notice them if only to point the way to a further line of inquiry.

One model is a society of independent producers where everyone owns or has the free use of as much land or other resources as he wishes to use. Such was the hypothetical position in the first stage of Locke's state of nature, where everyone had as much land as he could use and there was still 'enough and as good' for others. Whether a society of independent producers is envisaged as a pure household economy where nothing is produced for exchange, or as a simple exchange economy where products but not labour are put on the market, there is no net transfer of powers.

But although such a society is conceivable, and although approximations to it have existed at times when there was more free land than the population could use, no one would think that such a society is now generally possible. Advanced industrial societies cannot go back to handicraft and peasant production. They could not so sustain their present populations; probably not at all, certainly not at the material level of life their members expect. And the world's present underdeveloped societies, which until now have generally remained at a level of handicraft and peasant production (except for such large-scale production as was organized by and for outside capital), have recently formed a new level of expectations and are therefore determined not merely to reduce the transfer of powers involved in outside ownership but also to move beyond their own peasant and handicraft production. We may therefore say that a society of independent producers each owning his own means of labour is now out of the question.

The other model of society in which no net transfer of powers is necessary is the socialist model, in which no individuals own the means of labour of the whole society, and in which, therefore, no class of owners automatically gets a net transfer of some of the powers of the others. Such a society would, of course, be no more possible than the one we have just rejected unless it could sustain all its members at the material level which they have come to expect. But the reason why a society of independent producers could not now do this does not apply to any other societies. The society of independent producers has a built-in limit on its productivity, for by definition it cannot use any technology which requires larger units of capital equipment than each independent producer can operate by himself. A society not confined to independent producers is not subject to this limit; it can take full advantage of technological advances in productivity.

It must, like any society, ensure that a part of the powers of its members is spent on replacing and even increasing the social capital which is required to maintain or improve the level of production. But this is not in itself a transfer of powers from some men to others for the benefit of the others: it does not in itself, therefore, diminish anyone's human essence.

However, the fact that a socialist model contains no necessary transfer of powers does not in itself settle our problem. For we do not know and cannot demonstrate whether or not a socialist society necessarily contains some other diminution of each man's powers equal to or greater than the market society's diminution of powers. When we bring back into account what we set aside earlier in considering the utility-maximizing claim of liberal-democratic society, namely, the civil and political liberties which have been won in the market society and which have not been won so far in the practising socialist societies, the balance of advantage in terms of maximization of power is substantially altered. And whether civil and political liberties are considered as utilities, or whether they are considered as contributing directly to the opportunity to maximize individual powers, they clearly must be weighed in any judgement about the maximizing claims of a society.

The absence or severe restriction of civil and political liberties must be held, on the ethical concept of powers, to diminish men's powers more than does the market transfer of powers. But while the comparative record of liberal-democratic and practising socialist societies on civil and political liberties is clear enough, we cannot demonstrate that the lack of civil and political liberties in the socialist societies is inherent rather than attributable to the circumstances in which those societies were born and have developed.

Moreover we must weigh not only civil and political liberties but all the other freedoms which, on the ethical concept of powers, make up the total opportunity each man has to exert and develop all his natural capacities. One of the freedoms which is said to do this in the market society (and which does do it there for successful men), namely, the right of unlimited appropriation, is clearly not present in a socialist model. But this is a freedom for some which reduces the freedom for others, hence its absence is not obviously a net loss of freedom. The Marxian vision of the ultimately free classless society offers, of course, the greatest conceivable opportunity for each individual to use and develop his human attributes. But no society built on a Marxian revolution has yet achieved this vision, and we do not know if it can be done. And no liberal-democratic society, however politically strong a socialist movement there may be within it, has yet moved beyond the welfare state into a socialist model far enough for any judgement on the possibility that the diminution of human powers inherent in the market society can be discarded without losing other freedoms which are important in the maximizing of human powers.

In short, experience so far can neither validate nor invalidate the claim of liberal-democratic society to maximize men's powers in comparison with any other possible kind of society.

The analysis so far has proceeded on the assumption that it is theoretically possible to compare and weigh the claims of different kinds of society to maximize individual powers, on the ethical concept of powers. The difficulty has been our lack of knowledge about the inherent properties of the socialist model. This difficulty is insuperable at the present stage of our knowledge. We may therefore drop the assumption that an objective comparison is possible, and consider instead the subjective judgements about the comparative merit of liberal-democratic society that are actually made by the members of those societies.

The people in liberal-democratic societies have voted pretty consistently for a market society rather than a socialist society. It is worth considering on what judgements this choice may possibly have been based, and whether any of the judgements are likely to change.

Three possible bases for this choice, in increasing order of rationality, may be considered. First, the choice may be founded on nothing more than a failure to recognize the fact of the net transfer of powers in the market society. The transfer is likely to be, in the more affluent societies, obscured and overlaid by an appreciation of the comparatively high material productivity of those market societies. That it is so obscured is suggested by the negative correlation between the strength of socialist and communist votes in, and the affluence of, various Western nations. If this is the case, the voters' judgement can be expected to change in the measure that the material productivity of the most advanced socialist countries catches up with that of the capitalist countries.

Or, secondly, the choice of the voters in the liberal democracies may be founded on a value judgement that the civil and political liberties which they enjoy are worth more than any gain in their powers to be expected from the cancellation of the transfer of powers in a socialist society, and on the empirical judgement that they might lose those liberties in a socialist society. This judgement also may be expected to change, if and to the extent that the practising socialist societies find themselves able to institute more civil and political liberties as their ability to meet the material expectations of their peoples increases.

Or, thirdly, the choice of voters in the liberal democracies may be based on a value judgement that, while the transfer of powers is inevitable in a full market society, market freedoms (including freedom of enterprise and freedom of appropriation) are nevertheless a prerequisite of, or a substantial part of, the full enjoyment and development of the human essence. This is the most rational basis for that choice. Yet this judgement may also change if it appears that the assumptions on which it is based are of only transitory validity. I think it can be shown that this is so.

I want now to argue that the net transfer of powers in a free society is necessary only when the society has made certain assumptions about scarcity and desire, and that these assumptions have been historically necessary in liberal societies down to the present but are now becoming unnecessary and unrealistic.

5

To argue this case we must begin by looking more closely into the causes of the net transfer of powers. We must try to establish the set of factors whose conjuncture has historically required, and does logically require, a net transfer of powers. We are concerned only with the transfer in a free society. There is obviously a transfer also in slave societies, in feudal societies, and in colonial and other dependent societies which are tributary to an imperial power, but in all these cases the transfer can be explained simply as the result of superior military force. Our question is, how does the transfer come about in a free society, where no class or group is using open force to keep down another, and where everyone is free to make the best bargain he can in the market for his powers?

The immediate cause of the transfer in such a society is, as we have seen, that one set of people has got virtually all the capital and other resources, access to which is necessary for anyone to use and develop his human capacities. But when and how does this distribution of resources come about in a free society? It comes when the society has set up, as an incentive to get the productive work of the society done, the individual right to unlimited, or virtually unlimited, accumulation of property. It is then, and only then, that the natural inequality of individual capacities leads to the accumulation of virtually all the resources—the means of labour—in the hands of one set of people.

When, and why, does a society set up the right of unlimited accumulation as an incentive to production? The question needs to be asked, because, taking the world as a whole and through history, the right of unlimited individual appropriation has been the exception rather than the rule. A society sets up this right, I suggest, when the people (or the most active classes) make two value judgements. One (which is already included in our hypothesis of a free society, but may be restated here for completeness) is the preference for individual freedom of choice of work and reward rather than authoritative allocation of work and reward: without this value judgement men would be content with a hierarchical customary society. The other value judgement is the elevation to the position of one of the highest values, if not the highest value—as one of the chief purposes, if not the chief purpose, of man—an endless increase in productivity, or, which comes to the same thing, an endless battle against scarcity. Without this value judgement men would be content with a less strenuous society, and one with more moderate incentives.

The second value judgement, which I find implicit in Locke, became increasingly articulate in the eighteenth and nineteenth centuries.[6] What was new in this value judgement was the assumption of the rationality of unlimited desire. There had always been scarcity: men had always had to struggle with Nature to get a living. What was new was the assumption that the scarcity against which man was pitted was scarcity in relation to unlimited desire, which was itself rational and natural. Moral and political philosophers had from the earliest times recognized in mankind a strain of unlimited desire, but

[6] Hume, for instance, held that what distinguished man from other animals was 'the numberless wants and necessities with which [nature] has loaded him, and . . . the slender means which she affords to the relieving these necessities', and that in society 'his wants multiply every moment upon him'; the advantage of society was that it augmented man's powers to satisfy his numberless and multiplying wants (*Treatise of Human Nature*, Book III, Part II, Section II).

most of them had deplored it as avarice and had believed that it could, and urged that it should, be fought down. What was new, from the seventeenth century onwards, was the prevalence of the assumption that unlimited desire was rational and morally acceptable. When this assumption is made, the real task of man becomes the overcoming of scarcity in relation to infinite desire. Our second value judgement, then, can be stated as the assumption of the rationality and naturalness of unlimited desire.

It was this assumption, along with the other value judgement about freedom, which led, I suggest, to the setting up of the right to unlimited individual appropriation. For the only way that a free society could call forth the effort required in the unending battle against scarcity was the carrot, not the stick. And the right of unlimited individual appropriation was an admirable carrot. It moved man, the infinitely desirous creature, to continuous effort by giving him the prospect of unlimited command over things to satisfy his desire as consumer. Moreover, it could be seen as a way of moving man as a doer, an exerter of powers, for it authorized him to enlarge his powers by acquiring, in addition to his natural powers, command over the powers of others: property being, as the economists saw, not only command over things but also command over the powers of other men.

We may now summarize the logical chain that leads to the transfer of powers. The net transfer of powers in a free society is the result of the accumulation of the material means of labour in the hands of one set of people. This accumulation is the result of two factors: (a) the society's decision to set up a right of unlimited individual appropriation, and (b) the natural inequality of individual capacities. Of these two factors, I assume that (b) is inherent in any society short of a genetically managed one. Factor (a) I find to be the result of the society's double value judgement: (i) that individual freedom is preferable to authoritative allocation of work and reward, and (ii) that the chief purpose of man is an endless battle against scarcity in relation to infinite desire. Assumption (ii) can be restated as, or reduced to, the assumption that unlimited desire is natural and rational.

Putting the logical chain in the reverse order, and compressing it, we get: the acceptance, by the most active part of society, of the belief that unlimited desire is natural and rational *leads to* the establishment of the right of unlimited appropriation, which *leads to* the concentration of ownership of the material means of labour, which *leads to* the continual net transfer of powers.

In giving first place to the acceptance of the assumption about unlimited desire I do not mean to say that this change in ideas was the sole moving force. I do not enter into the general question of the primacy of ideas or material conditions. It is enough to argue that the acceptance of the assumption about unlimited desire was a necessary condition of the establishment of the right of unlimited appropriation. Without attempting here to assign weights and relations to all the forces which led to the emergence of the capitalist market society, it is enough to point out that a widespread acceptance of the assumption about unlimited desire was needed to justify the institutions of that society, particularly to justify the right of unlimited appropriation. The right of unlimited appropriation was needed as an incentive to increased productivity. An incentive to increased productivity was needed to make possible the increase of wealth (and power) which a new enterprising class saw in prospect for themselves. And to get *any substantial* increase in productivity then, it was necessary to recast the institutions in a way that could only be justified by postulating *infinite* desire. In short, the assumption of the rationality of infinite desire may be said both to have produced the capitalist market society and to have been produced by that society.

The point of drawing attention to the assumption of scarcity in relation to infinite desire, or of the rationality of unlimited desire, is that this assumption is in the twentieth century beginning to appear not to be permanently valid. It is beginning to appear that this assumption will not be needed to make a free society operate, and even that it will have to be dropped to allow our society to operate.

If this can be established, it offers some hope. For the root difficulty of our justifying theory is, I have argued, that the transfer of powers which is produced by the assumption about unlimited desire contradicts the moral principle implicit in the value judgement ((i) above) that individual freedom is preferable to authoritative allocation of work and reward.

The moral principle implicit in that value judgement is the principle that all individuals should be equally able to use and develop their natural capacities. The transfer of powers contradicts that principle because it denies the greater part of men equal access to the means of using and developing their natural capacities.

6

The chief new factor which seems to make the assumption about unlimited desire dispensable is the prospect now present in people's minds that scarcity can be ended once and for all by the technological conquests of nature that are now so rapidly advancing. The exploitation of new sources of energy and new methods of productive control of energy—automation and all that—seem capable of ending the need for incessant compulsory labour. Whether they will in fact do this, and whether they are capable of doing this within the framework of market institutions, are questions on which expert opinion is divided. But the vision of a society in which a fraction of the present compulsory labour can produce plenty for all is a vision not likely now to be extinguished by the disclaimers of experts. For the vision has taken shape at a time when two-thirds of the world is already in revolt against the market morality and searching for new ways of establishing human dignity, which they had already tended to identify with the ending of compulsory labour. This shift in value judgements in the other two-thirds of the world would not necessarily in itself have any great effect on Western liberal-democratic societies, were it not for the fact that the latter must compete in technological advance with the most advanced of the non-Western nations. The Western nations can therefore not afford to slow down their rate of technological change, and so can scarcely avoid reducing the need for work. The claims of leisure, of non-work in the sense of non-compulsive-labour, will thus increase at the expense of the claims of incessant productive work.

Against this it may be argued that there is another possible outcome of the technological revolution in the West, namely, that desires will multiply as fast as technological advance can meet them, so that society as a whole will have reason to work as hard as ever. This seems the more probable outcome to those who discount the compulsive transfer of powers. They point out that scarcity and plenty are relative to levels of desire, and that one can only properly speak of ending scarcity in relation to the present or some other finite level of desire. They then dismiss the possibility of ending scarcity, by postulating infinite desire as an innate quality of rational man.

But to make this assumption is, as I have argued, to mistake for an innate characteristic of man what was a historical novelty brought in by the needs of the capitalist market society. It was needed to justify the right of unlimited appropriation, which was needed as an incentive to increased productivity. To get any substantial increase in productivity then, as I have said, it was necessary to recast the institutions in a way that could only be justified by postulating infinite desire. To establish and justify a society which would give more men more opportunity to enjoy and to develop their powers it was necessary to postulate a degree of desire for material satisfactions which soon led to a society in which the enjoyment and development of men's powers were submerged under the aim of satisfying their supposed infinite desire for utilities.

I am suggesting that we have now reached, or have now in prospect, a level of productivity which makes it no longer necessary to maintain this perverse, artificial, and temporary concept of man. I am arguing that we are reaching a level of productivity at which the maximization of human powers, in the ethical sense, rather than of utilities or of powers in the descriptive sense, can take over as the criterion of the good society, and that in the present world climate it will have to be an egalitarian maximization of powers.

We saw that the notion of maximization of powers went with the concept of the essence of man as an exerter and developer of his uniquely human capacities. In any general moral or political theory based on this concept, what had to be maximized was *each* man's ability to realize his essence. What had to be asserted was the *equal* right of every man to make the best of himself. The conditions for this had never existed in any class-divided society before the market society. Nor did they exist in the market society once the right and the incentive of unlimited appropriation had taken effect, for this produced a new form of transfer of powers. The unequal properties acquired in market operations became the means by which some men increased their powers by acquiring the powers of others. The earlier moral idea of maximizing each man's human powers gave way to the market idea of allowing and encouraging each to try to maximize his power by engrossing some of the powers of others.

This kind of maximization of powers cannot serve as the criterion of a democratic society: it has no better standing than the maximization of utilities, of which it is only an ideological inversion (in the sense that it substitutes for the postulate of infinite desire for utilities a postulate of infinite desire for power over others).

I am suggesting that just as we can now do without the concept of man as an infinite desirer of utilities so we can do without the concept of man as an infinite desirer of power over others, and can install, with some hope of its realization, the concept of man as exerter and developer of *his own* powers.

But to say that we now can do without the concepts which have prevailed for the last two or three hundred years, and that we can install finally the more humane concept that was never possible till now, is not to say that we are likely to do so. The hitherto prevalent concepts may no longer be needed to spur our societies on economically, but they are deeply ingrained. The prospect of abundance makes it *possible* for us to drop the old assumptions, but does anything make it *necessary* for us to do so? I suggest that certain new social facts of the second half of the twentieth century do make it necessary.

One new fact is that the West no longer dominates the whole world. Another new fact is that the West no longer expects to impose its pattern of society on the whole world. It cannot do so militarily because of another new social fact, the development of nuclear weaponry. Since it cannot impose its pattern on the rest of the world, the most it can do is compete with the rest of the world. It can compete economically, but with present rates of growth the odds are that the West's comparative advantage will diminish. It can compete in political and civil liberties, in which the West is well ahead so far, but again the odds are that its comparative advantage will diminish: in the scale of political and civil liberties, the communist nations have nowhere to go but up, while the demands of the warfare state can very easily push the Western nations down.

The West will therefore, I think, be reduced to competing morally. It will, that is to say, have to compete in the quality of life it makes possible for its citizens. And in these egalitarian decades, the quality of life is to be measured in terms of the maximization of *each* person's powers.

The notion of moral competition between West and East is somewhat strange. For whose favour, it may be asked, are they competing? An obvious partial answer is, for the esteem of the third world, the recently independent, underdeveloped countries of Africa and Asia who have rejected liberal-democratic market values and institutions without embracing communist values and institutions. The third world is very numerous; it has arrived in the consciousness of the West; its poverty is already a burden on the conscience of the West. Yet both West and East are so confident of their technical and cultural superiority to the third world that their behaviour is unlikely to be determined by the notion of competing for its favour.

The question, for whose favour are West and East competing, is wrongly posed. The competition is not between West and East for the favour of any third party: it is between the leaders, the holders of political power, in both East and West, for the support of their own people. I do not mean that Western voters are likely suddenly to switch to communism, or the communist nations to liberal democracy; there is no evidence, and I think little likelihood, of such shifts. What is more probable is that the people in the West will demand a levelling up, that is to say, an end to the transfer of powers, and the people in the East a levelling up in civil and political liberties. Both are becoming technically possible.

And unless the leaders in the West are prepared to make or accept the fundamental change in the liberal-democratic justifying theory which is now possible, the West stands to lose. For the communist nations can take over, and are taking over, the technological advances in productivity which were created in the capitalist world: capitalism is no longer the sole source of productive power. And as they take over those advances, they will become more able to offer a kind of human freedom which the market society has to deny. In the measure that they reach abundance they will be able to move unimpeded to the realization of their vision, a society free of compulsive labour and therefore providing a fully human life for all. We shall not be able to move to this without the fundamental change in our theory which the prospective conquest of scarcity makes possible. If we do not now resolve the contradiction that has been built into our Western theory, the contradiction between equal freedom to realize one's human powers and freedom of unlimited appropriation of others' powers, or between the maximization of powers in the ethical sense and the maximization of powers in the descriptive market sense, we are unlikely to be able to compete.

ESSAY II

Democratic Theory: Ontology and Technology

1. *The Race Between Ontology and Technology*

THE notion of a race between East and West for technological superiority has been familiar since Sputnik. The notion of a competition between Eastern and Western ways of life, which can be stated as a competition between two sets of ethical values, is, if less precise and less specific, still familiar enough. The notion that the latter competition can be reduced still further to a competition between two ontologies, two views of the essence of man, is less familiar but will repay investigation. I want to suggest that there is now, as between East and West, not only a competition between technologies, and another competition between ontologies, but that these have set up, in the West at least, a fateful race between ontological change and technological change. I shall argue that our Western democratic theory—the theory by which we justify and so sustain our Western democratic societies—will fail to sustain those societies, unless we can revise its ontological base before it is faced with the effects of much more technological progress. My concern, then, is with the race between ontology and technology in Western democratic society and theory.

I shall argue that the ontological assumptions of our Western democratic theory have been, for something like a hundred years, internally inconsistent, comprising as they do two concepts of the human essence which are in the circumstances incompatible. One of these is the liberal, individualist concept of man as essentially a consumer of utilities, an infinite desirer and infinite appropriator. This concept was fitting, even necessary, for the development of the capitalist market society, from the seventeenth century on: it antedates the introduction of democratic principles and institutions, which did not amount to anything before the nineteenth century. The other is the concept of man as an enjoyer and exerter of his uniquely human attributes or capacities, a view which began to challenge the market view in the mid-nineteenth century and soon became an integral part of the justifying theory of liberal democracy. I shall argue further that changes now clearly discernible in our society, notably the technological revolution, make it possible to move away from this unstable theoretical position, but that this move, far from being an automatic consequence of social change, requires first, among political scientists, a theoretical understanding rooted in the social history of political theory and, concurrently or subsequently (but not much subsequently), a more widespread change in Western democratic ideology. I shall suggest, that is to say, that twentieth (and twenty-first) century technology will make possible the realization of the more democratic concept of man's essence; but that technological change in our lifetime, if left to operate by itself within the present social structure and guided only by our present ambivalent ontology, without a conscious reformulation of the concept of man's essence appropriate to the new possibilities, is as likely to prevent as to promote the realization of liberal-democratic ends. It is in this sense that I regard the race between ontological and technological change in our society as fateful.

2. *Western Democratic Ontology:* (1) *The Individualist Base*

To demonstrate that the assumptions about the essence of man on which our democratic theory rests are contradictory, we shall have to look at what I have called the social history of political theory in the last century or more, for the two now conflicting sets of assumptions rose at different times in response to different changes in the power relations of our Western societies. But we may start from a contemporary point about a distinguishing feature of Western democracy.

The first thing that emerges from any examination of contemporary Western democratic theory, as distinct from the communist theory of democracy and the various populist theories prevalent in much of the third world, is that the Western theory puts a high value on individual freedom of choice, not only as between political parties but also as between different uses of one's income, of one's capital, and of one's skill and energy. Western democracy is a market society, through and through; or, if one prefers to confine the term democracy to a system of government rather than a kind of society, Western democracy is *for* market society.

This observation from the contemporary scene of comparative so-called democratic systems and ideologies takes on fuller meaning when the Western concept of democracy is traced back a century and more. It is then seen that the roots of the contemporary Western or liberal-democratic theory are in the liberal market society and the liberal state, which emerged first in England as early as the seventeenth century, and in the liberal justifying theory, from say Locke to Bentham. As I have shown elsewhere,[1] that society and state and theory were well

[1] See my *The Real World of Democracy*.

established at least half a century before the franchise became at all democratic and democratic theory became at all respectable or intellectually tenable. The liberal market postulates were well entrenched before the liberal theory was transformed into liberal-democratic theory. Their entrenchment meant the entrenchment of a peculiar concept of man's essence. The pre-democratic liberal theory was based on a concept of man as essentially a consumer of utilities, an infinite desirer. This concept, clearly dominant in Benthamism, where it is displayed to perfection in James Mill's essay on *Government*, goes back through the classical economists, at least as far as Locke.[2]

The liberal theory, in its Benthamite form, specifically made the criterion of the good society the maximization of individual utilities, and made the essence of man the desire to maximize his utilities. Man was essentially a bundle of appetites demanding satisfaction. Man was a consumer of utilities. The Benthamite analysis was of course much more refined than to suggest that all the satisfactions or utilities the individual sought were material consumer goods: man's utilities included the pleasures of curiosity, of amity, of reputation, of power, of sympathy, of ease, of skill, of piety, of benevolence, and so on.[3] Nevertheless, when it came to the decisive question whether material equality or security for unequal property and profit was the more important, Bentham's answer was unequivocal: security for unequal property must outweigh the ethical claims of equality of property, even though he had just demonstrated, by invoking the law of diminishing utility, that equality of property was required in any society where each man was really to count as one in the calculation of aggregate utility. The reason for subordinating the claims of equality was that any regime of equality would destroy incentives to accumulation of capital and hence would prevent all increase of the aggregate of material goods available for the satisfactions of the whole society.[4] Man's good lay in the indefinite increase of the aggregate of material goods. It is clear from this reasoning that Bentham saw man as first and foremost an appropriator and consumer of material utilities.

Indeed, the first two postulates on which Bentham based his case for equality may be considered the bedrock of his whole idea of utility. These are (abstraction having been made 'of the particular sensibility of individuals, and of the exterior circumstances in which they may be

[2] On Locke's view, see my *The Political Theory of Possessive Individualism*, chap. V, sect. 3, ii (a). Hobbes, while holding that man was not by nature infinitely desirous, did maintain that man in market society was necessarily so (ibid., chap. II, pp. 41–5).

[3] Bentham: *Introduction to the Principles of Morals and Legislation*, chap. V; chap. X, sect. 3.

[4] Bentham: *The Theory of Legislation*, ed. C. K. Ogden (New York, 1931), p. 120.

placed', which abstraction Bentham said was amply justified): '1st. *Each portion of wealth has a corresponding portion of happiness*. 2nd. *Of two individuals with unequal fortunes, he who has the most wealth has the most happiness*'.[5] The maximization of wealth *is* the maximization of happiness, or at least is the *sine qua non* of maximization of utility. The centrality of the concept of man as consumer is sufficiently evident.

It may be objected that the concept of man as a consumer of utilities does not necessarily carry with it a postulate of *infinite* desire. Logically this may be so. But it can be seen that historically the postulate of infinite desire was required to justify the society of which man the consumer was said to be the centre.

The first society that postulated man as an infinitely desirous consumer of utilities was the capitalist market society that emerged in the seventeenth century in England. I do not mean that moral and political philosophers had never before then noticed the appetitive side of man or even postulated the infinitely desirous nature of some men. Many had done so. But they had generally noticed it only to deplore it and to urge its supersession by higher moral values. What I find new, from the seventeenth century on, was the widespread assumption that infinite desire was not only present in man but was also rational and morally allowable.

How may this new assumption be said to have been required by the new society? It was, I think, required in order to justify the change to certain new institutions which were required to realize the great increase of individual and national wealth (and of individual freedom) that was then seen to be possible. Let me try to establish this in two stages: (a) that new institutions, including a new system of incentives to productive labour, were required; (b) that the new assumption about the essence of man was required to justify these institutions.

(a) It will not I think be disputed that the system of capitalist enterprise (whether in its mercantilist, *laissez-faire*, or neo-mercantilist form) requires, by contrast with any previous system, an abandonment of authoritative or customary allocation of work and reward to individuals, and its replacement by freedom of the individual to use his energy, skill, and material resources, through contractual engagements, in the way that seems to him best calculated to bring him the greatest return. Nor will it be disputed that for this system to operate efficiently everyone in it must base his decisions on the calculation of his maximum return. Only so would the operation of the market produce the socially desirable result of maximizing the wealth of the nation.

The market system, then, requires that men act as maximizers of their utilities. This in itself could be expected to set up a disposition

[5] Ibid., p. 103. Italics in the original.

towards a concept of man as essentially a maximizer of his utilities, which implies a postulate of infinite desire. But as we shall see in a moment another requirement of the market system makes such a concept imperative.

The minimum institutions required for the system of capitalist enterprise are, first, legal contractual freedom to use one's person and property in the most gainful way one can see, and, secondly, a system of markets in which labour-power, capital, and land will continually find prices that will induce their proprietors to enter them in the productive process. These requirements, we should notice, can be met under a mercantilist system of state regulation of trade as well as under the perfectly free market of *laissez-faire*: a considerable amount of state regulation of trade and prices is quite consistent with the market system, for such regulation simply alters some of the terms of the calculation each individual must make, while leaving as the driving force of the whole system the individual actions based on those calculations.

But while a perfectly free market is not required to get the system going or to make it go, something more is required, by way of incentives, than merely freedom to seek the best return. What is needed, in a society which by definition cannot rely on traditional, patriarchal, or feudal obligations to work, and whose supporters, besides, see prospects of untold wealth under the new market arrangements if only people can be induced to exert themselves, is an institutionalized incentive to continuous exertion. Such an incentive can be, and was, provided by setting up a right of unlimited individual appropriation. The establishment of that right could be expected to move men to continuous effort by giving them the prospect of ever more command over things to satisfy their desires.

Whether this incentive ever did or could operate to induce continuous exertion by the bulk of the employed labour force may well be doubted. The seventeenth-century writers, including Locke, did not think it would. But then they did not think of the propertyless labouring class as fully human, or at least not as full citizens. The right of unlimited individual appropriation would, however, be an effective incentive to continuous exertion, and ingenuity, on the part of the small and middling independent proprietors as well as the capitalist enterprisers proper. And it was on these that the chief reliance was placed for increasing productivity. The employed work-force was expected to continue to be tractable, to work because they had to, on terms set by the market (aided from time to time by the Justices in Quarter Sessions). But the farmers, the manufacturers, and the merchants, the backbone of the new society, would respond to the incentive offered by the prospect of unlimited appropriation.

And it is difficult to see how any incentive short of the right of unlimited appropriation would bring this response. For what limits to the right of individual appropriation could be set? It would obviously have been useless to limit men's acquisition of property to the amounts required to maintain some customary standard of living for members of each traditional rank or class. It would have been equally useless to retain any such limits on the ways one could acquire wealth as were set by the old principle of commutative justice. Nor could the old principle of distributive justice have been retained as a limit on any man's acquisition, for the market system can permit no other criterion of a man's worth than what the market will give him. All these limits had to go, and there was no reason to think up other limits. Indeed, any other limit would presumably have to be justified in terms of some moral principle which would encroach on the market system, whereas the whole point was to get away from moral as well as traditional limits (as Locke did in nullifying the Natural Law limits on individual appropriation).

We conclude, then, that the institutions needed by the capitalist market society included, as an incentive to continuous effort, the right of unlimited individual appropriation.

(b) We have now to show that this in turn required the new assumption about the essence of man.

To justify, that is to find a moral basis for, the right of unlimited individual appropriation (and some justification was needed, for to assert this right was to jettison the hitherto prevalent Natural Law limits on property), it was necessary to derive the right from the supposed very nature or essence of man, just as the previous theories which had limited the right of appropriation had been derived from a supposed nature or essence of man.

The postulate that would most directly supply this derivation is that man is essentially an infinite appropriator, that is, that his nature can only be fully realized in his acquiring ownership of everything. But this postulate is unsuitable, if not untenable. Apart from the difficulty that, on this postulate, no individual could realize his essence while there were other individuals in the same universe, there is another difficulty, less logical but more operational. For what was required was not simply the postulate that men were like that, but that their being so was in accordance with Natural Law or morality. The postulate that was needed was one that would serve as the basis of a moral justification. It had to be one on which an acceptable moral theory could be built. It would have been too outrageous to postulate that love of wealth was not only natural but also the root of all good.[6]

[6] Hobbes, who came nearest to postulating man as an infinite appropriator (though he did not quite do so), got a bad press for it. Not until the late eighteenth

But if the postulate of man as infinite appropriator was too stark, there was another which appeared more moral and which would serve as well. This is the postulate that man is essentially an unlimited desirer of utilities, a creature whose nature is to seek satisfaction of unlimited desires both innate and acquired. The desires could be seen as sensual or rational or both. What mattered was that their satisfaction required a continuous input of things from outside. Man is essentially an infinite consumer.

This does not necessarily make man an infinite appropriator: he need not, in principle, seek ownership of everything in order to expect to consume at an ever-increasing level of satisfaction. And consumer satisfaction could even be represented (as it was by Locke) as a moral reward for honest effort, having nothing in common with *amor sceleratus habendi*.

However, while the postulate of man as infinite consumer does not necessarily make him an infinite appropriator, only a simple additional minor premiss is needed to convert him into that. The premiss required is merely that land and capital must be privately owned to be productive (a premiss which Locke, for instance, explictly made).[7] Then, to realize his essence as consumer, man must be an appropriator of land and capital. Man the infinite consumer becomes man the infinite appropriator. This conclusion was not usually drawn: the postulate of man as infinite consumer was enough.

A more accurate representation of the essential nature, not of man as such, but of man as shaped by capitalist market society, might have been found but for the fact that the theorists wanted to make statements about man as such, this being the only kind of statement that appeared to provide a secure foundation for a general justificatory theory. Had it not been for this, man might have been described straight away as an infinite appropriator not only of goods for consumption but of revenue-producing capital (which is what capitalist man essentially must be). But it was more fitting to the needs of a general moral theory to describe him, instead, as an infinite desirer of utilities, which could be taken to mean only a desirer of things for consumption. This would entitle him to unlimited appropriation of things for consumption. And by failing to make, or to emphasize, the distinction between property in things for consumption and revenue-producing property, the theory could be taken to justify unlimited appropriation of the latter as well.

I have argued so far that the concept of man as an infinite consumer was not only congruous with the behaviour required of men in

century had market morality become so respectable that Burke could refer to 'the love of lucre' as 'this natural, this reasonable, this powerful, this prolific principle . . .' (*Third Letter on Regicide Peace*, *Works*, Oxford World Classics edn., VI, p. 270).

[7] *Second Treatise of Government*, sections 35, 37.

market society, but was also needed to justify the right of unlimited appropriation, which was needed as an incentive to continuous effort in that society. I do not attempt to deal here with the question whether this concept was a conscious invention of thinkers who saw clearly that the market society could not be justified without such a concept. I simply propose that the need for such a concept did exist, and that this need was met in the body of liberal theory from Locke to Bentham. The concept is still with us: it is still needed in so far as our society relies on market incentives to get its main productive work done.

And we should notice one implication of the acceptance of the concept of man as an infinite consumer, an implication whose importance will be evident later in our analysis. If man's desires are infinite, the purpose of man must be an endless attempt to overcome scarcity. This is saying a good deal more than simply that scarcity is the permanent human condition, which was not at all a novel idea. There had always been scarcity, and until the rise of capitalism it had generally been assumed that there always would be. But the pre-capitalist assumption of the permanence of scarcity did not involve any idea that the rational man's purpose in life was to devote himself to trying to overcome it. On the contrary, it was more apt to result in resignation to scarcity as man's fate (scarcity being thought of as an absolute rather than a relative condition), and in moral theories denigrating a life of acquisition.

The new view of scarcity was quite different. In the new view, scarcity was indeed also thought to be permanent, but not because of any inability of men to increase their productivity, and not in any absolute sense. Scarcity now was seen to be permanent simply because, relative to infinite desire, satisfactions are by definition always scarce. What was new was the assumption of the rationality or morality of infinite desire. And as soon as this assumption is made, the rational purpose of man becomes an endless attempt to overcome scarcity. The attempt is endless by definition, but only by engaging endlessly in it can infinitely desirous man realize his essential nature.

3. *Western Democratic Ontology:* (2) *The Egalitarian Complement*

A second concept of the human essence was introduced at the time when the liberal individualist theory became democratized. The turning-point comes in the nineteenth century: it is clear in the contrast between John Stuart Mill and Bentham. By the middle of the nineteenth century it was apparent to perceptive observers such as Mill that the market society had produced a working class sufficiently politically conscious that the franchise could not be denied it much longer. At the same time the quality of life in the market society was seen by moralists as different as Mill and Marx, Carlyle and Saint-Simon, Ruskin and Green, the German romantics and the English Christian Socialists, to be little or nothing short of an insult to humanity. Those of the critics of market morality who still hoped to retain some of the values of liberal individualism thus thought it both politically expedient to moralize the clamant democratic forces before they were admitted to a share in political power, and morally right to assert a higher set of values than those of the market.

This meant asserting an equal right of every individual to make the most of himself. And it meant that the concept of man as essentially a consumer of utilities had to yield its pre-eminence, or at least its monopoly position: a concept of man as essentially an exerter and enjoyer of his own powers had to be asserted. Life was to be lived, not to be devoted to acquiring utilities. The end or purpose of man was to use and develop his uniquely human attributes. A life so directed might be thought of as a life of reason or a life of sensibilities, but it was not a life of acquisition. If we wished to express this concept of man's essence in terms of maximization we could say that man's essence is not maximization of his utilities but maximization of his human powers. Or we could say that man is neither an infinite consumer nor an infinite appropriator but an infinite developer of his human attributes.

The liberal-democratic thinkers who took this view—Mill and Green most notably—were of course going back to a much older tradition than the Locke-to-Bentham theory of man. They were, in a sense, exposing Locke-to-Bentham as a deviation from the Western humanist and Christian traditions that go back to the Greeks and to medieval natural law. They were reasserting the old values, and on a new and more democratic plane.

It might seem that this concept of man's essence as exerter and enjoyer of his own powers, and the assertion of the equal right of every individual to make the most of himself, would be a sufficient basis for a viable liberal-democratic theory. It could be claimed that a liberal individualist society, redeemed by these principles (the latter of which would be enforced by the sanction of the democratic franchise), would have the best of both worlds—the individual freedom of the liberal society plus the equality of a democratic society. This is, in effect, the claim made by Mill and Green and subsequent liberal-democratic theorists.

The claim has never been made good. The reason is that it has been impossible to jettison the Locke-to-Bentham concept of man, and impossible to combine it with the other concept of man.

The reason it has been impossible to jettison the concept of man as infinite consumer or infinite appropriator has already been suggested:

that concept is needed to provide the incentives and justify the power relations of a capitalist market society. The Western liberal democracies are still capitalist market societies. We still demand, as an essential freedom, the individual's freedom to choose how he will use his natural and acquired capacities and his acquired material resources (if any) with a view to maximizing his material utilities (including capital as well as utilities directly for consumption). And we still rely on the capitalist market incentive of a right of appropriation, no longer quite unlimited (for our tax structures generally set an upper limit) but with a limit so high as to be far beyond the reach of most men, and so, for them, virtually unlimited. So long as we rely on this incentive, we cannot dispense with the concept of man as infinite desirer, nor deny the rationality of infinite desire.

The proposition that our society is based on the assumption of infinite desirousness may seem to be controverted by the phenomenon of modern advertising. The purpose of mass advertising of consumer goods, its critics assert, is to create demand, that is, to create desires which otherwise would not exist. If the system has to create new desires by this stimulus from outside the individual, the system does not seem to be based on the assumption of infinite natural desire.

There is some substance in this objection, though not as much as first appears. We may grant that the purpose of advertising is to create a desire for a certain commodity (X's detergent) or, in the case of institutional advertising, for a certain category of goods or services (beer is best, wine is smart, worship in the church of your choice). The purpose is to create a desire which did not exist, or to increase the amount of desire which did exist, for these specific things. But this may be no more than an attempt to divert part of a given mass of desirousness from one product to another. If it is more than this, it appears to be an attempt to increase the mass of desirousness by artificial creation of desires for new things or for more things. This would not seem to be consistent with the assumption of innate infinite desire.

Yet on closer analysis it may be thought to be not only consistent with that assumption but actually based on that assumption. For what else are the advertisers assuming than what economic theory commonly assumes, namely, that every want satisfied creates a still further want, which is to assume that desire does automatically increase without limit, although by stages? The assumption is that the mass of desire is naturally ever increasing: the purpose of the advertiser is to capture some of the increment and make it a demand for his product. The assumption, after all, is that man is infinitely desirous.

Any discussion of this sort soon runs into the vexing question of the relative importance of innate and socially acquired desires. It is sometimes said that civilization consists in the acquisition and satisfaction of new desires. If it is assumed that it is man's nature to civilize himself (and some such theory of progress generally goes with that view of civilization), then infinite desire is not only good but is innate. The acquisition of new desires becomes an innate need. The line between innate and acquired desire disappears. So does any moral criterion for choosing between different patterns of desire.

Much of this difficulty comes from the way the question is put. If you start from the assumption that there is a permanent unchanging nature of man, then you are forced to subsume all changes, such as increase of desires, under his innate nature. If you drop that assumption, and assume instead that man changes his nature by changing his relation to other men and the material environment, the difficulty disappears. It can then be seen that man can in principle choose and impose what moral rules he wishes, and can change them as circumstances seem to him to call for. This is what men in different societies commonly have done. In the market society they created an image of man as infinite desirer and infinite appropriator, and set the moral rules accordingly. In reaction to the results of this, theorists began in the nineteenth century to try to replace this image with another one, and to propose a revised set of moral rules. The new image and morality have as good a claim as the market image and morality, or a better claim since they go back to a longer humanist tradition. Neither one can be judged by the principles of the other. And it is difficult to see how they can both be held simultaneously.

My apparent digression on advertising and ethics has brought me back to the point that had next to be considered. I had said enough, I hope, to show that, and why, it has been impossible to jettison the market concept of man as essentially an infinite consumer. I have still to show that it is now impossible to hold this concept simultaneously with more morally pleasing and now politically necessary concept of man as an exerter and enjoyer of his human capacities.

Let me say at once that the two concepts are not, in the abstract, logically contradictory or even logically incompatible. For it can be held that the maximization of utilities is a means to, rather than being opposed to, the maximization of human powers. What is incompatible about the two concepts may be put in either of two ways. First, what is opposed to the maximization of individual human powers is not the maximization of utilities as such, but a certain way of maximizing utilities, namely, a system of market incentives and market morality including the right of unlimited individual appropriation. For in such a market society, inequality of strength and skill (if nothing else) is bound to lead to greatly unequal holdings of property which effectively deny the equal right of each individual to make the best of himself. It is indeed a requirement of the capitalist system of production that capital be amassed in relatively few hands and that those left without any should pay for access to it by making over some of their powers to the owners. Thus in the capitalist market society the arrangements made to promote the maximizing of utilities necessarily prevent an effective equal right of individuals to exert, enjoy, and develop their powers.

Or we may put the point in a second way. What is incompatible with the concept of man as exerter, enjoyer, and developer of his powers, is not the concept of man as infinite desirer of utilities but the concept of man as infinite appropriator. For if man, to realize his essence, must be allowed to appropriate without limit he must be allowed to appropriate land and capital as well as goods for consumption. The same result as we saw a moment ago then follows: all the land and capital is appropriated by some men, leaving the rest unable to use their powers without paying part of them for access to the resources without access to which they cannot use any of their powers. This is necessarily the position in a capitalist market society. And indeed, as I suggested earlier, the real meaning of the postulate that man is essentially an infinite consumer was, historically, that he is essentially an infinite appropriator. What was needed was a postulate that would justify a right of unlimited individual appropriation. The postulate that man was essentially an infinite appropriator would have been simpler but would have been too stark a repudiation of Natural Law. It is presumably for this reason that it was not consciously entertained by most theorists or, if entertained, rejected. The less obnoxious postulate—man as infinite consumer of utilities—seemed to provide the justification that was needed, but we can see it now as a surrogate for man as infinite appropriator.

I have suggested two ways in which the concept of man as maximizer of utilities or infinite consumer and the concept of man as maximizer of individual human powers or as exerter, enjoyer, and developer of his human capacities can be seen to be incompatible. And I have argued that both concepts are contained in our Western democratic theory and that both have been needed by it, the first because we are still capitalist market societies, the second because our thinkers were (and are) morally revolted and our leaders were (and would be) politically endangered by the society that shaped and was shaped by the first concept alone.

Because Western democratic theory contains these inconsistent postulates, its condition is internally precarious. This might not matter, for we have made do with the theory in that condition for something like a century now, except that Western democracy from now on will have to face increasingly strong competition from the Communist nations (which are sustained by a different notion of democracy), and even, on a moral plane at least, from the underdeveloped nations of of the third world (which have a still different idea of democracy).

Moreover, we have to expect in the next few decades a technological change in the productive base of our society which will change our problem. I want now to argue that foreseeable technological change both requires and makes possible a change in our theory; that if the technological change is left to operate by itself in our present society it will aggravate our weakness, but that there is a possibility of utilizing it to cure the weakness of our society and our theory.

4. *Technology, Scarcity, and Democracy*

The most fundamental change in the political theory and, let us hope, in the ideology, of Western democracy which I believe to be both required and made possible by technological change is the rejection of the concept of man as essentially an infinite consumer and infinite appropriator (which I shall refer to, for brevity, as the market concept of man's essence). That change was, in an obvious sense already indicated, needed many decades ago, if only for theoretical tidiness. But the change has become more urgent now, because of the conjuncture of two changes in our society, namely, the increasingly democratic temper of the world as a whole, and the technological revolution of our time. The two changes are not unrelated.

The rejection of the market concept of man's essence is increasingly needed now because, as I have argued, that concept, as it is entrenched in our present society, is incompatible with the equality of individual right to make the most of oneself which is now being demanded by the increasingly democratic temper of the world as a whole. Given that change in temper, and given the competition for world influence and power between Western and non-Western systems, it is probable that the continuance of Western societies combining individual liberties and democratic rights depends on those societies providing their members with an equal right to realize their essence as exerters, enjoyers, and developers of their individual human capacities. For this is the concept of man's essence avowed in the theory and ideology of both the communist and third worlds. If the realization of this concept in the non-Western worlds were to remain only a millenarian hope for their people, the matter would have no immediate implications for the West.

But it is here that the technological revolution of our time makes a difference. By the technological revolution I mean the discovery and application of new sources of energy, and new methods of control of the application of energy and of communication in the widest sense. This revolution is not confined to the West. It is shared by the most advanced of the non-Western nations. And it can be expected to bring them up to a level of productivity where they can begin to realize the Marxian vision of man freed for the first time in history from compulsive labour.

Thus for the non-Western nations, the technological revolution brings closer the realization of their concept of the human essence. For them, technology assists ontology.

What of the Western nations? Here too the technological revolution *could* provide the means of realizing the democratic concept of the human essence (which is fundamentally the same as the Marxian concept). It could, that is to say, by releasing more and more time and energy from compulsive labour, allow men to think and act as enjoyers and developers of their human capacities rather than devoting themselves to labour as a necessary means of acquiring commodities. At the same time the technological revolution could enable men to discard the concept of themselves as essentially acquirers and appropriators. For as we have seen, that concept was needed as an incentive to continual exertion of human productive energy and continual accumulation of capital. These incentives will no longer be needed. The problem will not be to enlist men's energies in the material productive process, but to provide alternative outlets for those energies; not to accumulate ever more capital, but to find socially profitable uses for future accumulation at anything like the rate to which we have become accustomed.

The technological revolution in the West thus offers the possibility of our discarding the market concept of the essence of man, and replacing it by a morally preferable concept, in a way that was not possible when previous generations of liberal-democratic thinkers, from John Stuart Mill on, attempted it. But the technological revolution by itself cannot be relied on to do this. Its immediate effect is likely rather to impede this. Before we consider why this is so, we should look at one logical objection that may be made about the possibility of discarding the market concept of the essence of man.

Can we just play about with these postulates of the essence of man, rejecting one because it does not suit our moral values and setting up another because it does? Do we not have to demonstrate the truth or falsity of the postulates, and have we done so? I think we do not have to, and certainly we have not done so. All we have demonstrated is that the postulate of man as essentially consumer and appropriator was brought into Western theory and ideology at a certain historical period and that it did fill a certain need (in that it provided a justification of capitalist market relations). This does not in itself demonstrate either the truth or the falsity of the postulate.

But the truth or falsity of the postulate is not in question. For it is not entirely a factual postulate, however much it may be presented as such. It is an ontological postulate, and as such, a value postulate. Its basic assertion is not that man *does* behave in a certain way (although it may make this assertion), but that his *essence* can only be realized by that behaviour. An assertion about man's essence is surely a value assertion. One can agree that man as shaped by market society does behave in a certain way, and even that man in market society necessarily behaves in a certain way, but this tells us nothing about the behaviour of man as such and nothing about man's essence.

Since postulates about essence are value postulates, they may properly be discarded when they are seen to be at odds with new value judgements about newly possible human goals. The discarding, now, of the postulate of man's essence as infinite consumer, infinite appropriator, infinite antagonist of scarcity, comes within the category of allowable discards. The rejection of the market concept of man's essence is thus logically possible as well as now technically possible.

But there is one great difficulty. The technological revolution in Western nations, if left to develop within the present market structure and the present ideology, would have the immediate effect of strengthening the image of man as infinite consumer, by making consumption more attractive. As technology multiplies productivity, profitable production will require the creation of new desires and new amounts of desire. (What will be required may properly be described as *creation* of new desire, in spite of what I said above about advertising not creating new desire, if we reject, as I have argued we should reject, the factual accuracy of the postulate that man as such is naturally infinitely desirous.) Since profits will increasingly depend on creating ever more desire, the tendency will be for the directors of the productive system to do everything in their power to confirm Western man's image of himself as an infinite desirer. Efforts in that direction are evident enough in the mass media now. Thus in the West the immediate effect of the technological revolution will be to impede the change in our ontology which it otherwise makes possible and which I have argued is needed if we are to retain any of the values of liberal-democracy.

What then should we do? I hope that as political theorists we may widen and deepen the sort of analysis here sketched. If it stands up, we shall have done something to demolish the time-bound and now unnecessary and deleterious image of man as an infinite consumer and infinite appropriator, as a being whose rational purpose in life is to devote himself to an endless attempt to overcome scarcity. Scarcity was for millennia the general human condition; three centuries ago it became a contrived but useful goad; now it is dispensable, though we are in danger of having it riveted on us in a newer and more artificial form. We should say so. If we do not, the liberal-democratic heritage of Western society has a poor chance of survival.

ESSAY III

Problems of a Non-market Theory of Democracy

IN the preceding essays I proposed a recasting of liberal-democratic theory by dropping from it the market assumptions about the nature of man and society and building on the more democratic assumptions which are also contained in it. The central defect of the justificatory theory of liberal democracy was found to consist in its attempt to combine two concepts of man, and to make both of the corresponding two maximizing claims: the claim to maximize utilities and the claim to maximize powers in the sense of ability to use and develop essentially human capacities. Reasons were given for thinking that it is now becoming possible for liberal-democratic theory to drop the first concept (man as consumer) and the first maximizing claim, and to base itself increasingly on the second concept of man (as essentially a doer, an actor, an enjoyer, and developer of his human attributes) and the second maximizing claim.

Any attempt to rebuild a democratic theory on this basis raises a new range of questions. For example, can the concept of power as ability to use and develop essentially human capacities be made precise enough to be of any use? Can we assume that all men's essentially human capacities can be exercised not at the expense of each others'? Can the ability to exercise these capacities be sufficiently measured to entitle us to make its maximization the criterion of a fully democratic society?

Such questions are not easy. If their difficulties flowed entirely from our formulating democratic theory as a matter of maximizing powers, we might be well advised to abandon that formulation. But it will be seen that the difficulties are inherent in any democratic theory: our formulation simply enables them to be seen more clearly and dealt with more openly.

In exploring these questions, the first task is to clarify the central concept: power as ability to use and develop human capacities. I shall come at this by examining (in section 1 of this essay) the contrast between that concept of power and the one more usually employed in political theory. In section 2, the concept of 'essentially human capacities' is further considered and is shown to be both less and more demanding than appears at first sight. Sections 3 and 4 take up problems of the measurement of powers. In section 3, I argue that a man's power, in the sense required by a democratic theory, must be measured in terms of impediments to the use and development of his human capacities and must be measured as a deficiency from a maximum rather than (as utility is commonly measured) in relation to a previously attained amount. Section 4 examines what are to be counted as impediments and how they are to be measured, and shows that the 'net transfer of powers' is not, as my previous treatments had let it be understood to be, a sufficient measure of the impediments. Finally, in section 5, I consider how powers, unlike utilities, can be aggregated, and conclude that the difficulty of so doing arises only in the *transition* to a fully democratic society, and is not insuperable.

1. *Two Concepts of Power: Extractive and Developmental*

In the first essay I distinguished between two concepts of human power, one of which was central to the democratic humanist ideal and the other to the classical liberal individualist tradition. The first was called an 'ethical' concept: it was a man's power seen as his ability to use and develop his essentially human capacities. The second was the 'descriptive' concept of a man's power as his present ability to procure satisfactions by whatever means. The point of that distinction was to show that as soon as one thinks of a man's power in the ethical sense it becomes apparent that his power must include his access to the means of using his capacities, and that his power is diminished, and some of it transferred to others, by lack of such access,[1] whereas those who neglect any considerations of human essence or essentially human capacities commonly fail to see any such diminution or transfer, since they measure a man's power *after* that has taken place.

The distinction there drawn remains useful. But it is not entirely satisfactory, for it diverts attention from a very important fact, and it raises one question which it leaves incompletely answered.

It diverts attention from the fact that a man's access to the means of using his capacities is a component part of his power *whether or not* his power is seen to have an ethical dimension. The fact that access is integral to a man's power is only *seen* when the ethical dimension is seen, but access is integral in any case. The *amount* of a man's power, in the most neutral descriptive sense, always depends on his access to the means of exerting his actual capacities.

The question raised but incompletely answered by the distinction between the ethical and descriptive concepts of power is the question, precisely what kind of power is diminished or transferred by lack of

[1] The same point was made earlier in *The Political Theory of Possessive Individualism: Hobbes to Locke* (Oxford, 1962), p. 56, and *The Real World of Democracy*, p. 43.

access to the means of using capacities? There is no difficulty about what is *diminished*. That is obviously a man's power in the ethical sense: he loses some of his ability to use and develop his own capacities under his own conscious control for his own human purposes. But this cannot be what is *transferred*, for clearly no one can transfer to another his ability to use his own capacities under his own control. Equally clearly, what is transferred cannot be a man's power in the descriptive sense as that has been defined, for that power is measured *after* any transfer.

What is transferred is not caught by either of the two concepts proposed so far. This is not surprising, for they are not two categories of power: they are two ways of looking, from two different standpoints, at the same power—the ability to use human capacities to do or to produce what people want to do or produce. What is transferred is some of a man's ability to use his capacities in a neutral sense, abstracted from any consideration of *whose* purposes that exercise of his capacities serves, his own or another's. What is transferred is some of his ability to do things and make things. That power, if it serves his purposes, is part of his ethical power; if it does not serve his purposes it is what is transferred. The same ability to use the same capacities is counted as ethical power in the one case and as transferred power in the other.

Since neither 'ethical' nor 'descriptive' powers, as defined, are what is being transferred, it is evident that those two concepts alone are not enough to categorize the 'net transfer of powers'.[2] We may say, then, that while the distinction drawn hitherto between the ethical and descriptive concepts of a man's power is valuable, it is nevertheless insufficient. It is valuable in indicating why no transfer is seen by those who employ only the descriptive concept, and in pointing out that the descriptive concept, because it embodies no standard of essentially human needs or purposes, is an inadequate one for use in a democratic theory. But those two concepts together are not by themselves sufficient for a fuller analysis of the problems of democratic theory.

Of the two, the ethical concept remains essential: without it, or something like it, no fully democratic theory is possible. But a name other than 'ethical' is perhaps more appropriate for purposes of further analysis of the place of the concept of power in a democratic theory, if only because the emphasis which that term gives to the qualitative character of the concept tends to obscure the fact that the concept is quantitative as well, that the *amount* of that power that men have is what is important in a democratic theory. Since that power is defined as

[2] The concept of the 'net transfer of powers', previously formulated in *The Political Theory of Possessive Individualism* (pp. 56–7), in *The Real World of Democracy* (pp. 40–3), and in Essay I of this volume (pp. 10–14, 16 ff.), is further developed later in this essay (below, pp. 64–66).

a man's ability to use and develop his capacities, it may concisely be called a man's *developmental power*.

The 'descriptive' concept of power, useful as it is, will not carry our analysis much further. We need, in addition to it, a more precise one which will allow us to separate the two components of which a man's power may consist: his ability to use his own capacities, and his ability to use other men's capacities. The latter ability is power over others, the ability to extract benefit from others. We need a name for it. I shall call it *extractive power*. It is central to an understanding of the liberal individualist tradition, and so deserves close attention.

A man's extractive power is evidently not identical with the whole of a man's power in the general descriptive sense, for the latter includes whatever ability he may have to use his own capacities as well as whatever ability he may have to extract benefit from the use of others' capacities. But as we shall now see, the individualist tradition from Hobbes to James Mill did, increasingly explicitly, treat the two as virtually identical: the whole of a man's power was seen as nearly equivalent to his extractive power. We shall see also that, with the transformation of classical utilitarianism into modern pluralist empirical theory, part of this insight was lost.

Most of the literature of modern political science, from its beginnings with Machiavelli and Hobbes to its twentieth-century empirical exponents, has to do with power, understood broadly as men's ability to get what they want by controlling others. Hobbes put it succinctly in 1640: after defining a man's power as his ability to produce some desired effect, and hence as his faculties of body and mind and such further powers as by them are acquired, he concluded: 'And because the power of one man resisteth and hindereth the effects of the power of another: power simply is no more, but the excess of the power of one above that of another.'[3] Having thus made every man's power contentious and comparative, he went on in effect to make it consist of each man's power over others, by showing that man in his market-like model of society can secure power in comparison with others only by getting power over others.

The reduction of power to power over others had become even more explicit by the nineteenth century. The high point was reached in the propositions James Mill announced in 1820 as undisputed: 'The desire . . . of that power which is necessary to render the persons and properties of human beings subservient to our pleasures, is a grand

[3] *Elements of Law, Natural and Politic*, Part 1, chap. 8, sections 3 and 4. The same point is made, though less noticeably, in *Leviathan*, chap. 10, paragraphs 1 and 2, where a man's power ('his present means to obtain some future apparent good') is stated to consist of the *eminence* of his faculties of body or mind and the further powers acquired by such eminence.

governing law of human nature . . . The grand instrument for attaining what a man likes is the actions of other men. Power, in its most appropriate signification, therefore, means security for the conformity between the will of one man and the acts of other men. This, we presume, is not a proposition which will be disputed.'[4]

The increasingly explicit reduction of a man's power to power over others should not be ascribed to carelessness or lack of rigorous consistency of definition on the part of the theorists. It may better be seen as a reflection of the changing facts. With the growth and predominance of capitalist market society it became increasingly the case that the whole of a man's power was nearly equivalent to his extractive power. In a fully developed capitalist society the two come to much the same thing. For, at least in the classical economists' model of a fully competitive capitalist market economy, the relation between owners and non-owners of land and capital puts each member of both categories in the position of having his whole power nearly equivalent in amount to his extractive power. This can be seen by a simple analysis.

(a) Those who in a market society have no land or capital have no extractive power.[5] They also may be said to have, at any given time, no power (or only negligible power) of any other kind. For their productive power, their ability to use their capacities and energies to produce goods, has continuously to be sold to someone who has land or capital, and sold for a wage which goes to replenish the energy which makes their capacities saleable next week. They are left continuously with no productive power of their own. If they have any leisure, and any energy left for leisure pursuits, they have indeed some power left, some ability to use and develop their own capacities for themselves. But in the classical capitalist model, with wages always tending to a subsistence level and energies tending to be fully absorbed by the

[4] James Mill: *An Essay on Government*, section IV (ed. E. Barker, Cambridge, 1937, p. 17).

[5] This is strictly true only for a model of a *lawful* market society in which there is no private violence, corruption, or misuse of office (governmental or non-governmental), for all of these do of course give extractive power regardless of ownership of capital. The amount of such extractive power, as distinct from the amount due to ownership of capital, in any actual market society is impossible to calculate. But since present capital is partly the product of past private violence and misuse of office, and since current gains from unlawful extractive power tend to be consolidated as capital, the amount of extractive power based on capital may be allowed to be at any time an approximation to the whole amount of extractive power. One other non-capital kind of power may be noticed and dismissed as irrelevant here. Lawful and proper use of office gives some personal power to those with leadership and organizational talents. But if it is lawful and proper, i.e. used in the interests of those on whose behalf it is exercised and subject in some degree to their control, it is not extractive.

productive work for which the energies have been purchased, the amount of such power could be treated as negligible. Thus the whole power of each non-owner could be taken to be virtually the same amount as his extractive power: the latter is zero, the former is negligible.

(b) Those who have the land and capital have extractive power. In a full capitalist society, with its substantial concentration of ownership of capital and productive land, a few men have extractive power over many; hence each of the few has extractive power equivalent to the whole (or virtually the whole) power of several other men. The greater the concentration of capital,[6] the greater the proportion of each owner's entire power consists of his extractive power. This can be readily seen if we follow James Mill in expressing the amount of benefit a man is able to extract from others as the (whole or fractional) number of men he is able to 'oppress'.[7]

Thus we may calculate, treating capital as extractive power, that if, for instance, all the capital were owned by 10 per cent of the people, each of the owners on the average would have extractive power equivalent to virtually all the powers of 9 other men. Or, to come nearer to the usual distribution in capitalist society,[8] if two-thirds, say, of all the capital is owned by 5 per cent of the people, then each of those owners on the average has an extractive power equivalent to virtually the whole power of 2/3 of 19 other people, i.e. of about 12 other people. Smaller owners (those among the other 95 per cent of the people, who between them own the other 1/3 of the capital) have of course less extractive power. There is also the complication that some extractive power is normally being transferred continuously from smaller to larger owners, as for instance from tenant farmers or other tenant entrepreneurs to landlords, and from any except the largest entrepreneurs to creditors; but this does not affect the total amount of extractive power of owners.

If, as seems probable, the order of magnitude of the extractive power is in the neighbourhood of 9 (each owner of capital, on the average,

[6] For brevity, 'capital' is used to include land used for production.

[7] James Mill: *An Essay on Government*, section VIII (Barker ed., p. 50). Equating the vote with political power, and political power with power over others, Mill pointed out that if more than half the people had the vote, each voter would have 'something less than the benefit of oppressing a single man', and that if two-thirds of the people had the vote each voter 'would have only one-half the benefit of oppressing a single man'.

[8] Cf. J. E. Meade: *Efficiency, Equality and the Ownership of Property* (London, 1964), p. 27. It is there estimated that 75 per cent of 'total personal wealth' in the U.K. in 1960 was owned by 5 per cent of the population. Although 'personal wealth' is not identical with capital and productive land, the distributions are presumably not very different.

having an extractive power equivalent to virtually the whole power of 9 other men), then much the largest part of the whole amount of the power of each owner is his extractive power. If we assume that the natural capacities of the members of the two classes are roughly equal (i.e. that, setting aside the advantages or handicaps people start with by being born into an owning or non-owning class, the capacities of the members of the two classes are not significantly different), it follows that, on the average the whole power of each member of the owning class consists of one part of his own natural power plus nine parts of his extractive power. So, the extractive power of the owners is nearly equivalent to their entire power.

Thus, in a full capitalist model, the whole power of everyone is nearly equivalent to his extractive power. Each non-owner's whole power is near zero, and his extractive power is zero. Each owner's whole power is about 9 parts extractive power to 1 part non-extractive power. How clearly the classical economists and Utilitarians saw this is a matter of conjecture. The increasingly explicit identification of a man's whole power with his extractive power, culminating in James Mill's formulation, does correspond to the increasingly near actual equivalence of the two as unqualified competitive capitalist society was reaching its zenith. Later in the nineteenth century as capitalism began to go on the defensive ideologically, the acknowledgement and the very perception of extractive power declined.[9] It is still present, though modified, in John Stuart Mill; later it disappears almost entirely.

When we move on to the twentieth-century empirical political theorists we find the same assumption that the only significant power in any political view is one man's or one group's power over others. Thus Laswell and Kaplan write in 1950: 'power in the political sense cannot be conceived as the ability to produce intended effects in general [the reference is to Bertrand Russell's definition of power], but only such effects as directly involve other persons: political power is distinguished from power over nature as power over other men'.[10] So Easton in 1953: power is 'a relationship in which one person or group is able to determine the actions of another in the direction of the former's own ends . . . [Power] is present to the extent to which one person controls by sanctions the decisions and actions of another'.[11] So Friedrich in 1963: '[political] power is always power *over* other men'.[12] So Dahl in 1964, defining power as one kind of influence, namely '*coercive influence*', defines influence as 'a *relation among actors* in which one

[9] Cf. below, p. 72, and Essay XI.
[10] Lasswell and Kaplan: *Power and Society* (New Haven, Conn., 1950), p. 75.
[11] David Easton: *The Political System* (New York, 1953), pp. 143–4.
[12] Carl J. Friedrich: *Man and his Government* (New York, 1963), p. 160.

actor induces other actors to act in some way they would not otherwise act'.[13]

The current empirical theorists are on the whole less perceptive about political power than were the classical political theorists from Hobbes to Mill. They see that political power is power over others, but generally they do not see (as the earlier theorists had seen) that power over others is, in a market society, mainly extractive power of the sort just analysed; nor do they see that political power is the means of consolidating the extractive power of the owners of land and capital. Perhaps because the empirical theorists have been so concerned to map out a political science independent of political economy, or perhaps because they are trying to set up a framework of analysis which will be valid for all kinds of society, not merely for capitalist market societies, they generally overlook the extent to which in the latter societies political power is a means of maintaining a system of extractive power. They recognize of course that wealth is sometimes used to get political power and that political power is sometimes used to get economic power, but they do not treat these relations as central to the nature of political power. They move within a pluralistic model of society which has no use for the axiom of earlier statecraft 'with men we shall get money and with money we shall get men'. Far from treating political power as primarily a means of consolidating extractive power, they are apt to insist on a disjunction between the two. Thus Friedrich rejects Hobbes's definition of a man's power as his 'present means to obtain some future apparent good' because it does not distinguish between power and wealth, whereas he holds that 'it is operationally important today to draw this distinction in order to differentiate political from economic concerns and thus politics from economics'.[14] The extreme separatist position is stated, and endorsed, by Easton in his reference to 'a long line of [modern] writers who see that the characteristic of political activity, the property that distinguishes the political from the economic or other aspect of a situation, is the attempt to control others'.[15] There could hardly be a clearer indication of the distance the empirical political theorists have put between themselves and the reality of power, than this assumption that political power *differs* from economic power in being power over others.

The trouble with the current empirical theorists' concept of power may be stated as follows. Instead of starting, as Hobbes and James Mill did, from an analysis of a man's power, showing how it amounts to power over others, and then moving on to political power as one kind of

[13] Robert A. Dahl: *Modern Political Analysis* (Englewood Cliffs, N.J., 1964), pp. 50, 40.

[14] Friedrich: *Man and his Government*, pp. 159–60.

[15] Easton: *The Political System* (2nd ed., 1971), p. 115.

power over others presumptively closely related to and interdependent with other kinds, they start by looking for a concept of *political* power, and look first for characteristics which distinguish it from other kinds of power. They see that political power is power over others, the ability to make others do what you want. Then, looking for differentiae of political power, they are apt to fasten on the state's monopoly of physical coercive power. What is interesting then is the means by which those who have this political power manage to maintain it. Attention is focused on the *source* of the power-holders' power: how do they recruit and renew their power? What are the conditions for the maintenance of a stable system of inputs to and outputs from political power? Hence the main interests of current empirical theory: analysis of models of democratic elitism, pluralist equilibrium analysis, systems analysis. What is lost sight of is that political power, being power over others, is used in any unequal society to extract benefit from the ruled for the rulers. Focus on the *source* of political power puts out of the field of vision any perception of the necessary *purpose* of political power in any unequal society, which is to maintain the extractive power of the class or classes which have extractive power.

We cannot say, then, that the current empirical theorists follow their Utilitarian forbears in treating the whole of a man's power as nearly equivalent to his extractive power. They do not do so, since they neither start from a concept of a man's whole power nor recognize the fundamental category of extractive power. Yet they still do treat political power as power over others.

We may say at least that power has been treated for the last three centuries, by all those who have considered themselves political realists, as power over others. Power as control over others has been treated as a central, it not the central, fact of political society. It has been taken as an observed phenomenon, and generally as a necessary phenomenon. It has been assumed that all human beings more or less desire power, and that in any society some men have more power than others. The questions that have been (and are) asked are: how is power to be measured, where and in what proportions is it located within given societies, and (if the theory is, like Hobbes's and James Mill's, prescriptive and not merely empirical) how can power be directed to, or prevented from frustrating, certain social goals held to be desirable?

Power as control over others may thus be the subject both of empirical study which tries or pretends to be value-free, and of admittedly prescriptive study. Most political scientists would admit to some moral concern over the uses to which power is put, however separate they may try to keep such concern from their empirical studies. So they will treat power as a force which is at best ethically neutral, but more likely harmful unless channelled and confined by political institutions and ultimately by beliefs about political rights and obligations. Power, because it is seen as control over others, is certainly not seen as something whose increase or maximization is desirable in itself.

Indeed it is generally assumed that it cannot be increased, that the total amount of power within one set of individuals or groups (e.g. within one nation-state or within one system of nation-states) is a constant quantity. For if power is defined as control over others, one man's or one group's power can apparently be increased only at the expense of others'. The competition for power is seen as a zero-sum game: the total amount of power cannot be increased except by increasing the population. We should notice at once that this is a fallacious deduction.

To define power as control over others does not entail that the aggregate amount of power in a given population cannot be increased. For power as control over others is generally desired and used in order to extract some benefit from the controlled for the controller. The amount of power may therefore be measured by the amount of benefit extracted. If a more efficient method of control is devised enabling the old or a new controller to extract more benefit than before from the controlled, e.g. by making them work harder and produce more, the amount of power within a given population is increased. This has been a frequent occurrence in history: it has been the commonplace of colonial administration, and the normal concomitant of industrial revolutions. Contemporary political science has generally neglected this feature of power as control over others (which we may call the variable-extractive dimension of power): if it thinks of power as an amount at all rather than as simply a relation, it tends to treat it as a constant amount in a given population. This makes equilibrium analysis easier.

Of course, if power is defined not as control over others but simply as ability to get what one wants, without the stipulation that this is to be got by controlling other men, the aggregate in any society can be increased by increasing men's control over Nature. This approach is implicit in some of the current theory of political development and modernization. The power of a whole society is defined as its ability to attain its goals. So defined, the aggregate power of a society can be increased, not at anyone's expense, by a societal reorganization, e.g. modernization of a tribal society, which increases the society's control over Nature. But by and large, modern political science continues to treat power as control over other persons, as it has done from the beginning. That is the phenomenon it chiefly studies.

No one will deny the importance of power as control over others. It will, and should, remain a central concern of political science. One might wish that those political scientists who concern themselves with power in that sense would not succumb so far to the scientific blandishments of games theory and systems analysis as to treat power as a zero-sum game and so overlook the variable-extractive function of power. And one might wish that those who are concerned with political modernization theory would not so often neglect the humanly extractive function of power over others in favour of the non-humanly-extractive function of control over Nature. These shortcomings of current empirical approaches to politics might be remedied if more attention were given to the other concept of power: power as ability to use and develop essentially human capacities. It is true that the purpose for which it was introduced into liberal theory was to reform, rather than explain, nineteenth-century society: it was clearly part of a value theory. But an understanding of it now should help us to explain, as well as to evaluate, twentieth-century liberal-democratic society.

Indeed, some understanding of the developmental concept of power is now useful for understanding the controversies and conflicts over extractive powers. For the two concepts are in fact synthesized in some political movements of our time which any political science worth the name must try to comprehend: analysis of the developmental concept of power thus appears valuable not only for a justificatory theory of democracy but also for any adequate contemporary political science. It would be a pretty thin political science that did not attempt to deal with the concepts of power which now inform or motivate the political actions of a considerable and apparently increasing proportion of human society outside, and (if less obviously) within, the West. Recognition and study of the realignment of forces in the political world of the second half of the twentieth century ought not to be confined to a branch of political science called area studies or comparative government; it should be brought into a central theoretical position. Since political science as we know it has always been a Western affair, no doubt it is not easy for it to expand its horizon to take in new phenomena occurring elsewhere, except in the form of area studies and the like, which is to treat concepts that are foreign geographically as foreign intellectually. But the effort must be made if political science is to be of any importance in the world of the late twentieth century. To argue that is not to belittle the continuing study of power in the usual extractive sense. The prevailing relations of control and subordination both in Western and non-Western societies obviously need not merely continuous scrutiny but the most thorough scrutiny that can be devised. But if it is to be thorough it should not be conducted in pluralist or behaviouralist blinkers, which are apt to shut out new phenomena of some importance even within the Western world.

The emergence of new phrases in common speech is not an infallible indication of the emergence of new phenomena. Yet it should give us pause that in the last decade the social fabric of Western liberal democracies has been torn by new movements which have taken, or accepted, such names as 'black power' and 'student power'. No very thorough acquaintance with these movements is needed to see that what they are demanding is, in varying proportions, a hybrid of the two kinds of power. The power they seek is a cross between (i) power as the ability to control others (or not to be controlled by others), so as to increase their share of the satisfactions now available but now distributed unfavourably to them, and (ii) power as the ability to exercise and develop their human capacities in ways and to an extent they believe to be not possible for them, or for anyone, within the framework of existing society, whether they designate existing society as the consumer society, or as capitalist, imperialist, technocratic, bureaucratic, gerontocratic, or (comprehensively) alienated. They may be derided as wishing to opt out of society, or resisted as threatening to disrupt or take over existing societies. But they cannot be disregarded by any realistic political science.

In so far as the power they demand is the ability to use and develop what they sense as presently unusable or denied human capacities, they are the ideological reflection within Western societies of the ferment that has been at work for some time now in much of Eastern Europe and Asia and Africa. In so far as the power they demand is the ability to become the controllers instead of the controlled, they are the practical imitators of the revolutions in that other two-thirds of the world. But whatever the mixture is, the phenomenon has surely made itself sufficiently evident, even within the West, to set a new requirement for Western political science. We must attend to the developmental concept of power, and the democratic claim to maximize that power, if our political science is to be analytically adequate. My main concern here, however, is with the importance of the developmental concept of power in any modern justificatory theory of democracy.

To discuss democratic theory as a claim to maximize men's developmental powers may seem perverse in view of the failure of John Stuart Mill and Green and their followers to build a coherent liberal-democratic theory around their developmental concept of power. Is it worthwhile pursuing the implications of that concept of power? I think it is, on two grounds. First, their failure need not be attributed to any weakness in the concept but, as I have argued, to contradictions in the liberal-democratic society which are now capable of being resolved.

Secondly, I would argue that the developmental concept of power remains, if not essential, at least the most serviceable for the building of any adequate democratic theory in the late twentieth century. Let me put a preliminary case for this view by arguing that what *is* essential to a modern democratic theory can most efficiently be formulated in terms of the developmental concept of power, the test of efficiency being how fully the formulation permits the implications of the essential principle to be drawn out, and the difficulties of its application to be faced.

What is essential in a modern democratic theory? As soon as democracy is seen as a kind of society, not merely a mechanism of choosing and authorizing governments, the egalitarian principle inherent in democracy requires not only 'one man, one vote' but also 'one man, one equal effective right to live as fully humanly as he may wish'. Democracy *is* now seen, by those who want it and by those who have it (or are said to have it) and want more of it, as a kind of society—a whole complex of relations between individuals—rather than simply a system of government. So any theory which is to explicate, justify, or prescribe for the maintenance or improvement of, democracy in our time must take the basic criterion of democracy to be that equal effective right of individuals to live as fully as they may wish. This is simply the principle that everyone ought to be able to make the most of himself, or make the best of himself. I am saying that this not only *was* the principle introduced into predemocratic liberal theory in the nineteenth century to make it liberal-democratic, but that it is now an essential principle of any democratic theory. Moreover I would argue that this principle requires (as Mill and Green thought it did) a concept of man as at least potentially a doer, an exerter and developer and enjoyer of his human capacities, rather than merely a consumer of utilities.

We may here notice and dispose of one apparent difficulty about this concept of man. It may be allowed that some men (especially as shaped by modern market society) might, given the greatest freedom, wish to be no more than consumers of utilities. But it must be allowed that some do wish to be active exerters and developers and enjoyers of their human capacities. And it must be allowed that the others are potentially such. It follows that all must be treated as at least potentially such, by any theory that asserts the right of each to live as fully as each may wish; and we have seen that any democratic theory must assert this. It may be added, although this is not essential to the case just made, that the notion of man, and society, as *developing* entities, is probably more widely held now than even in the late nineteenth century. We live, and are likely for some time to live, in an age of development: man is, for the most part, seen as a striving being.

I conclude that any adequate twentieth-century democratic theory, since it must treat democracy as a kind of society and must treat the individual members as at least potentially doers rather than mere consumers, must assert an equal effective right of the members to use and develop their human capacities: each must be enabled to do so, whether or not each actually does so. To state such a principle is not enough. It should be stated in such terms as allow all its implications to be drawn out clearly, and its difficulties to be faced directly. The formulation I have offered, of democracy as a claim to maximize men's powers in the sense of power as ability to use and develop human capacities, seems to me to have the advantage by this test.

The following sections of this essay attempt to make good this claim, by examining some hitherto insufficiently examined implications and difficulties of formulating democratic theory as the claim to maximize men's powers in the developmental sense of power. In so far as this claim can be made good, this formulation of democratic theory will serve as a basis for a critical look at some of the leading current justificatory theories of liberal democracy. Such criticism is offered in Essays IV and V.

2. *Power and Capacities*

The concept of power which I describe as the developmental concept defines a man's power as his ability to use and develop his supposed essentially human capacities. Before we examine some implications of the concept, attention should be drawn to another change in terminology now introduced. In previous references[16] to the ethical (now developmental) as well as to the descriptive concept of power I have used the term 'a man's powers'. It will I think be better now to put this in the singular, and to refer to 'a man's power' (retaining the plural only for 'men's powers'). This will help to avoid a confusion between a man's *power* (understood as his *ability* to exercise his human capacities), and the capacities themselves. One naturally speaks of capacities in the plural, since they are discernibly of several sorts;[17] and it is all too easy to use 'powers' interchangeably with capacities if both are used in the plural. Yet there are two different things here, whatever names we give them, and the difference is important when we are thinking of quantities. For the amount of a man's capacities—physical, mental, and psychic—is neither the same as, nor necessarily correlated with, the amount of his ability to use them. The latter depends on present external impediments; the former on innate endowment and past external impediments.

It is a man's ability to exercise his capacities which I have called a man's powers, and which I now propose to call a man's power, chiefly in order to mark the difference between power and capacities. The political theorists who introduced the developmental notion of power

[16] Essay I, 'The Maximization of Democracy', section 3.
[17] See below, pp. 53–4.

did not always make a clear distinction. Both Mill and Green were apt to use 'powers' to mean what I am calling capacities.[18] The use of 'powers' to mean latent powers, i.e. capacities, is perfectly intelligible, but it leaves us without a distinct word for actual power, i.e. actual ability to exercise one's capacities. It therefore seems best to keep 'power' for the actual ability to exercise one's capacities, and to use 'capacities' for what is there to be exercised.

The usefulness of the developmental concept of power clearly depends on the adequacy of the concept of 'essentially human capacities'. To put such an imprecise term in our definition may seem to beg a lot of questions. Yet a concept of power which is to be of any use in a justificatory democratic theory must contain a notion of essentially human capacities. Indeed any ethical theory, and therefore any justificatory political theory—whether idealist or materialist, and whether liberal or not and democratic or not—must start from the assumption that there are specifically or uniquely human capacities different from, or over and above, animal ones. Whether the existence of specifically human capacities is attributed to divine creation, or to some evolutionary development of more complex organisms, it is a basic postulate. It is an empirical postulate, verifiable in a broad way by observation. It is at the same time a value postulate, in the sense that rights and obligations can be derived from it without any additional value premiss, since the very structure of our thought and language puts an evaluative content into our descriptive statements about 'man'.[19]

But this leaves open the question, what are these human capacities? In 'The Maximization of Democracy' I proposed that, while men's human attributes might be variously listed, they could 'be taken to include the capacity for rational understanding, for moral judgement and action, for aesthetic creation or contemplation, for the emotional

[18] e.g. Mill's approving quotation of Humboldt's statement: 'the end of man . . . is the highest and most harmonious development of his powers to a complete and consistent whole' (J. S. Mill: *On Liberty*, chap. III): and Green's definition of 'freedom in the positive sense' as 'the liberation of the powers of all men equally for contributions to a common good' (*Liberal Legislation and Freedom of Contract*, *Works*, III.372), and his references to 'the free exercise of his powers' and 'the free play of the powers of all' (*Lectures on the Principles of Political Obligation*, sec. 216). Sometimes Green used capacity and power as identical terms, e.g. where in consecutive sentences he described freedom as 'a positive power or capacity of doing or enjoying something worth doing or enjoying' and as 'a power which each man exercises through the help or security given him by his fellow-men . . .' (*Liberal Legislation* . . . , *Works*, III.371).

[19] Cf. H. L. A. Hart: *The Concept of Law* (Oxford, 1961), pp. 188–9; and Isaiah Berlin: 'Does Political Theory Still Exist?', in P. Laslett and W. G. Runciman (eds.): *Philosophy, Politics and Society* (*Second Series*, Oxford, 1962), pp. 26–7.

activities of friendship and love, and, sometimes, for religious experience'.[20] And of course the capacity for transforming what is given by Nature is presupposed in this view of men as essentially a doer, a creator, an exerter of energy, an actor;[21] this is broader than, but includes, the capacity for materially productive labour. It is evident that such a list could be extended or rearranged in many ways. One might add the capacity for wonder or curiosity; one might treat the capacity for religious experience as subsumed under one or more of the others; one might add the capacity for laughter (though not, perhaps, if one agreed with Hobbes's account of laughter);[22] one might add the capacity for controlled physical/mental/aesthetic activity, as expressed for instance in making music and in playing games of skill. But some such list as this does I think give the gist of what the liberal-democratic theorists have meant when they have thought of the human capacities whose development or fulfilment was their highest value. And some such list is surely essential to any democratic theory.

Here it may be objected that the very looseness of any such list renders the idea of essentially human capacities unusable. At the very least, it may be thought, the capacities should be shown to be in an ordered relation, with one as the first principle and the others as derivative: we can have *homo faber* or *homo sapiens* or *homo ludens* but not a hodge-podge of all these or more. I do not think that this objection can be sustained when the idea of capacities is being used in a democratic theory. For when capacities are postulated in a democratic theory, the postulate must include a further assumption which incidentally makes hierarchical ordering unnecessary. The further assumption, which at first sight is a staggering one, is that the exercise of his human capacities by each member of a society does not prevent other members exercising theirs: that the essentially human capacities may all be used and developed without hindering the use and development of all the rest.

Now to describe as the essentially human characteristics only those ones which are not destructively contentious is of course to take a fundamentally optimistic view. That view has always been at the root of the democratic vision, and indeed of the liberal vision: one has only to think of the Encyclopedists, with Condorcet as the limiting case. Men's very visible contentiousness might be attributed to intellectual

[20] Above, p. 4.

[21] Cf. J. S. Mill: 'all human action whatever, consists in altering, and all useful action in improving, the spontaneous course of nature' ('Nature', in *Three Essays on Religion:* in *Collected Works*, Vol. X, ed. J. M. Robson (Toronto and London, 1969), p. 402.

[22] Hobbes: *English Works*, Vol. II, as quoted below, Essay XIV, p. 240.

error or to scarcity: both conditions were assumed to be removable. That men if freed from scarcity and from intellectual error (i.e. the ideologies inherited from ages of scarcity) would live together harmoniously enough, that their remaining contention would be only creative tension, cannot be proved or disproved except by trial. But such a proposition is basic to any demand for or justification of a democratic society. The case for democratic *government* ('one man, one vote') can indeed be made sufficiently on the opposite assumption: in a thoroughly contentious society everyone needs the vote as a protection. But the case for a democratic *society* fails without the assumption of potential substantial harmony. For what would be the use of trying to provide that everyone should be able to make the most of himself, which is the idea of a democratic society, if that were bound to lead to more destructive contention?

It must therefore be a postulate of any fully democratic theory that the rights or freedoms men need in order to be fully human are not mutually destructive. To put this in another way: it must be asserted that the rights of any man which are morally justifiable on any egalitarian principle are only those which allow all others to have equal effective rights; and that *those are enough* to allow any man to be fully human. They are not the same as the rights anyone might like to have. They do not amount to Hobbes's (self-defeating) natural right of every man to any thing. To translate this from terms of right into terms of power: the power which a democratic theory requires to be maximized is the ability of each to use and develop those of his capacities the use and development of which does not prevent others using and developing theirs. His *human* capacities are taken to be only those; and those—the non-destructive ones—are taken to be enough to enable him to be fully human.

The postulate of the non-opposition of essentially human capacities may be too good to be true. But it is necessary to any fully democratic theory. It is not often stated explicitly, perhaps because it appears to be contradicted by all experience. All societies, including those with democratic systems of government, exhibit perennial contention between opposed desires of their members. Democratic governments are thought to have enough to do in keeping such contention within bounds, and rationing the objects of opposed desires in some tolerable way. No doubt this is so as long as there is scarcity of such objects. A fully democratic society is only possible when both genuine and contrived scarcity have been overcome. But the belief that they can be overcome is at the heart of democratic theory. In any case, the postulate of non-opposition of essentially human capacities cannot be said to be contradicted by experience, for it is asserted of the capacities that would be held to be human in a society as yet nowhere realized. I shall return to this question later,[23] after more attention has been given to questions of scarcity.

We may now notice two further points about capacities and their exercise. The first is that the concept of human capacities is, in a democratic theory, quantitative as well as qualitative. For the goal in a democratic theory is to let these capacities reach their fullest development, which can only be conceived as a quantity. Thus a man's capacities must be understood to be the *amount* of his combined and co-ordinated physical, mental, and psychic equipment, whether as it actually exists at a given time or as it might exist at some later time or under certain different conditions.

There is a rich source of confusion here. No fewer than three different quantities are liable to be confused in the one notion of a man's capacities: (i) his actual present capacities; (ii) the supposed capacities he might have developed up to the present if society had placed no impediments in his way; (iii) the supposed greater capacities he could develop during his whole life if society placed no impediments in his way. It is easy for a liberal-democratic theory to slip from one to another of these meanings. For if one is thinking of an ideal liberal democracy (i.e. one in which society placed no impediments in anyone's way), (i) and (ii) would be the same, and (iii) would be automatically reached. But in anything short of the ideal, (i) is less than (ii) for some men, and less by different amounts for different men, depending on the different impediments they have confronted; and (iii) is not automatically reached by some men.

The other point to be noticed about the concept of human capacities is that their exercise, to be fully human, must be under one's own conscious control rather than at the dictate of another. This is required by the concept of human essence which holds that a man's activity is to be regarded as human only in so far as it is directed by his own design (an assumption as old as Aristotle's *to logon echon*). To say this is not of course to say that a man should refuse to acknowledge himself to be a social animal who can be fully human only as a member of society. It is rather to say that the rules by which he is bound should be only those that can be rationally demonstrated to be necessary to society, and so to his humanity. Or it may be put that the rules society imposes should not infringe the principle that he should be treated not as a means to other's ends but as an end in himself. With all its difficulties, this is at bottom simply the assertion of the dignity of man.

It may still be asked whether a liberal-democratic concept of men's powers must include the development, as well as the full use, of men's present capacities. Must a liberal-democratic theory in claiming (and a

[23] Below, pp. 74.

liberal-democratic state in seeking) to maximize men's powers, claim to maximize the future development, as well as the present use, of each man's capacities? At first sight it might seem enough to claim only to maximize the use of each man's present capacities; indeed this by itself would be a considerable claim and a considerable endeavour. But a democratic theory must assert an equal right of individuals to develop their capacities to the fullest: an equal right merely to use the capacities each has at a given time is not equality as between those whose capacities had been stunted by external impediments and those whose capacities had not been so stunted.

Finally we should notice that this view of capacities and their development, while it does assume that all men are at least potentially exerters and developers of their essentially human capacities, and does therefore treat the development of capacities as a process which would go on if society placed no impediments in anyone's way, does not imply that society is only an impeding agent. It does not deny that society is also a positive agent in the development of capacities. It does not deny that every individual's human capacities are socially derived, and that their development must also be social. Human society is the medium through which human capacities are developed. A society of *some* kind is a necessary condition of the development of individual capacities. A *given* society, with all its enabling and coercive institutions, may be judged more of a help than a hindrance, or more of a hindrance than a help, at any given time. Societies have usually been both, in varying proportions. If my analysis concentrates on the hindrances in modern market societies, it is because this is what requires most analysis if we are to find a way through from a liberal market society to a fully democratic society. The objective is to find a form of society which will be more of a help and less of a hindrance: a help in new ways, without the present hindrances. We must start from the hindrances, but this is in no way to say that society is nothing but a hindrance.

3. *The Measurement of Powers*

Having seen (in section 1) that any adequate twentieth-century theory of democratic society must assert an equal effective right of the members to use and develop their essentially human capacities, treating all the members as at least potentially doers rather than mere consumers, and that this principle may be stated as the claim that democracy maximizes men's ability to exercise those capacities (which ability we define as their power), and (in section 2) that a democratic theory must postulate that the essentially human capacities are ones, the exercise of which by any one does not prevent their exercise by others, we have now to look at some problems of maximizing powers.

To formulate democratic theory as the claim that democracy maximizes men's powers is to require that their powers be measurable, at least in terms of greater or less. How is a man's power, defined as his ability to use and develop his human capacities, to be measured? And how can the powers of all the members of a society be added together to give a total (which is what is claimed to be maximized)? There is less difficulty about either of these operations than might be supposed. I shall consider the question of measurement of one man's power in this and the following section of the essay, and the question of aggregating all men's powers in section 5.

A man's power, in the sense required in a democratic theory, is to be measured in terms of the *absence of impediments* to his using his human capacities. For we have seen that a democratic theory rests on the assumption that everyone is at least potentially a doer, an actor, a user and developer of his capacities. His *ability* so to act, which is what democracy claims to maximize, is at its maximum when there are no external impediments to such action. His ability is diminished by the amount of impediments. His ability is therefore measured as greater or less by the lesser or greater amount of impediments.

We shall examine shortly what are to be counted as impediments. But it should be emphasized here that the amount of a man's power must, in any democratic theory, be measured against a maximum, not (as is usually done with the measurement of utilities) against some previously attained amount. Liberal theory customarily measures utilities against a bench-mark of a previously attained amount. This is perfectly appropriate when man is taken to be essentially a consumer: his power is increased by the amount of his increased command of utilities. It is all too easy for liberal-democratic theory to carry this standard of measurement over to the measurement of power in the developmental sense. But it is not an appropriate standard for the measurement of men's powers in a democratic theory; indeed it is not even a proper way to measure utilities when men are seen as primarily doers and only incidentally consumers.

Both these points can be readily demonstrated. A democratic theory must measure men's present powers down from a maximum rather than up from a previous amount because it asserts that the criterion of a democratic society is that it maximizes men's present powers. Consequently the standard by which the theory must judge the democratic quality of any society, and by which its claim that any particular society is democratic must be tested, is how nearly it attains the presently attainable maximum (i.e. the maximum level of abilities to use and develop human capacities given the presently possible human command over external Nature). How nearly a society attains that maximum can only be established by measuring the deficiency, if any, from the maximum. Utilities also must be so measured as soon as men are seen as primarily doers, exerters, and enjoyers of their human capacities, and only instrumentally consumers. For utilities then become mere means to using and developing human capacities (instead of, as in classical liberal theory, capacities being mere means for acquiring utilities). Utilities as mere means to powers must then be measured in the same way as powers, i.e. measured down from a maximum.

That democratic theory must logically measure men's powers down from a maximum is not always seen by liberal-democratic theorists. The early liberal-democratic theorists were more aware of it than current ones often are. Mill and Green, breaking away from classical liberal utilitarianism, and realizing that their own socicty fell far short of maximizing men's powers, were apt to measure the quality of society by its deficiency from that maximum. Twentieth-century liberal-democratic theorists, less crusading and more defensive, are apt to argue that present liberal-democratic societies, with slight reforms, would attain the maximum (or that an easily realizable theoretical model of liberal-democratic society *does* attain it).[24] Seeing little or no deficiency from the maximum now, they see no need to measure powers down from a maximum. So they can easily slip back into the classical liberal habit of measuring up from a previous level.

4. *Impediments and their Measurement*

A man's power in the sense required in a democratic theory is, I have argued, to be measured in terms of the absence of impediments to his using his human capacities. What then are to be counted as impediments?

We can dismiss at once those physical impediments which cannot be altered by any action of society. The force of gravity, the obduracy of materials, any innate limitations of the human frame, are indeed impediments to men doing what they might wish. But a social or political theory can only be concerned with impediments which are socially variable.

What then are the socially variable impediments to each man's using and developing his human capacities, which liberal democracy would have to minimize in order to realize its aim of maximizing men's powers? There are more of them than liberal theory has traditionally emphasized. They may be deduced from the human condition under three headings.

(i) *Lack of Adequate Means of Life*

Since every exercise of a man's capacities is an exertion of energy,

[24] See the positions taken by Chapman and Rawls, discussed in Essay IV.

such exercise requires that a man should have energy, and therefore that he should have a continuous intake of the material means of maintaining his energy. Since it is not just physical energy but also psychic energy that is required, this calls for a supply of the material prerequisites for his taking part in the life of the community, whatever the level of its culture may be, as well as for food and shelter. Lack of this is an impediment.

(ii) *Lack of Access to the Means of Labour*

Since every exercise of a man's capacities requires materials to work on or work with, it requires access to such resources. This applies both to the materially productive exercise of capacities (which requires land and/or capital), and to the materially non-productive but equally important exercise of capacities in which activity is not a means of producing utilities but a satisfaction in itself: man as actor must have something to act on or with. Lack of access to such material is an impediment. This impediment may be described as *lack of access to the means of labour* if we take labour in its broadest sense as exertion of human energy.

(iii) *Lack of Protection Against Invasion by Others*

Since every exercise of a man's capacities requires that he should not be invaded or subdued by others while or because he is exercising these capacities, lack of protection against such invasion is an impediment.

Of these impediments, the third can be removed, or reduced, so far as that can be done by social action, by the state guaranteeing civil liberties and providing protection of the person and of such personal property as the society allows. This normally is done, more or less well, by liberal-democratic states. There are certainly many and recurrent problems about this—where should the limits of permissible individual liberty of action be set? what minority rights should be protected?—but the problems are not in principle insoluble if there is agreement on the general principle of the equal right of every individual to use and develop his capacities so far as this does not interfere with others using and developing theirs. It is with these problems that traditional liberal theory has been mainly concerned.

But the other two impediments present difficulties of quite a different kind, which have not been as much explored. Their removal or reduction requires a supply of the material means of life, and access to material resources on which and with which to work. What if the supply, and the resources, are inadequate to provide for everyone? This is the problem of scarcity. We may consider in turn (a) scarcity of the means of life and (b) scarcity of the means of labour.

(a) *Scarcity of the Means of Life*

The niggardliness of Nature has commonly been considered, not only by economists, as a fixed datum. Nature, it has been admitted, could indeed be made to yield more, by human ingenuity and labour, but never enough to meet all human wants, since wants were observed (or assumed) to increase with every increase in the means of meeting them. In that view, scarcity of the means of life (that is, of the means to a full life) is an invariable natural phenomenon, from which it would follow that our first impediment could not be removed or reduced.

On closer examination it can be seen that this is not so. Material scarcity is scarcity relative to some standard of material wants, and the standard assumed in the view that scarcity is a permanent natural phenomenon is not the same as the standard appropriate to a democratic theory.

In the former view, which is implicit in the classical individualism of the seventeenth to nineteenth centuries and in classical political economy, the standard of wants from which scarcity is measured is the amount of material goods supposed to be actually desired at a given time by all the members of a given society at its then level of culture. The amount has to be *supposed* to be actually desired; it cannot be *shown* to be so, since the only indicator in a market society is the amount of desire of those who have the money to buy the goods. The classical theorists generally seem to have assumed that everybody else actually desired at least the comfortable material level the theorists themselves enjoyed, or perhaps the even higher level that they themselves might aspire to enjoy. On this assumption it was reasonable to conclude that actual wants were greatly in excess of goods available. And from their own experience and observation in a rapidly advancing commercial and industrial society the theorists could easily make the further assumption that material wants naturally tended to increase with every increase in the material productivity of the society, without limit.

I have argued in the preceding essays that this notion of man as infinite desirer or infinite consumer is itself a culturally determined concept which was needed to get capitalist enterprise into action, but is not needed, and has no warrant, once capitalism has become mature. But the point here is that this standard of supposed or projected actual wants is not the same as the standard of wants entailed in a liberal-democratic theory which justifies liberal-democratic society as maximizing men's ability to use and develop their essentially human capacities and which assumes that men are essentially not consumers but doers. In such a liberal-democratic theory, the standard of material wants from which scarcity is to be measured is the amount of material goods required to enable everybody to use and develop fully his human capacities (rational, moral, aesthetic, emotional, and productive in the broadest sense). This bears no assignable relation to the amount needed to meet the supposed or projected actual wants of men culturally conditioned to think of themselves as infinite consumers.

We simply do not know what men's 'actual' wants are, even in the liberal-democratic society which is supposed to come nearest to expressing them. What we do know is that, in the liberal-democratic market society, neither the economic market nor the political market measures men's actual wants accurately or adequately. Demand, in the economic market, measures only the wants that have money to back them. The demand which is transmitted by the market-like processes of indirect democracy (in both the cabinet and presidential models) is always diluted and often negated by the operation of the party system and of the bureaucracy, not to mention the power of money in the public opinion industry. The increasing disenchantment with indirect democracy and the increasing desire for something called participatory democracy may be cited as evidence that the political market does not, and is increasingly seen not to, register actual wants. The same disenchantment and desire suggest also that the wants now catered for are no more 'actual' than those not catered for.

The standard of wants appropriate to a democratic theory, then, is different from the standard generally assumed in the liberal theory. But does it not also, like the liberal standard, tend to shift upwards without limit? It is true that the full development of human capacities, as envisioned in the liberal-democratic concept of man—at least in its most optimistic version—is infinitely great. No inherent limit is seen to the extent to which men's human capacities may be enlarged. But there is no reason to think that such indefinite enlargement requires an indefinite increase in the *material* prerequisites. On the contrary, the extent to which an advanced society makes individually owned material increases the main criterion of social good militates against its recognizing the importance of equal development of the essential human capacities.

The great increase in productivity brought about by the technological revolution of our time, and the further increases in prospect, do not in themselves end scarcity. No increase in productivity, however great, will end scarcity while people continue to see themselves as infinite consumers. A comparatively modest increase in productivity, or no increase at all in the present productive capacity of the economically most advanced nations, would end scarcity if people came to see themselves (as the justifying theory of liberal democracy must assume them to be) as doers, exerters, enjoyers of essentially human capacities. The economically least advanced nations will indeed need substantial increases in their productivity to overcome the absolute shortage of the material means of life, but they will not need to reach or approach the productivity of the most advanced except in so far as they are caught up in the market societies' present consumer mentality.

The difficulty to be overcome within the advanced liberal democracies is not primarily material but ideological. For though our liberal-democratic justifying theory does contain (and does require) the assumption that man is essentially an enjoyer and exerter of his human capacities, it also still contains (but does not now require) the opposite assumption, inherited from classical liberal individualism, that man is essentially an infinite consumer. It is only on the latter assumption that scarcity is permanent. Yet now, since the emergence of modern technology, we should be able to see that scarcity, whatever it was for many millennia, is not an invariable natural phenomenon but a human construction. We do not yet sufficiently see this. We still think, like nineteenth-century liberal democrats, that the problem is to redistribute scarcity. It is true that scarcity still is very unfairly distributed, less so now within each advanced Western nation than Mill saw it to be a century ago,[25] but more so as between advanced and underdeveloped countries. But the most advanced problem now is not to redistribute scarcity but to see through it: to see that it is not an invariable natural phenomenon but a variable cultural one. Scarcity of the means of life, then, is a socially variable impediment.

(b) *Scarcity of the Means of Labour*

Scarcity of material resources (land, raw materials, implements) on which and with which men can exert their energies, is also a human construction, though of a different kind. This scarcity is not due to the amount of capital being fixed, nor to its being necessarily always short of what is required to enable everyone to use and develop his capacities, for neither of these is the case. The amount of accumulated capital in modern societies tends to increase continually. And one cannot say that the amount of resources must always be short of what is needed, unless one assumes that consumer demand for the products of the use of those resources is infinite, which assumption I have argued is untenable.

The fact that in the most advanced capitalist economies the existing capital resources are rarely fully employed is not strictly relevant, for this shows only that, as the system operates, the resources are generally greater than the amount the entrepreneurs think it profitable to use

[25] '. . . the produce of labour . . . apportioned as we now see it, almost in an inverse ratio to the labour—the largest portions to those who have never worked at all, the next largest to those whose work is almost nominal, and so in a descending scale, the remuneration dwindling as the work grows harder and more disagreeable, until the most fatiguing and exhausting bodily labour cannot count with certainty on being able to earn even the necessaries of life . . .' (J. S. Mill: *Principles of Political Economy*, Book II, chap. I, sect. 3, *Collected Works*, Vol. II, ed. Robson (Toronto and London, 1965), p. 207).

fully, which amount depends on (among other things) their estimate of the effective demand for the product, and this as we have seen is not necessarily the same as what is needed for the use and development of everyone's capacities. Nor is it relevant that material resources may properly in one sense be said to be scarce as long as entrepreneurs will pay something for them. This is the kind of scarcity economists have in mind when they see economic decisions as choices between alternative uses of scarce means. But this also is scarcity in relation to uses which entrepreneurs expect will yield a profit, that is, in relation to demands that are maintained or created by the entrepreneurial society itself, with its image of man as infinite consumer. No doubt in any foreseeable socialist society also, decisions will still have to be made, however democratically or bureaucratically, about alternative uses of material resources, and so long as this is so the resources may be said to be scarce, in the economists' sense. But this is not to say that the resources are therefore less than enough to enable everyone to use and develop his human capacities.

There is indeed one resource which is absolutely limited in any country, namely, the extent of the land (and water) surface. And with present and probable future population densities it may be said that there is and always will be a scarcity of this, such that society somehow must make choices between various sorts of land utilization—for food production, for building, for recreation, and so on. This scarcity is not entirely a human construction though it is so to the extent that it is a result of uncontrolled land use for profit. But the shortage of this natural resource is not self-evidently such that the amount must always be less than what is needed to enable everyone to use and develop his capacities.

The scarcity of material resources which is fundamental in any democratic theory is that which is felt by those who have none, that is, by those who have none of their own and no free access to any other, on which and with which to work. This distribution of material resources is a human construction. And it is fundamental to any democratic theory because it diminishes some men's powers. The fact is that those who do not own, or have free access to, the resources which are their necessary means of labour, have to pay for the access with a transfer of part of their powers. And, as we shall see, their powers are diminished by more than the amount of the transfer.

Let us be clear what the transfer of powers comprises.[26] Most simply, what is transferred, from the non-owner to the owner of the means of labour (i.e. of the land and capital), is the non-owner's ability to labour, i.e. his ability to use his own capacities productively, during the time contracted for. The owner purchases that ability for a

[26] Cf. above, pp. 40–1.

certain time and puts it to work. The ability, the labour-*power*, is transferred. The actual work is *performed* by the non-owner. But in a very real sense the actual work is *owned* by the owner of the capital. He, having purchased the other's ability to labour, has the rights of ownership in the labour that is actually performed. He of course controls the performance; he determines how the energies purchased are to be applied. He also owns the product, including the value added to the materials by the work. And he owns that value added by the work *because* he owns the labour; that is to say, his moral and legal property right in the value added by the work is grounded in his having purchased a property in the labour. Locke got it neatly: 'the Turfs my Servant has cut . . . become my *Property* . . . The *labour* that was mine, removing them out of that common state they were in, hath *fixed* my *Property* in them.'[27] Because the servant's labour is *my* labour, the product is mine.

What is transferred, then, is both the ability to work and the ownership of the work itself; and, consequently, the value added by the work. The only *measure* of the net transfer of powers which is provided by the market is the excess of the value added by the work over the wage paid; these material factors are the only factors that the market can measure. The importance of this limitation will appear shortly.

The transfer of powers is a continuous transfer between non-owners and owners of the means of labour, which starts as soon as and lasts as long as there are separate classes of owners and non-owners; not a momentary transfer occurring at the time of that separation. Once the separation has taken place, the non-owners of capital must transfer their labour-power repeatedly (week by week or month by month or whatever the contractual period is), so that the transfer is continuous. In other words, the continuous transfer of powers is a result of, but is not to be confused with, the cumulative specific legal transfers of ownership or rights in land and capital that had been made at assignable times in the past, by whatever mixture of conquest, force, fraud, and fair market dealing.

The amount of the continuous transfer of a man's power, the amount he has to pay for access to the means of labour, I have previously described as the amount by which his power is diminished. That, it must now be said, is an understatement of the diminution. To show the extent of the understatement it will be convenient to distinguish between *productive* and *extra-productive* power. A man's productive power (or labour-power, as I have used that term) is his ability use his

[27] *Second Treatise of Government*, sect. 28. Locke, holding that almost the whole value of any commodity was created by labour, maintained that the labour entitled its owner to the whole value of the commodity. For Marx's view, see Essay VII, penultimate paragraph.

energies and capacities in the production of material goods. His extra-productive power is his ability to use his energies and capacities for all other purposes, that is, his ability to engage in activities which are simply a direct source of enjoyment and not a means of material production.

The amount of the continuous transfer of power can now be seen to fall short of the whole diminution of a man's power in two respects: it leaves out part of the diminution of his productive power, and it leaves out the whole of any related diminution of his extra-productive power. Let us look at these in turn.

First, the transfer leaves out of account part of the amount by which a man's productive power is diminished by virtue of his lack of access to the means of labour. For the amount of power transferred can be only the amount that is given up by the seller *and received* by the buyer. The amount received by the buyer can only be measured in material terms: it is the amount of exchange-value (whether in money terms or real terms) that can be added by the work to the materials on which it is applied, and be realized in the value of the product. Since that is the only amount that is both given and received, it is the whole amount of the transfer. But that leaves out of account the value that cannot be *transferred* but is nevertheless *lost* by the man who, lacking access, has to sell his labour-power, namely, the value of the satisfaction he could have got from using it himself if he had been able to use it himself. The possibility of this satisfaction is denied to the man who has to sell his labour-power (at least to the extent that the way he is required to use his capacities differs from the way he might have chosen to do, which for most sellers of labour-power is something like the whole extent). But the possibility of this satisfaction is an integral part of a man's power as a democratic theory must define it, that is, of his ability to use his capacities and exert his energies humanly, in accordance with his own conscious design. The seller loses this satisfaction-value, but it is not transferred to the buyer.

In other words, although the seller indeed transfers the whole of his labour-power, the whole control of his productive capacities, for the contracted time, he can transfer only part of the value it would have had if he had been able to keep it; the rest of that value is simply lost, and is lost by virtue of the fact that he has to sell. If he were able to keep his labour-power and use it himself, its value would be the satisfaction value *plus* the value which its application added to the materials on which it was applied. Only the latter value can be transferred; that is precisely the value that is transferred from seller to buyer when labour-power is sold; and that is the amount that the market measures. Thus the amount transferred is only part of the amount lost by the seller: the transfer does not measure the whole diminution of his productive power.

The second respect in which it is an understatement to treat the payment for access to the means of labour as measuring the whole amount by which a man's power is diminished by lack of access, is that the payment for access to the means of labour measures only (some of) the resulting diminution of a man's *productive* power. It leaves out of account the possible effect on his *extra-productive* power, that is, his ability to engage in all sorts of activities beyond those devoted to the production of goods for consumption, to engage in activities which are simply a direct satisfaction to him as a doer, as an exerter of (and enjoyer of the exertion of) his human capacities, and not a means to other (consumer) satisfactions. Yet a man's extra-productive power is, by the democratic concept of man's essence, at least as important as his productive power. Even when we have taken into account the absolute *loss* of human value brought about by the control of a man's own productive capacities being lost to him, as well as the market-measured amount of the current *transfer* of the material value of his productive power, and the two together are treated as the measure of the deficiency in a man's productive power, this still is no measure of the deficiency in a man's whole power, his whole ability to use and develop his capacities.

For the presumption is that the way one's capacities are used in the process of production will have some effect on one's ability to use and develop one's capacities outside the process of production. A man whose productive labour is out of his own control, whose work is in that sense mindless, may be expected to be somewhat mindless in the rest of his activities. He cannot even be said to retain automatically the control of whatever energies he has left over from his working time, if his control centre, so to speak, is impaired by the use that it made of him during his working time. Any such diminution of a man's control over his extra-productive activities is clearly a diminution of his power over and above the amount of the transfer.

Before concluding the argument on impediments and their measurement we should consider the possibility that a change in men's productive powers might be offset by an accompanying change in their extra-productive powers. It might be argued (and this argument is implicit in some liberal theories[28] which seek to reconcile capitalist market society with democratic values) that when men's extra-productive powers are brought into account there may be a gain in their whole power in spite of the diminution of their productive power.

Suppose—and this is historically a realistic supposition—that the separation of labour-power and capital has the effect of increasing the

[28] e.g. Chapman's, discussed in Essay IV.

level of productivity, so that less exertion of human energy is needed to provide an acceptable level of material means of life, thus leaving more energy for the extra-productive use and development of capacities. The men whose productive power had been diminished by their loss of access to capital might then be said to have had their extra-productive power increased; and it could be supposed to have been increased by more than the amount of their loss of their productive power, thus leaving a net increase in their power.

This kind of calculation, typically utilitarian, overlooks the unreality of dividing a single human being's activities into two separate parts as if they had no effect on each other. Such a calculation not only separates analytically, productive and extra-productive uses of capacities, but treats them as independent variables. It sets up two profit-and-loss accounts, one for each of the two departments into which the operations of the maximizing individual (now dividual) are separated, and adds them together to get a net profit or loss. This does some violence to the human individual. But we cannot on those grounds dismiss any such calculation out of hand. For the market society in fact does just this violence to the individual: he is compelled to see himself as thus divided, and to make that kind of calculation.

Let us grant, then, that changes in the amounts of men's productive and extra-productive powers may be balanced. Let us grant also the historical accuracy of the supposition that capitalism, which requires the separation of labour-power and capital, and hence a continuous transfer of powers, has, by inducing technological progress, on the whole released some human energies for other than productive uses (a proposition which Mill, for one, would not grant).[29] It still does not follow that there could be, in spite of the transfer of powers, a net increase in men's powers in the sense required by the liberal-democratic theory. For as we have seen, the democratic concept of man's essence requires that men's powers be measured by their deficiency from a supposed present maximum, not by their increase over some previous level. Historical comparisons are beside the point.

This is not a trick of definition. It is simply another way of saying that democratic theory requires that gains in productivity and leisure be treated as gains made by, and to be enjoyed by, the whole society, and that therefore the reckoning of men's ability to use and develop their capacities must be made, at any time, against the standard of what that society as a whole can at that time afford to do by way of enabling all its members to use and develop their capacities.

[29] 'Hitherto it is questionable if all the mechanical inventions yet made have lightened the day's toil of any human being' (J. S. Mill: *Principles of Political Economy*, Book IV, chap. 6, sect. 2 (*Collected Works*, Vol. III, ed. Robson, p. 756)).

To demonstrate that men's present powers are greater than they would otherwise be because of the present separation of labour-power from capital, and in spite of the consequent continuous transfer of productive powers, one would have at least to show that the system of production based on that separation is more productive (and more productive of the kinds of goods needed to enable people to use and develop their extra-productive capacities) than any other presently feasible system. Attempts are made from time to time to show this, but in any sober view of the comparative growth rates of capitalist and socialist economies, and of the kinds of goods that are produced (and the kinds of consumer demands that are contrived) by capitalist economies, such attempts are unconvincing.

Moreover, one would have to show that the deficiency in most men's power because of their lack of control over their own productive labour (which lack is inherent in capitalist organization) does not carry over into lack of a controlling mind or will—the mindlessness I referred to above—in their extra-productive pursuits, and so to a cumulative deficiency in their power as a whole. The overall deficiency, or changes in it, cannot simply be measured by looking at changes in the length (or length and intensity) of the working day (or week). There is no simple linear relation between them, although there may be a discontinuous relation between them. A reduction of the working week from, say, sixty to forty hours may not result in any perceptible reduction of the overall deficiency. A reduction from forty to, say, ten hours a week, even though the ten hours remained mindless, might release so much time and energy as to offset, or more than offset, the debilitating effects of the mindless work. But whether it did so or not would depend on other factors, especially whether or not men had ceased to conform to the image of themselves as essentially consumers.

No simple case can be made, then, for there being an overall increase in men's powers as a result of the increase in productivity and leisure accompanying the separation of the means of labour from labour. The presumption remains that the human powers of the non-owners are diminished by their lack of conscious control over their productive and other activities.

We may notice finally an apparent difficulty about the measurability of impediments and hence of a man's power. I have argued that liberal-democratic theory must treat a man's power, in the developmental sense, as a quantity, and must measure it in terms of external impediments to the exercise of his human capacities, that is, impediments to the maximum attainable in principle at any given level of social productivity and knowledge. One impediment, namely, lack of access to the means of labour, has been shown to diminish a man's power in three respects. First, it sets up a continuous net transfer of the material value of the productive power of the non-owner to the owner of the means of labour, the amount of which transfer, in each of the repeated transactions, is the excess of the value added by the work over the wage paid. Second, it diminishes each non-owner's productive power beyond that market-measured amount, by denying him the essentially human satisfaction of controlling the use of his own productive capacities: this value is lost, not transferred. Third, it diminishes his control over his extra-productive life. Of these three deficiencies in a man's power, the first is numerically measurable and is in fact measured by the market. The other two are not so measurable.

It may seem, then, that in recognizing the last two deficiencies we have made it impossible to measure the whole deficiency. But this is not so. For the last two are measurable in the only sense required by a democratic theory. They can be seen to be greater or less in different individuals, and greater or less for classes of individuals in different models of society. Since those deficiencies are the result of lack of access to the means of labour they can in principle be increased or decreased for any class of individuals by the society altering the terms on which access is to be had. And increase or decrease is the only degree of quantification needed by a democratic theory, whose claim is to increase (or provide the maximum) ability to use and develop human capacities.

We are left, however, with the question whether increases and decreases in the powers of all the individual members of a society can be added together to reach an aggregate which can be shown to be greater or less under one set of arrangements than under another. If we cannot do this we cannot speak of the maximization of powers within a whole society.

5. *The Maximization of Aggregate Powers*

We may begin by noticing that the well-known logical difficulty of maximizing aggregate *utilities*[30] does not apply to maximizing *powers*, in the developmental sense of powers. The difficulty about maximizing utilities is that it involves estimating whether changes in the distribution of different goods between persons would add more satisfaction for some persons than it would subtract from them and from others. One would have to be able to add and subtract changes in the amount of satisfactions or utilities enjoyed by different persons. One would therefore have to have a single measuring scale on which to compare utilities between persons. But this is impossible in principle, since the measure of satisfactions is inherently subjective: each person's judgement of his

[30] Above, p. 7.

own satisfaction is unique, and is incommensurable with others' judgement of theirs.

This difficulty does not apply to the maximization of powers. For a man's power, defined as the quantity of his ability to use and develop his human capacities, is measured by the quantity of external impediments to that ability, which is not a subjective quantity. It is indeed true that each person's judgement of the direct satisfaction he gets or would get from different exercises of his own capacities is a subjective judgement, and is incommensurable with others' judgement about theirs, just as incommensurable as are different persons' judgements about any utilities. But what has to be measured here is not the satisfaction they get from any exercise of their capacities but their *ability* to exercise them. And that depends on the quantity of external impediments, which quantity is objectively though not always numerically measurable. The basic logical difficulty of inter-personal comparison of satisfactions is thus irrelevant to the maximization of powers.

Nevertheless, there may still remain a difficulty about the conception of maximizing powers. What if the increase of some men's powers (ability to use and develop their essentially human capacities) is possible only by a reduction of others'? This need not generally be the case with powers in the developmental sense, though it is generally so for powers in the extractive sense. Some general rules which increase some men's developmental powers also increase, or at least do not decrease, everyone else's. This is most evident in relation to our third category of impediments, the direct invasion of one man by others. An improvement in the laws, or the enforcement of the laws, against the direct invasion of one man by another, affects everyone in the same direction. What increases my protection against you increases your protection against me. No man's power to use his human capacities is diminished, but every man's power is increased, by laws which prevent the direct invasion of one man by another.

But a change in the rules governing access to the means of labour or in the rules governing the distribution of the means of life, that is, a general change in the first or second category of impediments, might alter in opposite directions the ability of different individuals to use and develop their human capacities.

The most important case to consider is a change in the terms of access to capital in the direction of more nearly equal access. That would reduce the net transfer of powers, and increase the ability of those who had had inferior access. It would reduce the controlling and extractive power of those who had had superior access. It would also reduce their developmental power, their ability to use and develop their essentially human capacities, *if* the full exercise of those capacities could be shown to require the level of control of resources, or the level of income and leisure, which they had had by virtue of their extractive power. But this cannot generally be shown, for the income and leisure resulting from extractive power are not automatically conducive to the development of essentially human capacities. The presumption, I think, is to the contrary. I should argue that they can be so conducive only in a special case, or in what was once but is no longer the general case. A century or two ago, and for centuries before that, it could honestly be held that the cultivated man was the extractive man: that without a class which lived by its extractive power there could be no development of human excellence. Even that proposition was sometimes denied in the earlier centuries, notably by the spokesman of the yeomanry and small independent enterprisers in seventeenth-century England.[31] But generally, until the nineteenth century, it could reasonably be maintained that, with the apparently inexorable material scarcity, there could be no significant development of human capacities except by members of an extractive class. Spokesmen of that class might be quite conscious, as Adam Smith and Burke, Diderot and Bentham were, that the developmental power they valued was based on extractive power, but, in the circumstances of confined economic productivity they saw about them, they judged that this was inevitably the price of any human progress.

In the twentieth century, however, which even the pessimistic now see as an era of potential plenty, this is no longer the case. The justification of extractive power by developmental power no longer holds. The only case where it might still be argued that income and leisure resulting from extractive power can be conducive to the extractor's developmental power is when he lacks any consciousness that his income and leisure are being extracted from others. That was the position of most of the extractors in the nineteenth century, and they were supported in that position by the nineteenth-century economists, who could argue that capitalist enterprise was so productive that everyone was better off, and who could quite lose sight of the transfer of powers it involved. It is still the position of some twentieth-century liberals, who thus offer moral support to the continuance of at least a modified extractive power. Their inability to see the transfer of powers or the extractive power may be traced to their still thinking of men as infinite consumers, whose essential human wants are best served by a system highly productive of consumer goods, rather than as essentially exerters and developers of their uniquely human capacities. I have argued that this position is increasingly untenable in the twentieth century. Those who find it untenable will also think that the extractors' lack of consciousness of the extractive base of their own income and leisure is now

[31] Notably the Levellers, cf. *Political Theory of Possessive Individualism*, chap. III.

scarcely consistent with a fully human use of their capacities: in other words, that their power can scarcely be called developmental power. At least, on the assumption which I have argued is required in any fully democratic theory, namely, that essentially human capacities are only those which can be exercised without denying or impeding other men's exercise of theirs, activities which were seen to be made possible only by the exercise of extractive power could not be called an exercise of essentially human capacities.

Nevertheless, the extractors themselves, or at least their liberal supporters, still regard their power as developmental power, as ability to use and develop their human capacities. Let us therefore pursue the question on that assumption. Let us set aside any dehumanizing or counter-humanizing effect of the extractive basis of a man's power and treat his whole power as developmental power. We are back then at the position that a change in a society's arrangements about access to the means of labour in the direction of more nearly equal access, which would reduce the extractive power of those who had had superior access, would reduce their developmental power. Moreover, having set aside any counter-humanizing effects of extractive power, we should have to assume that on the whole those who had had a superior position had enlarged their own human capacities. And it could be presumed that the full exercise of those enlarged capacities would require the continuance of the level of income and leisure they had had by virtue of their extractive power. Thus a reduction of their extractive power would be a reduction of their higher-than-average developmental power. Clearly, then, a change to more nearly equal access to the means of labour, which would increase the developmental powers of those who had had inferior access, would decrease the developmental powers of those who had had superior access, and the decrease would be in enlarged powers. This is a genuine difficulty for a democratic theory which sets as its goal the maximization of powers of the members of a society as a whole, at least if the necessary step of moving towards equal access to the means of labour is contemplated before there is general agreement that developmental power is inconsistent with extractive power.

The difficulty amounts to this: we do have to make inter-personal comparisons, to add and subtract quantitative changes in different persons' powers. It is a real difficulty, but not an insuperable one. We have already seen that inter-personal comparison of powers, unlike inter-personal comparison of utilities, is not impossible in principle. How great is the difficulty of weighing some men's decrease against some men's increase of powers?

In the first place we should notice that the difficulty arises at all only in the *transition* from an unequal to a more nearly equal society (or indeed from an unequal to an even more unequal society). It would not arise in a society which had already established equal access to the means of life and the means of labour. For the difficulty consists in having to weigh against each other some men's increase and some men's decrease caused by a given change in the institutions, and the only change that can bring about simultaneous decreases and increases is a change in the level of extractive power, that is, in the permitted extent to which some have power over others for the former's benefit. But extractive power is a function of unequal access to the means of labour and of life: extractive power can only be maintained (short of permanent military occupation) by maintaining unequal access. In a society which has achieved equal access, there is no extractive power. In such a society, men's developmental powers might still be increased, but this increase would be achieved by increased command over external Nature, not (by the hypothesis of equal access) by increased command over others. An increase in the ability of any persons to use and develop their capacities would not be accompanied by a decrease for any others. The problem of weighing decreases against increases would not be present.

When this is understood, it can be seen that there is no inconsistency between (i) our recognition that in certain circumstances a change which increases some men's ability to exercise their human capacities may decrease others', and (ii) the assertion, made earlier,[32] that it is a necessary postulate of a fully democratic theory that the exercise of his essentially human capacities by any member of a society does not hinder any other members exercising theirs. The two positions are consistent in that the possible opposition of the exercise of capacities recognized in (i) is to be found only in the transition to a fully democratic society, not in a fully democratic society; whereas (ii), although asserted perfectly generally, could be realized only in a fully democratic society (in which extractive powers, which by the democratic concept are not required for the exercise of essentially human capacities, are reduced to zero).

The postulate of the non-opposition of the use of essentially human capacities appears, in the light of this analysis, to be less presumptuous and more tenable than it may have seemed when first stated. For it comes down to the postulate that a fully democratic society cannot permit the operation of any extractive power, and that a society without any extractive power is possible. The serious difficulty about a democratic society is not how to run it but how to reach it.

We are left, then, with the difficulty of weighing increases against decreases of developmental powers in any move from a society of unequal access to the means of life and labour to a society of equal

[32] Above, p. 55.

access. The difficulty, we saw, was that the beneficiaries of extractive power in an unequal society may be assumed to have developed their human capacities further than the non-beneficiaries could have done, so that any reduction of their extractive power and hence of their command of resources and leisure would reduce their developmental power, their ability to use and develop their already expanded capacities fully. The question is whether such a loss would be as great as the others' gain.

The question can be answered, and is answered in the negative, on two grounds. First, in the society of unequal access, as we have seen, those who lacked access had their powers diminished by *more* than the amount of the net transfer, i.e. by more than the amount extracted. They were continuously losing more of their powers than those who had access were gaining. There was an absolute loss of human powers. In the postulated move to a society of equal access this loss would disappear. Those who had lacked access would gain not only the amount of power which had been extracted and transferred from them (which is all that those who had had superior access would now lose) but would gain, in addition to that, the human power which had been absolutely lost. Thus the aggregate gain would be greater than the aggregate loss. Secondly, we must notice that the gains and losses are in abilities to use *and develop* human capacities fully. By hypothesis, the beneficiaries of extractive power in the unequal society have developed their capacities further than have the non-beneficiaries. Now even if we assume that there are differences in different men's maximum capacities (an assumption which some liberals would not make),[33] we cannot know at the given time what those differences are. But the presumption must surely be that the capacities of those who had had inferior access to the means of life and labour would be more underdeveloped, would have more deficiency to make up, than the capacities of those who had had superior access. A move to more nearly equal access, which is a move to more nearly equal ability to use and develop capacities, will therefore be expected to bring more gain than loss in the aggregate ability to develop human capacities. In short, to equalize access, which is to equalize developmental powers, is to maximize developmental powers.

A final difficulty may be noticed about the concept of maximization of powers. All these calculations of gains and losses, it may be objected, are much too mechanical. They purport to deal with ability to use and develop essentially human capacities, but they do so only in terms of the

[33] Cf. Adam Smith: 'The difference of natural talents in different men is, in reality, much less than we are aware of . . . The difference between the most dissimilar characters, between a philosopher and a common street porter, for example, seems to arise not so much from nature, as from habit, custom, and education' (*Wealth of Nations*, Bk. I, chap. 2, penult. para.).

external impediments to that ability. What, it may be asked, of internalized impediments? What of the phenomenon of men hugging their chains? And what of those who have become slaves of their own possessions? No such internalized impediments, it is true, are directly taken into the calculus of maximization as set out here. And clearly, in any operational view, they are of great importance, as thinkers from Rousseau to Marcuse have pointed out.

To this objection the first reply must be that the impediments were external before they were internalized, that they could only be internalized because they already existed as external impediments. The external impediments, palpable, rooted in class, remain basic and deserve the first attention. This is not of course a sufficient reply to the objection. For it does not follow that the internalized impediments will disintegrate in the measure that the external impediments are shown to be no longer required by or consistent with civilized society. They must not only be *shown* to be no longer required, they must be *seen* to be no longer required, and seen so by the very people in whom they have been internalized, before any action sufficient to remove or reduce the external impediments can be expected.

We appear to be in a vicious circle: neither kind of impediment can be diminished without a prior diminution of the other. It may be so. It may be that the impediments have been so internalized, backed by all the resources of those who think it their interest to reduce men to infinite consumers, that there is no way out, or no way short of an indefinite destruction of some of the freedoms essential to a fully human society. But this is not necessarily so.

It may also be that the process of reciprocal reinforcement of external and internal impediments, which has been going on in one way or another since the beginning of modern market society, can work reciprocally in reverse. A partial breakdown of the political order (national or international) of the market society, or a partial breakthrough of consciousness, might either of them put the process in reverse, setting off the other, provided that the other was ready to respond. Partial breakdowns of the political order have become frequent in market societies, and can be expected to continue so. Pressures against the image of a man as consumer, and against the cult of economic growth at whatever cost to the environment and the quality of life, are also building up, so that a sufficient partial breakthrough of consciousness is not out of the question. In these circumstances it seems well worthwhile to press rational analysis of the external impediments, which are analytically more manageable than internalized impediments, in the hope of contributing to the breakthrough of consciousness, and so to a cumulative reciprocal reduction of both kinds of impediment, and a cumulative realization of democracy.

ESSAY IV
Revisionist Liberalism

THE preceding essays are I hope sufficient to demonstrate (i) that the traditional justificatory theory of liberal-democracy is in some disrepair; (ii) that this is due largely to its attempt to carry into the period of mature capitalist society a combination of market postulates and egalitarian humanist principles which were not strictly tenable together even when first compounded a century or more ago, and which are now more evidently incompatible; and (iii) that a non-market democratic theory which retains the ethically valuable liberal principles is, although not without difficulties, conceivable.

I should put it, on the basis of Essay III, that the difficulties of any non-market theory of democracy which can still significantly be called liberal, are demanding but not insuperable: this will be argued further in Essay VI in the context of the political theory of property. But it will be appropriate now to consider some current attempts to reformulate liberal-democratic theory while retaining market principles. I shall suggest that the difficulties of these attempts *are* insuperable.

There is a considerable range of reformulations of liberal-democratic theory which might be discussed under the head of revisionist liberal theory. It could properly include the current empiricist theories of democracy, for although superficially they are of a different order from the justificatory liberal theories they seek to replace, claiming (as they do) to be explanatory only, they are in effect justificatory as well. They offer, as realism, a savage revision, almost obliteration, of the democratic content of traditional liberal-democratic theory, with a view to reformulating its liberal market content: it is revisionist liberalism at its most extreme,[1] though a travesty of what used to be thought of as democracy.

However, I shall not attempt to review here either the empirical theory or the current counter-attack on it, which is being ably conducted by a number of penetrating critics.[2] My main concern will be with some of the principles of leading contemporary normative theorists who are reformulating something like the traditional liberal-

[1] Except for Milton Friedman's liberalism, discussed in Essay VII.

[2] Mostly in journal articles, many of them conveniently brought together in three recent collections: Charles A. McCoy and John Playford (ed.): *Apolitical Politics, a Critique of Behaviouralism* (New York, 1967); William E. Connolly (ed.): *The Bias of Pluralism* (New York, 1969); Henry S. Kariel (ed.): *Frontiers of Democratic Theory* (New York, 1970).

democratic theory. But I shall begin by drawing attention to one merit of the prevailing empirical theory which is generally overlooked: for all its shallowness, the empirical theory has a valuable lesson to teach the would-be revivers of traditional liberal theory, a lesson which is usually lost behind their urgent concern about the empiricists' assault on moral values.

1. *The Lesson of Empiricism*

The empirical theory of democracy, which has become the prevalent view, was first clearly formulated by Schumpeter[3] in 1942, and is now conveniently typified by Dahl.[4] The empiricists mounted a heavy attack on what they called the 'traditional' or 'classical' theory of democracy, by which they meant the liberal-democratic theory, traced back variously but generally typified by John Stuart Mill.

There is no doubt about the violence done to the traditional theory by what we may call the Schumpeter-Dahl axis. The traditional theory of Mill, carried over into the twentieth century by such writers as A. D. Lindsay and Ernest Barker, gave democracy a moral dimension: it saw democracy as developmental, as a matter of the improvement of mankind. The Schumpeter-Dahl axis, on the contrary, treats democracy as a mechanism, the essential function of which is to maintain an equilibrium. I have argued elsewhere that the Schumpeter-Dahl theory is wholly inadequate as a general theory of democracy in the twentieth century, and even as a general theory of Western democracy.[5] But here I want to suggest that the violence it has done to the traditional theory is salutary, or will be if it drives the proponents and reformulators of traditional theory to re-examine its assumptions.

Let us be clear, to begin with, in what this violence consists. The model of democracy that has been raised to orthodoxy in American political science is indeed destructive of the original liberal-democratic idea. It is counter-democratic (by the older concept of democracy) in that it empties out, as being normative, unrealistic, or utopian, the egalitarian and developmental moral ideal of the original liberal-democratic theory, and accepts as an adequate model (and proclaims as the only accurate model) of democracy, a competition between two or more élite groups for the power to govern the whole society. Democracy is held to be consistent with, and even to require, a low level of citizen participation: only so, it is said, is the political system likely to stay in equilibrium. Democracy is reduced from a humanist aspiration to a

[3] Joseph A. Schumpeter: *Capitalism, Socialism, and Democracy* (New York, 1942).

[4] Robert A. Dahl: *A Preface to Democratic Theory* (Chicago, Ill., 1956).

[5] See my *The Real World of Democracy*, and Essays IX and X below.

market equilibrium system. And although the new orthodox theory claims scientific neutrality, its value judgement is clear enough: whatever works, is right—that is, whatever enables the existing class-stratified society to operate without intolerable friction is best.

This is indeed a striking reversal of the original nineteenth-century liberal-democratic theory. It is an even more striking departure from the truly classical concept of democracy, democracy as it was understood from Plato to the early nineteenth century, when both the supporters and opponents of democracy were clear that democracy was the cry of the oppressed, their claim for recognition as equally human beings. Both in the classical concept of democracy and the so-called 'traditional', that is, the liberal-democratic nineteenth-century concept, democracy was seen as a means by which, or a society in which, all men could enjoy and develop their human capacities. All this is rejected as irrelevant by the exponents of the new American orthodoxy. For them, democracy is simply a means by which men as they are now can register their wants as political consumers in the political market.

We should, however, not be too hasty in condemning this view. Shallow it certainly is. But it builds on, and thus reveals, one of the two contradictory assumptions that lie at the root of the traditional liberal-democratic theory. Perhaps the exponents of the new orthodoxy should not be blamed, but praised, for having drawn out the logical consequences of one of the assumptions of traditional liberal-democratic theory, and thus having revealed, however unconsciously, the grave weakness in that theory. The weakness may be stated in various ways. I have stated it in the previous essays as a failure to differentiate between two concepts of power, or between two concepts of the essence of man. The now traditional theory, when it was new (in the nineteenth century), tried, I have said, to introduce a new (or reintroduce an old, pre-Hobbesian) concept of the power of a man as his ability to use and develop his uniquely human capacities, but, so strong was the Utilitarian bias, it could not give up the concept of a man's power as his ability to command the services of others. Or, to put the same point in a different way, it tried to introduce, or reintroduce, a concept of man as essentially a doer, an exerter, and enjoyer of his human attributes, and yet was unable to break away from the Utilitarian liberal concept of man as a consumer of utilities, for whom a share of power of any sort (wealth, or the power to command the services of others) is valued primarily as a means to a future flow of utilities to him from outside himself.

The latter is precisely the concept of man that is taken for granted by the new twentieth-century orthodoxy. The Schumpeter-Dahl axis is based on the implicit postulate that man is essentially a consumer of utilities, and it proceeds by assuming that any realistic and honest liberal-democratic theory will treat men so. The point is, of course, that where and when and in so far as men *do* behave as consumers rather than exerters, democracy *is* reduced to a means of letting people have some indirect say in who gets what, when, and how: in that case, the Schumpeter-Dahl model makes very good sense. The trouble with the traditional liberal-democratic theory is that, while it has always asserted a nobler democratic concept of man, it has also accepted a model of society which entails that men behave as consumers.

If twentieth-century exponents and revisers of traditional liberal-democratic theory are to rescue democratic theory from the behavioural axis, they will have to re-examine the ambivalent model of man and society that lies at the root of the traditional theory. The empirical theorists will have done some service to the retrieval of democratic theory if it is seen that their *reductio ad absurdum* of democracy is simply the logical outcome of their sticking to the postulate that man is essentially a consumer. This has not yet generally been seen. It has been missed by most of those who are now seeking to revise and reinstate something like the traditional liberal-democratic theory. Two of those who may be called revisionist liberals in the full normative sense, whose work has recently attracted considerable attention, are John W. Chapman and John Rawls. Their effective reformulations of liberal theory deserve our attention now.

2. *Chapman's Revisionist Liberalism*

Professor Chapman has expounded and examined various implications of a modern theory of liberal democracy in a series of articles,[6] a full appreciation of which is beyond the scope of this essay. But one of his articles—'Natural Rights and Justice in Liberalism'—demands notice here because it is, in direct confrontation of my views, an effort to demonstrate the theoretical and moral coherence of liberalism, and because it does so with considerable economy, employing a theoretical model of a liberal society which can be fairly precisely examined.

His case is that a practicable model of a liberal democratic society can be constructed in which 'the principles of justice, the criteria of economic rationality, and the claims of moral freedom may be conceived as theoretically consistent' (p. 35); or, that a liberal theory based on a

[6] Notably: 'Justice and Fairness', in Carl J. Friedrich and John W. Chapman (eds.): *Justice, Nomos VI* (New York, 1963); 'Natural Rights and Justice in Liberalism', in D. D. Raphael (ed.): *Political Theory and the Rights of Man* (London, 1967); 'Voluntary Associations and the Political Theory of Pluralism', in J. Roland Pennock and John W. Chapman (eds.): *Voluntary Associations, Nomos XI* (New York, 1969); 'The Moral Foundations of Political Obligation', in J. Roland Pennock and John W. Chapman (eds.): *Political and Legal Obligation, Nomos XII* (New York, 1970).

principle of equal natural rights of the individual is capable of accommodating 'the criteria of economic rationality, the claims of moral freedom, and the principles of justice' (p. 42). Although these three terms are not precisely defined, their meaning is fairly clear.

The criterion of economic rationality he takes to be the 'optimum allocation of resources, including persons', the optimum allocation apparently being that which maximizes the production of the utilities (goods and services) in the proportions actually demanded by consumers in accordance with 'the principle of consumers' sovereignty' (p. 35).

'The claims of moral freedom' he equates with 'men's [equal] rights to make the best of themselves' (p. 35), that is, with the claim to let men equally realize their human capacities. Chapman is thus in effect arguing that there is no necessary inconsistency, within a liberal theory, between the maximization of utilities and the maximization of men's equal powers.

'The principles of justice' are not fully stated but appear by implication. The main principle which he seems to endorse is the negative principle he quotes from Rawls: 'inequalities are arbitrary [i.e. unjust] unless it is reasonable to expect that they will work out for everyone's advantage' (p. 33). This is also phrased: 'any degree of inequality, in order to qualify as just [,] must optimize' (p. 39); to optimize being to provide 'optimum allocation of resources, including persons' (p. 35), i.e. the allocation which maximizes the production of utilities in the proportions actually demanded by consumers (or, in accordance with the principle of consumers' sovereignty). Justice not only *permits* such inequality but *requires* it: a reduction of inequality which would hinder that optimum allocation 'would produce injustice' (p. 35). The first principle of justice thus appears to be the distribution of benefits which maximizes benefits in accordance with the principle of consumers' sovereignty.

It is not entirely clear how far Chapman here accepts Rawls's principle. He had in an earlier paper[7] criticized Rawls's concept of justice as inadequate in that it reduced justice to reciprocal agreement and thus denied that there are any 'rights so fundamental that they cannot be bargained away', such as 'the right to moral freedom'. He complained that 'Rawls's concept of justice has swallowed the concept of rights.' Chapman in the present paper guards himself against such narrowness by setting up 'equal moral freedom' alongside justice, rather than by broadening Rawls's concept of justice: he seems to find the latter acceptable provided it is supplemented by a separate principle of moral freedom. One might, in turn, complain of Chapman that, as I

[7] 'Justice and Fairness', pp. 166–7.

shall argue, his concept of economic rationality swallows up (or at least vitiates) his concepts both of justice and of moral freedom.

A second principle of justice is also defined negatively: a system is unjust if 'the material well-being of the few is purchased at the expense of the many' (p. 30), or if it is 'invasive' (p. 34), i.e. permits one to gain at the expense of another. Thus the second principle is that justice requires that no one shall gain at the expense of another.

Chapman is willing to grant that, historically, liberal societies may have been invasive. We are agreed that, in his words, 'a class system based on private property, [where] wealth, power, and authority all mesh together for the benefit of the classes in which they are concentrated . . . is "invasive", oligopolistic, and unjust in that the well-being of the few is purchased at the expense of the many, even as, Rousseau would say, the welfare and moral freedom of all suffer' (p. 30). But Chapman argues 'that a liberal society, whatever may have been the historical case, is not as a matter of principle morally defective or incoherent' (p. 35). He thinks it is possible to have a liberal society based, as I have taken it to be based, on private ownership of capital and market incentives (for his ideal liberal society is based on these), without invasiveness or injustice. Accordingly, he finds my model of 'possessive market society', with its inherent contentiousness and invasiveness, unconvincing as a statement of the necessary relations of any liberal-democratic capitalist society. He is therefore not persuaded that, as I have argued, any liberal-democratic theory which retains and justifies capitalist market relations must be internally inconsistent.

In order to show the possibility of a non-invasive liberal market society, he offers, in place of my inherently invasive model, another model (in two variants) of a theoretically conceivable liberal society in which the claims of economic rationality are said to be consistent with the claims of moral freedom and the principles of justice, and in which he sees no transfer of powers or invasiveness.

Consider an economy in which returns to capital are taxed from the owners, in part invested, and the remainder distributed in the form of free public services available to all. Assume further that there is full equality of opportunity, unrestricted competition for the position of 'owner', which is now rather that of 'manager', and that both workers and owners receive their marginal value productivity and are compensated for disutility. Their incomes would not be equal, and the differential would reflect not only differences in productivity but also the equalizing increase in real incomes from the free services. This inequality is now seen as being dictated by the requirements of economic rationality. It would hardly seem appropriate to say that it 'measures' a 'transfer' of 'powers'. On the contrary, the 'powers' of both workers and owners have been mutually enhanced; the income inequality performs an allocative function; it is the result of processes which are both competitive and optimizing. (p. 29)

We notice that this model stipulates private ownership of capital, and also the economic rationality of a capitalist system, i.e. a competitive market for capital and labour, in separate hands, which distributes rewards to both according to the marginal productivity of the units of capital and labour actually employed in profitably meeting consumer demands. The model would produce unequal incomes, but these are said not to be due to any transfer of powers, and not to be invasive.

Now if this model is to reconcile economic rationality, the claims of moral freedom, and the principles of justice, it must do at least three things. (a) It must show that its economic rationality does not necessarily produce a net transfer of powers[8] from non-owners to owners, for this transfer would offend against the principle of moral freedom and the second principle of justice. (b) It must show that its economic rationality does not entail any other kind of economic relation between non-owners and owners which would offend against the principle of equal moral freedom. And (c) it must show that its distributive justice is consistent with the principle of equal moral freedom. Chapman's model fails on all three counts, as I think must any model that stipulates private ownership of capital and treats justice as primarily a matter of distribution of income. We may look at each of the three counts in turn.

(a) In order to eliminate from his model the invasiveness of a net transfer of powers, Chapman stipulates that 'returns to capital are taxed from the owners' and, after allowance for socially desirable reinvestment, are distributed as free public services. It is not clear whether this means that the whole amount of returns to capital is taxed away or only some part of them. But in neither case could the claims both of economic rationality and of justice be satisfied.

If, as seems more probable (in view of his suggestion on p. 34 'that one would wish to recover, so far as is practicable, and to redistribute intra-marginal rents'), he means that only part of the returns to capital is taxed away, economic rationality could still operate but his principle of justice would not be satisfied, since the part not taxed away would still be the product of a transfer of powers from non-owners to owners, which is unjust in that it is one man gaining at the expense of another.

If on the other hand he means that the whole returns to capital are

[8] The concept of a 'net transfer of powers' was set out in my *The Political Theory of Possessive Individualism*, pp. 56–7, and *The Real World of Democracy*, pp. 41–4, and is reconsidered in Essays I (at pp. 10–14, 16 ff) and III (at pp. 64–66) above. Chapman appears not to have understood it fully; only the first of those statements of it was available to him when he wrote.

taxed away (which would cancel the income shift resulting from the net transfer of powers), how could economic rationality in his society of private capital possibly operate? A system which rewards owners according to the marginal productivity of their capital, and then taxes the reward away, is *not* effectively rewarding them according to the marginal productivity of their capital. Consequently, it does not appear to meet the criterion of economic rationality. At one point, indeed, Chapman seems to grant that the requirements of economic rationality and of justice are inconsistent: in a variant of his model (p. 34) he assumes that in an ideal liberal society it would be necessary 'to correct for justice the distribution of income implied by economic rationality', though he apparently holds that 'the criteria of economic efficiency' are not 'sharply' but 'merely marginally' incompatible with justice (loc. cit.). And he clearly holds that this 'marginal' incompatibility can be overcome by income transfers made by a welfare state.

It is difficult to see how this could be done. How could the market perform its function of allocating resources optimally among different uses (which economic rationality expects it to do, by rewarding owners proportionally to their success in employing their resources optimally) when the rewards of whatever size are reduced to zero?

(b) But suppose that this hurdle is surmounted. Suppose, which is not inconceivable, that capitalists would go on investing, and trying to invest optimally, even with a zero effective rate of return, just for the sake of controlling the game. The position then would be that they would continue to control the game. The society would still be, in Chapman's sense, which is the important sense, oligopolistic. His stipulations that there must be full equality of opportunity and unrestricted competition for the position of owner do not help his case. For, apart from their being doubtfully consistent with unequal ownership of resources, they are in any case irrelevant to the existence of oligopoly. They do not alter the fact that there would be a class of owners, and that it would control, by virtue of its ownership, the allocation of human resources as well as material resources. 'Genuine equality of opportunity' does not, in a system based on private ownership, do away with classes: it does not 'enforce the absence of those non-competing groups known as classes', as Chapman assumes it would do (p. 31); it simply allows more mobility between classes.

Economic rationality in a system of private ownership of capital requires that owners be rewarded for using their resources, or allowing them to be used, in the production of goods wanted by the members of the society considered as consumers. The more rationally the owners are so rewarded, the more concentrated their control will become. To see this, we must look at both possible meanings of Chapman's stipulation that returns to capital are taxed away.

(i) If less than all the return to capital is taxed away, the normal process of capital accumulation through investment of profits continues, and capital tends to become concentrated in fewer and larger corporations. In spite of, or rather because of, the well-known diffusion of ownership of corporate stocks in an affluent society, the control of the capital remains concentrated: the more diffused among many small holders the shares of a corporation are, the easier it is for a few substantial holders who own only a small fraction of the whole to control it all.

(ii) If *all* the returns to capital are taxed away, there are still two possible outcomes, depending on what is counted as 'returns to capital'. It would make a great deal of difference whether this included all profits, or whether part of profits was counted as the reward for enterprise or risk-taking, not as returns to capital. Again, it would make a considerable difference whether the returns to capital were counted after allowance for reinvesting out of profits *only* the amount needed to replace the real capital used up or depreciated in producing that profit, or whether any investment out of profits for purposes of *expanding* the enterprise were allowed before returns to capital were calculated. If some of the profits were retained as being, in either of these ways, not 'returns to capital', the outcome would be the same increasing concentration as in the case where less than all the returns to capital is taxed away.

Although Chapman does not specify which of the possible constructions of 'returns to capital' he has in mind, it seems most probable that it would not include reward for enterprise; and it would be most in keeping with his general market model if 'returns to capital' also excluded profits reinvested for expansion of production, since the merit of the model is supposed to be that it does maximize productivity.

However, even if his stipulation that returns to capital are taxed away means that all profits are to be taxed away, the tendency to concentration would still operate. True, if no firm could retain any of its profits, the successful firms could not reinvest any of theirs: capital could not become more concentrated in that way. But in that model, some firms would, in the normal course of competition in efficiency at meeting (or at creating and meeting) consumer demands, fail. They will either go out of business or will be taken over by their more successful competitors. In either case, the mass of capital becomes more concentrated. Nor could the place of the failed capitalists be taken by thrusters coming into the game. Even if they could borrow enough capital to get into the game, they could not move up because, by hypothesis, all their profits are taxed away. So, in a model where all profit is taxed away, the outcome would still be an increasing concentration of capital.

In short, whether part or all of the return to capital is taxed away, the tendency towards increasing concentration of control by owners of capital will prevail. Thus, economic rationality in a system of private ownership of capital perpetuates social oligopoly.[9] And this oligopoly offends against the claims of moral freedom even if the transfer of income resulting from the transfer of powers which the separation of ownership from labour generates is assumed to be entirely counteracted by welfare-state transfers in the opposite direction. For the claims of moral freedom, as Chapman states them, require not only that there be no net transfer of powers, but also that there be no oligopolistic concentration of power to determine the kind of work and conditions or work the non-owners must do. But such concentration of power is inherent in any model based on private ownership of capital.

(c) Chapman's principle of distributive justice is, if I have understood it correctly, inconsistent with his principle of equal moral freedom. For his first principle of justice requires a distribution of benefits in accordance with not merely economic rationality but capitalist economic rationality; and capitalist rationality entails, as I have shown previously, unequal ability (as between owners and non-owners) 'to make the best of themselves', i.e. unequal moral freedom. That his principle of justice is confined within the limits of capitalist rationality can readily be seen.

Although his principle of justice is stated with complete generality —'inequalities are arbitrary [i.e. unjust] unless it is reasonable to expect that they will work out for everyone's advantage'—when he applies the principle, 'advantage' turns out to mean advantage not in comparison with *any* other arrangement but only with any other arrangement within the limits of capitalist economic rationality. We can see this by examining his crucial argument about the case where a reduction of inequality would produce injustice. The argument runs as follows. In the model of an ideal liberal society, in which the distribution of income has been corrected for justice by welfare-state redistribution (but not corrected so far as to interfere substantially with economic rationality, or to interfere at all with the pattern of ownership of resources), incomes would still be unequal. But any attempt at further equalization would produce injustice. Why? Because 'economic theory suggests that more equalization would hinder optimum allocation of resources, including persons, and would therefore encroach on the principle of consumers' sovereignty . . .' (p. 35). The economic theory that suggests this is the theory that presupposes competitive

[9] His variant model of an ideal liberal society (p. 34), which includes economic rationality but excludes 'all forms of monopolistic and oligopolistic advantage', is thus internally inconsistent.

markets in labour and privately owned capital. The whole demonstration depends on comparison of possible distributions of income within the limits of capitalist economic rationality. This of course says nothing to the question whether some other system of production and distribution could provide greater distributive justice, i.e. be more to everyone's advantage.

Chapman's model thus not only fails to reconcile his principles of economic rationality, equal moral freedom, and justice; it also fails as a justifying theory for a market-based liberal democracy. The latter failure may be ascribed to his confusing two concepts of man, in the best liberal-democratic tradition. He sees, rightly, that a liberal-democratic society must claim that it provides its members with an equal ability to make the best of themselves—this is his equal moral freedom. This implies a concept of man as exerter and developer of his human capacities. But his principle of justice embodies the concept of man as consumer: it is concerned primarily with the distribution of *income*, that is to say, with the distribution of utilities between men as consumers. This is not the same as the distribution of men's ability to use and develop their human capacities, which is the substance of men's moral freedom. Yet Chapman appears to equate them: he refers to an encroachment upon the principle of consumers' sovereignty as an encroachment 'by implication upon men's rights to make the best of themselves, upon moral freedom to the extent that this is expressed in economic activity' (p. 35). This is to confuse men's economic activity as producers with their economic activity as consumers. But his principle of equal moral freedom is not satisfied by a principle of distributive justice of income. For his equal moral freedom is the equal right of individuals to make the best of themselves. It requires, therefore, not only equal rights as consumers (or, which is all Chapman can allow, such approach to equality of income as is consistent with economic rationality), but also something like *control* of the exercise of their capacities. No liberal-democratic justifying theory can hope to be adequate in our time unless it considers people primarily as exerters and enjoyers of their human capacities, rather than as consumers of utilities.

3. *Rawls's Distributive Justice*

Professor John Rawls, in the course of a close and protracted examination of justice,[10] has set out a model of a liberal-democratic

[10] In a series of papers published in the last decade: 'Justice as Fairness' in Peter Laslett and W. G. Runciman (eds.): *Philosophy, Politics and Society, Second Series* (Oxford, 1962); 'The Sense of Justice', *Philosophical Review* (1963); 'Constitutional Liberty and the Concept of Justice', in C. J. Friedrich and J. W.

society which he believes satisfies the concept of justice for which he argues. His main concern is to show that a 'natural rights' or 'contractarian' concept of justice is preferable to a utilitarian one: it is only as part of his case for the former that he tries to show that it can be embodied in a set of institutions which best satisfy common-sense notions of justice, and so sets up a model of a just society. The model, as we shall see, is essentially a liberal-democratic capitalist welfare state.

I do not propose to add to the general critical treatments his work has already called forth,[11] which are mainly concerned with his central case for a contractarian concept. My concern is specifically with the adequacy of the model he offers as satisfying his principles of justice, and with one of the assumptions which determine the model and limit his particular principles of justice. For it is the model and the assumption which put him, whether or not he so intended, among (and indeed in the forefront of) the revisionist liberals. Rawls's argument is so elegant that the narrowness of some of his postulates may easily be overlooked. But when examined they appear inadequate to a justifying theory of liberal democracy in much the same way as are Professor Chapman's.

Rawls sets out, as basic moral principles which a 'constitutional democracy' should (and he believes can) satisfy, two principles of justice: 'first, each person engaged in an institution or affected by it has an equal right to the most extensive liberty compatible with a like liberty for all; and second, inequalities as defined by the institutional structure or fostered by it are arbitrary unless it is reasonable to expect that they will work out to everyone's advantage and provided that the positions and offices to which they attach or from which they may be gained are open to all.'[12] These are offered as principles by which should be judged the basic structure of any society, including 'the political constitution and the principal economic and social institutions

Chapman (eds.): *Justice, Nomos VI* (New York, 1963); 'Distributive Justice', in Peter Laslett and W. G. Runciman (eds.): *Philosophy, Politics and Society, Third Series* (Oxford, 1967); and 'Distributive Justice: Some Addenda', in *Natural Law Forum*, Vol. 13 (1968). His forthcoming book, developing these papers, is not available as this is written.

[11] e.g. Charles Fried: 'Justice and Liberty', in *Justice, Nomos VI* (1963); J. W. Chapman: 'Justice and Fairness', ibid.; Robert Paul Wolff: 'A Refutation of Rawls' Theorem on Justice', *Journal of Philosophy* (1966); J. O'Connor: 'Wolff, Rawls, and the Principles of Justice', *Philosophical Studies* (1968); D. Emmett: 'Justice', *Aristotelian Society, Supplementary Volume XLIII* (1969); Michael Lessnoff: 'John Rawls' Theory of Justice', *Political Studies* (1971); Robert L. Cunningham: 'Justice: Efficiency or Fairness', *The Personalist* (1971).

[12] 'Distributive Justice', p. 61. In this and subsequent references to Rawls's work, the page references are to the volumes cited in note 10.

which together define a person's liberties and rights and affect his life-prospects, what he may expect to be and how well he may expect to fare'.[13] The two principles of justice are not claimed to be the *only* principles by which a society should be judged. 'Justice is not to be confused with an all-inclusive vision of a good society; it is only part of such a conception.'[14] But justice is clearly a very important part. And although he says that there is no need to consider his two principles 'as *the* principles of justice',[15] one of his concerns, as he develops his argument, is 'how to interpret these principles so that they define a consistent and complete conception of justice'.[16] And he can make the fairly comprehensive claim for his contractarian theory of 'justice as fairness': 'Analogously [with Aristotle's belief that "participation in a common understanding of justice makes a *polis*"], one might show that participation in the understanding of justice as fairness makes a constitutional democracy.'[17]

My concern, as I have said, is not with Rawls's central case that a contractarian theory of justice is preferable to a utilitarian one. I want chiefly to consider the adequacy of the model of a liberal-democratic society which he constructs from and justifies by his principles of justice. But we should notice first an assumption he makes which drastically limits the scope of his whole inquiry.

He proposes and defends his principles of justice as criteria for judging the moral worth of various distributions of rights and income *only within a class-divided society*. His explicit assumption is that institutionalized inequalities which affect men's whole life-prospects are 'inevitable in any society'; and he is referring to inequalities between *classes* by income or wealth.[18] It is with these supposedly inevitable basic inequalities that 'the two principles of justice are primarily designed to deal'.[19] Or, as he puts it again, 'differences in life-prospects arising from the basic structure are inevitable, and it is precisely the aim of the second principle to say when these differences are just'.[20]

The assumption that such class division is inevitable does narrow his principles severely. Although his first principle calls for equal liberty and equal opportunity, the second, which is what is novel in his theory and gives it its distinction, is designed to show when class inequality in life-prospects is justified. Principles of justice designed to show when

[13] 'Distributive Justice', p. 62.
[14] 'Justice as Fairness', p. 133.
[15] 'Justice as Fairness', p. 133.
[16] 'Distributive Justice', p. 61.
[17] 'Constitutional Liberty and the Concept of Justice', p. 125.
[18] 'Distributive Justice', p. 62. (Cf. his example of the entrepreneurial class and a class of unskilled labourers, ibid., p. 67.)
[19] 'Distributive Justice', p. 62.
[20] 'Distributive Justice', p. 71.

class inequalities are just do not go very deep. Of course, on his inevitability assumption, that is as deep as they can go. But the assumption is not self-evidently valid. A classless society, in his sense of class, that is, a society without classes which determine what the life prospects of their members are, is not unthinkable and not in principle impossible.

It may be that the difference between us here is about what is necessarily involved in the existence of classes unequal in income or wealth. Rawls, if I understand him rightly, thinks they are consistent with a substantial equality in liberty and personal rights, in any society, including a capitalist market society. I have argued, on the contrary, that these are inconsistent in a capitalist market society, where class-inequality of income or wealth is the result and the means of an inequality in power which reaches to the liberties, rights, and essential humanity of the individuals in those classes.

Non-capitalist models which utilize or permit differences of income or wealth are of course possible, and may result in classes by income or wealth. But these need not create unequal liberties and rights since they are not necessarily either the result or the means of domination, of gaining at the expense of others. Rawls's principles of justice, applied to such a society, would probably make very good sense. But as we shall see, he applies them to a capitalist society, where they become a charter for revisionist liberalism. I shall return to this point after looking at Rawls's model of a currently feasible just society.

The model which Rawls proposes as satisfying his two principles of justice is a constitutional democracy in which

> the government regulates a free economy in a certain way. More fully, if law and government act effectively to keep markets competitive, resources fully employed, property and wealth widely distributed over time, and to maintain the appropriate social minimum, then if there is equality of opportunity underwritten by education for all, the resulting distribution will be just.[21]

The kinds of government regulation, taxation, and income transfers, required to keep the economy competitive, to modify the results of a purely competitive market distribution by considerations of need and a decent minimum standard, and 'to prevent the concentrations of power to the detriment of liberty and equality of opportunity'[22] are sketched briefly. The mainspring of the system is private capitalist enterprise operating through free markets in labour and capital: it is stipulated that competitive markets, only 'supplemented' by government

[21] 'Distributive Justice', p. 69.
[22] 'Distributive Justice', p. 71.

operations, 'handle the problem of efficient allocation of labour and resources'.[23]

In this society there will still be inequality, not only as between individual incomes but between the life-prospects of members of different classes. The class inequality is held to be just if it is in accordance with Rawls's second principle. Thus he asks, what can justify the inequality in life-prospects between 'the son of a member of the entrepreneurial class (in a capitalist society)' and 'that of the son of an unskilled labourer'? He assumes that this inequality will remain even in his modified capitalist model: it will be there 'even when the social injustices which presently exist are removed and the two men are of equal talent and ability; the inequality cannot be done away with as long as something like the family is maintained'.[24]

The inequality is justified by Rawls's second principle if lessening the inequality would 'make the working man even worse off than he is'. And the presumption is that 'the inequality in expectation provides an incentive so that the economy is more efficient, industrial advance proceeds at a quicker pace, and so on, the end result of which is that greater material and other benefits are distributed throughout the system'; hence, to lessen the inequality is to lower, or at least prevent raising, 'the life-prospects of the labouring class'.[25]

It follows, for Rawls, that the welfare-state transfer payments which are required to mitigate the inattention of a market economy to considerations of need and decent minimum standards (and any other state regulation of the free play of the market) must be limited to the point at which they will not interfere with the efficiency and growth of the productive system. Such a limit is reached when the taxes required to finance transfer payments 'interfere so much with the efficiency of the economy that the expectations of the lowest class for that period no longer improve but begin to decline',[26] presumably by reducing the incentives of the entrepreneurial class.

[23] 'Distributive Justice', p. 70. A remark in a later article ('Distributive Justice: Some Addenda', p. 56) suggests an extraordinary misunderstanding of what his free market system entails: he refers there to his assumption 'that the economy is roughly a free market system, *although the means of production may or may not be privately* owned' (emphasis added). But if the means of production were not privately owned, his market model would not operate at all: his stipulation of 'a free economy' in which competitive markets do the primary allocation of labour and resources and which would distribute the whole product in a way that 'ignores the claims of need altogether' ('Distributive Justice', p. 70) surely requires the incentives attached to private ownership of capital.

[24] 'Distributive Justice', p. 67

[25] 'Distributive Justice', p. 67.

[26] 'Distributive Justice', p. 74.

It thus appears that Rawls, like Chapman, is assuming capitalist economic rationality, and is dealing with justice only within the limits imposed by it. His postulates about the requirements of capitalist rationality are more realistic than Chapman's in two respects: he assumes that any capitalist society will still be a class-divided one; and he assumes that inequality of income will always be necessary in such a society as an incentive to efficient production and that, therefore, welfare-state transfer payments must be limited to an amount which will still leave one class better off than another.

Yet there is a sharp limit to Rawls' realism. He does not see that the class inequality in his market system is bound to be an inequality of power as well as of income, that it allows one class to dominate another. In his earliest construction he could ask us to suppose a society whose members 'are sufficiently equal in power and ability to guarantee that in normal circumstances none is able to dominate the others' and could refer to this as part of 'the typical circumstances in which questions of justice arise'.[27] In his later model of a competitive market society, however, he does assume a tendency for concentration of wealth, and does see that this can be concentration of power detrimental to equal liberty and equality of opportunity, but he considers that it is so only when inequalities and concentrations of wealth go beyond a certain limit: one of the functions he assigns the government is 'to prevent this limit from being exceeded', but the limit would specifically still permit class differences in life-prospects.[28] Where the limit lies is a question on which, he tells us, 'the theory of justice has nothing to say.'[29] That is indeed the case with a theory of justice which does not recognize that in a competitive market system where capital and labour are in separate hands, all capital, whatever its degree of concentration, is power which controls and impedes the lives of others. Capital in that society is extractive power, and the extractive power of the owners of capital diminishes the developmental powers of the non-owners.[30]

The shortcoming of this theory of justice is not in its inability to say where the limit should be set to the concentration of wealth to prevent it becoming an undesirable and unjust concentration of power; it is in its thinking that wealth (the accumulation of capital) only becomes detrimental power (detrimental to equal liberty and equality of opportunity) beyond a certain level of concentration.

It thus appears that Rawls's principles of justice, as they would operate within his model of a market society, are internally inconsistent. His first principle requires continual income transfers from the upper to

[27] 'Justice as Fairness', pp. 138, 139.
[28] 'Distributive Justice', p. 71.
[29] 'Distributive Justice', p. 71.
[30] As shown in Essay III.

the lower class, and also requires various steady governmental interferences with the normal market tendencies towards concentration of capital. The transfers and the interferences must not, by his second principle, exceed a limit at which their amount would reduce the efficiency and productivity of the economy; and the limit must be low enough to maintain the incentive system of classes with different life prospects. If a limit on transfers and interferences low enough to comply with the second principle could be high enough to prevent the concentration of capital from exceeding *its* limit, namely the point at which accumulations of private capital become 'concentrations of power to the detriment of liberty and equality of opportunity' (which limit is required by the first principle), then his two principles would be consistent. But it is impossible to find a limit on transfers and interferences low enough to do the one thing and high enough to do the other. There has to be *some* limit on transfers and interferences, to comply with the second principle; but if there is *any* limit on transfers and interferences, they will not prevent concentrations of private capital detrimental to equal liberty and equality of opportunity, since *any* accumulation of private capital is detrimental to equal liberty and equality of opportunity. Put otherwise, the limit on transfers and interferences cannot coincide with the limit on accumulation of capital, because the limit beyond which accumulation of capital becomes detrimental to equal liberty and equality of opportunity is zero, whereas the limit on transfers and interferences cannot, by the second principle, be zero.

Rawls sees some inconsistency in his principles when he writes: 'the principle of fair opportunity can only be imperfectly carried out, at least as long as we accept the institution of the family . . . It is impossible in practice to secure equal chances of achievement and culture for those similarly endowed . . .';[31] but since he is still attributing the difficulty to the institution of the family rather than to the institution of capitalist market incentives, it cannot be said that he sees the full contradiction.

We must notice also that, quite apart from this difficulty, Rawls's model does not fully satisfy his own second principle—that inequalities are just if they can be expected to work out to everyone's advantage. For we must ask, advantage compared with what? Rawls rejects as unsatisfactory any comparison with a hypothetical state of nature or with 'any past state of society other than a recent one', and prefers 'comparisons defined by currently feasible changes'.[32] But his currently

[31] 'Distributive Justice: Some Addenda', p. 58.

[32] 'Distributive Justice', p. 63. I agree that historical comparisons are irrelevant (for the reason given in Essay III, p. 68, cf. 58), but wonder why Rawls would allow comparisons with 'a recent' state of society.

feasible changes are confined to those possible within the limits of his capitalist market model. He cannot be said to have shown that his model is the most just, since all possible models not run on principles of capitalist rationality are ruled out.

We may notice finally that Rawls's notion of advantage is limited in another way. The advantage of which he speaks is the advantage to men *as consumers*. It leaves out of account the relative advantage to men in all their other aspects, as exerters and developers of all their human capacities. It is true that he assumes 'the various liberties of equal citizenship':[33] civil liberties, equal political rights, and equality of opportunity (equality of educational opportunities, and free choice of occupation). But, apart from the inadequacy of any provisions for equality of opportunity in a society where, by his postulates, there must be inequality of life-prospects for members of different classes, one may ask whether all of these provisions, along with the advantage to men as consumers, could make up for the disadvantage of men as exerters of all their capacities which is inherent in the work situation of employees in a system of capitalist rationality.

I think it is proper to conclude that any theory, such as Chapman's and Rawls's, whose horizon is for the most part bounded by the supposed wants of man as consumer,[34] or which makes the satisfaction of those wants the main ingredient of moral freedom or of maximization of powers, is not adequate as a liberal-democratic theory, however adequate it might once have been as a liberal theory.

[33] 'Distributive Justice', p. 69.

[34] Rawls indeed does point out that the problem of distributive justice 'is not a problem of distributing given amounts of income or batches of goods to given individuals with certain patterns of tastes and wants' but rather 'a problem of distributing or assigning rights in the design of the general systems of rules defining and regulating economic activities' ('Constitutional Liberty and the Concept of Justice', p. 117, n. 5). But this is still to treat men as consumers. Justice 'is a set of principles for choosing between the social arrangements which determine this division [i.e. 'how the greater benefits produced by their joint labours are distributed'] ('Distributive Justice', p. 58). And 'the chief problem of distributive justice' is 'that concerning the distribution of wealth as it affects the life-prospects of those starting out in the various income groups' (ibid, p. 67).

ESSAY V

Berlin's Division of Liberty

SIR Isaiah Berlin's celebrated and influential *Two Concepts of Liberty*[1] is significantly different from the work of the revisionist liberals discussed in the previous essay. Berlin is not enamoured of economic rationality. Since he does not put it high on the list of liberal values, he is not caught up in contradictions between it and justice and freedom. Yet philosophically he is very much in the liberal-individualist tradition, to which, indeed, he has given new impetus. He has sharpened that tradition by his insistence that liberty amounts to the permitted range of individual potential choices, by his separation of this 'negative' liberty from all varieties of 'positive' liberty, and by his warning against positive liberty on grounds both of its liability to become an engine of oppression and of its embodying false assumptions about the human condition.

His treatment of positive liberty, and the division he makes between positive and negative, cannot be disregarded in any attempt to construct a democratic theory along the lines of maximization of human powers, for it is evident that his positive liberty, in what I take to be its basic sense, is very much the same as the concept of maximization of powers. Thus if his case against positive liberty is sustained, a democratic theory built on the maximization of powers could have little claim to embody genuine liberal values.

I shall suggest that the division Berlin makes between negative and positive liberty will not bear the weight he puts on it, ultimately because each of the two concepts is defined in a way which neglects or understates the role of those impediments whose importance I have sought to demonstrate in Essay III, namely, lack of access to the means of life and the means of labour. I shall argue (in section 1) that his negative liberty is, for that reason, too narrowly conceived, and that it is at bottom a mechanical, inertial concept of freedom which is fully appropriate only to a complete market society.

In section 2, turning to the concept of positive liberty, I point out that Berlin has fused three different things in his concept of positive liberty, and I suggest that his distinction between negative and

[1] Oxford, 1958; reprinted with revisions in *Four Essays on Liberty* (Oxford, 1969), which has a valuable Introduction expanding many of the ideas of the original essay. Page references to the text of *Two Concepts of Liberty* are to the revised text in the *Four Essays*.

positive liberty is valid only for two of the three senses of positive liberty, so that the full distinction he makes is not well established. Specifically I shall argue that while there is indeed a clear and important distinction between negative liberty and one of his senses of positive liberty (the right to participate in the sovereign authority), and a self-evident distinction between negative liberty and one other of his senses of positive liberty (the debased form which imposes 'rational' freedom on those said to be not fully rational), there is no such clear distinction between negative liberty and the apparently basic sense of his positive liberty (conscious self-direction). This will take us to the central question, whether positive liberty in its basic sense is so liable to be transformed into its debased form that the whole concept of positive liberty had better be abandoned. It is of course Berlin's main thesis that it should be abandoned. He is deeply concerned with the frightening claims that are made in the name of positive liberty, claims made increasingly in our century by movements and governments which, in the name of some ultimate freedom, deny present freedom. And because he finds that this denial of freedom not only has followed historically, but does follow abstractly, by an easy though sometimes false logic, from the concept of positive liberty, he recommends in effect that we should abjure that concept and stick to negative liberty, or, as he has put it in the amended text of *Two Concepts*,[2] to 'pluralism, with the measure of "negative" liberty that it entails', as 'a truer and more humane ideal . . .'

The case is powerfully argued. But I think that positive liberty can, and should, be rescued from the reproach to which he subjects it. I shall argue that the debased form of positive liberty (the imposition of 'rational' freedom) is not, either logically or historically, a necessary or even a presumptive outcome of the basic idea of positive liberty but emerges (when it does) from a conjunction of two other factors: a failure by theorists to see positive liberty in terms of absence of impediments to men's developmental powers,[3] and a failure by the holders of political power to deal with the practical impediments. This at least is what appears if one starts from the position implicit in my analysis of power, i.e. that liberty is the absence of humanly imposed impediments, and that these impediments include not only coercion of one individual by another, and direct interference with individual activities by the state or society (beyond what is needed to secure each from invasion by others), but also lack of equal access to the means of life and the means of labour. Berlin starts from a narrower position: in effect he leaves out the last category of impediments. He is, I think, more nearly entitled

[2] At p. 171. His reason for the amendment is set out in the Introduction at p. lviii, n. 1.

[3] As defined in Essay III, at pp. 41–2.

to do so in respect of his negative liberty than in respect of positive liberty, but even in respect of negative liberty the virtual omission of those impediments does not appear to be justified.

Finally, having argued (in section 1) that his concept of negative liberty is unworkably narrow, and (in section 2) that his concept of positive liberty is confusingly wide and dangerously abstract, I consider (in section 3) whether a more useful division of liberty might be found. I shall argue that the purpose which Berlin's division was intended to serve, i.e. the protection of liberty against its perverters, would be better served if the division were made not between 'negative' and 'positive' but between what I shall call 'counter-extractive' and 'developmental' liberty.

1. *Negative Liberty*

Berlin's discussion of negative liberty follows immediately after his description of liberty or freedom (he uses the terms interchangeably) *per se* as absence of coercion: 'to coerce a man is to deprive him of freedom' (p. 121).

Coercion, in the context of negative liberty, 'implies the deliberate interference of other human beings within the area in which I could otherwise act' (p. 122): a man is not said to be coerced by his natural inabilities but only by inabilities imposed on him by the actions of other men or arrangements made by other men. Berlin's main point here is well taken: in ordinary language, a man's freedom is said to be denied only when he is prevented by other human agencies—by the actions of other men or by the laws and institutions set up by other men—from doing what he might want to do. In ordinary language, certainly in the ordinary language of the English liberal tradition, which is the language of negative liberty, freedom is not anything as subtle as, say, the recognition of necessity: it is simply the absence of coercive interference by the state or society or other individuals. Yet Berlin's presentation of this point contains one stipulation and one assumption that may be questioned. It is not evident that the stipulation is proper in a definition even of negative liberty, nor that the assumption is justified historically or logically.

(a) The stipulation is that only *deliberate* interference constitutes coercion or deprivation of liberty. Deliberate interference clearly includes any direct menace or invasion of one individual by another, and those laws and institutions which forbid certain actions. It may also properly be taken to include all the social pressures making for conformity with which Mill was so concerned. It is broad enough to include also the relation of dominance and subservience between owners and non-owners in a class-divided society, *provided* that the poverty and dependence of the latter are ascribed to arrangements deliberately made and enforced for that purpose by the former. But the stipulation of deliberate interference does not, as I understand it, leave room for including in coercion a relation of dominance and subservience which may be an unintended, but which is a necessary, result of arrangements made and enforced by a class of owners. Yet if institutions such as the laws of property and contract coerce non-owners incidentally and unintendedly, they still coerce them, and the coercion is still the result of arrangements made by other human beings. Can this sort of unfreedom properly be written off?[4]

One might perhaps argue that its omission is justified on the ground that Berlin's negative liberty is explicitly modelled on the concept of liberty which was dominant in Mill and the classical English political philosophers, and that they did leave that sort of unfreedom largely out of account. Negative liberty, in that tradition, comprises mainly the absence of (and requires guarantees against) two kinds of interference: (i) interference by the state, or by the pressures of social conformism, with what each individual wants to do, at least within the widest possible area of action consistent with all others having the same freedom; and (ii) invasion of any one individual by another. If everybody is to have freedom (ii), nobody can be left completely free of interference by the state: this is why freedom (i) has to be stated as absence of interference only within a certain area of individual activities. Negative liberty 'is simply the area within which a man can act unobstructed by others' (p. 122). Proponents of negative liberty seek to establish, and to widen as far as possible, the area within which each individual is secure from interference by others, and especially by the state or the society: 'some portion of human existence must remain independent of the sphere of social control'; lines must be drawn 'for keeping authority at bay' (p. 126).

This is a most perceptive statement of the classical English liberal view of liberty. There is no doubt that Mill neglected or repudiated as

[4] The stipulation of deliberate interference is somewhat relaxed in the Introduction to *Four Essays* where he says: 'absence of [social or political] freedom is due to the closing of such doors [my potential choices] or failure to open them, as a result, intended or unintended, of alterable human practices, of the operation of human agencies; although only if such acts are deliberately intended (or, perhaps, are accompanied by an awareness that they may block paths) will they be liable to be called oppression' (p. xl). This seems to allow that unintended interferences may count as deprivations of liberty, though not as the highest degree of deprivation, namely 'oppression'. But Berlin has not treated this remark as requiring any alteration of the text, which still reads 'coercion implies the deliberate interference of other human beings' (p. 122). And one of the factors determining the extent of a man's freedom is 'how far [his possibilities of choice] are closed and opened by deliberate human action' (p. 130, n. 1).

an important source of unfreedom the capitalist property institutions whose necessary but not necessarily intended result was the coercion of the non-owning class. In the essay *On Liberty* he neglected them: he was almost entirely concerned with direct interferences, by the state and the pressures of social conformity, with everyone's liberty. Elsewhere, where he did deal with class institutions as a source of unfreedom, as he did explicitly in the *Political Economy*, he still did not attribute the unfreedom of the working class to the necessary but not necessarily intended result of the property institutions of capitalism. He did not regard that unfreedom as a necessary result of capitalist institutions at all. He was outspoken about the lack of freedom of the working class in nineteenth-century England,[5] and he attributed it directly to the monopoly of ownership by the ruling class. But that monopoly he saw as a continuing effect of the original pre-capitalist forcible seizure of the land, maintained by the subsequent failure of the ruling class to alter the laws of landownership and inheritance so as to permit 'industry' to smooth out the distribution of ownership.[6] Thus Mill saw the present unfreedom of the working class as due to a past deliberate action by others plus subsequent neglect: as due, we might say, to the present owning class's sins of omission rather than of commission. Whether Mill regarded their inaction as deliberate is not entirely clear. Probably he did.

In any case, we may say that Mill certainly regarded the unfreedom of the working class as the result of arrangements made by others, and probably as the result of deliberate current inaction of others. But he certainly did not see it as the necessary, even though unintended, result of the property institutions essential to capitalism. In this he was perhaps less clear-sighted than Bentham, who did apparently see this.[7] But it is fair to say that Mill and the classical English liberal tradition in general either neglected, as sources of unfreedom, the possibly unintended but necessary effects of capitalist property institutions, or

[5] 'The generality of labourers in this and most other countries have as little choice of occupation or freedom of locomotion, are practically as dependent on fixed rules and on the will of others, as they could be on any system short of actual slavery . . .' (J. S. Mill: *Principles of Political Economy*, Book II, chap. 1, sect. 3, (*Collected Works*, Vol. II, ed. Robson, Toronto and London, 1965, p. 209)).

[6] 'The social arrangements of modern Europe commenced from a distribution of property which was the result, not of just partition, or acquisition by industry, but of conquest and violence: and notwithstanding what industry has been doing for many centuries to modify the work of force, the system still retains many and large traces of its origin' (Ibid. (*Collected Works*, Vol. II, p. 207)).

[7] 'In the highest stage of social prosperity, the great mass of citizens will have no resource except their daily industry, and consequently will be always near indigence' (Bentham: *Principles of the Civil Code*, Part First, Chap. XIV, section 1 (in Bentham: *The Theory of Legislation*, ed. C. K. Ogden, p. 127)).

regarded them as more than offset by the utility-maximizing effect of capitalist enterprise.

Berlin has therefore some warrant in Mill and the classical English liberal tradition for neglecting as a source of class unfreedom the unintended but necessary results of the property arrangements made by others. In so far as Berlin's negative liberty is simply the classical English concept he may be held to be justified in leaving out necessary though not necessarily intended (and in that sense not deliberate) effects of capitalist property institutions. But we may still ask whether a concept of liberty adequate for the twentieth century can afford to neglect all that Mill and the classical English liberal tradition neglected.

(b) The other question raised by Berlin's presentation of negative freedom as simply the absence of interference by other human beings is distinct from the question whether the poverty or dependence of a subordinate class is an intended result of class arrangements. It is the logically prior question whether such poverty and dependence are the result of other people's actions or arrangements *at all.* Berlin assumes that they may not generally be so. He implies that this causal relation cannot be presumed: it is only imputed by those who accept certain social and economic theories. 'It is only because I believe that my inability to get a given thing is due to the fact that other human beings have made arrangements whereby I am, whereas others are not, prevented from having enough money with which to pay for it, that I think myself a victim of coercion or slavery. In other words, this use of the term depends on a particular social and economic theory about the causes of my poverty or weakness' (p. 123). He adds, in a note, that this forms a large element 'in some Christian and utilitarian, and all socialist, doctrines'.

But to say that poverty is properly described as an impediment to liberty only on some particular social and economic theory which ascribes poverty to human arrangements is to imply that there are other social and economic theories, equally credible, which do not do so. But are there in fact any theories of any standing, since the rise of capitalist market society, which do not attribute the poverty of the poor, at least in part, to arrangements made by other human beings? Vulgar proponents of free enterprise, it is true, sometimes do not make this attribution, but suggest or imply that the poverty of the poor is entirely their own fault, being due either to their laziness or to some accident of their physical or mental underendowment. But free enterprise theories of any standing from Adam Smith and Bentham to Mill and Green (with the possible exception of Malthus) have recognized that it is indeed arrangements made by other human beings (as well as differences in native abilities and industriousness) that determine the distribution of wealth and poverty. Different ones of them have attributed the distribution to different combinations of factors, and have seen different possibilities of change, and different justifications—natural law, utility, etc.—for what they would not change; but none of them has been in any doubt that the arrangements had been made by a set of human beings.

However, we need not rest on the views of the classical economists. We may simply point out, as an evident general proposition, that the distribution of access to the means of labour is a matter of social institutions: land and capital may, at the decision of a society, or of those who control it, be held in common, or owned individually, or held in any combination of these ways; and property in land and capital may be subject to any or no limits on amounts and ways of acquisition. It is surely equally clear that the difference between individuals' access to the means of labour is an important determinant of their incomes. No one doubts that in a capitalist market system differences of native ability and industriousness (and luck) also lead to differences in income: the more so, the freer (i.e. less monopolistic) the system is. But native ability, industriousness, and luck cannot account for all the differences in income so long as differences in access also prevail. And of course it is not differences in income alone that are in question. It is not a matter only of whether I can *get* what I want but also of whether I can *do* what I want. And, as I have argued[8], differences in access are at least as important in determining what I can do as what I can get. On these grounds we may conclude that the unequal access to the means of life and labour inherent in capitalism is, regardless of what particular social and economic theory is invoked, an impediment to the freedom of those with little or no access. It diminishes their negative liberty, since the dependence on others for a living, which deficiency of access creates, diminishes the area in which they cannot be pushed around.

We may conclude that a formulation of negative liberty which takes little or no account of class-imposed impediments, whether deliberate or unintentional, is not entirely adequate.

In his defence and elaboration of the concept of negative liberty in the Introduction to the *Four Essays*, Berlin makes what seems to be a reply to such criticism, but is not. He there makes explicit what he had originally left unstated, that the oppression and deprivation of the working class under nineteenth-century *laissez-faire* made their legal freedoms 'an odious mockery' (p. xlvi). He emphasizes his awareness that to keep a whole class or a whole people in poverty and ignorance, or to shut them out from the benefits accumulated by a dominant class,

[8] In Essay III, at pp. 66–7.

is to render their liberty hollow.[9] But he insists that this is to deprive them not of liberty but of some of the conditions of liberty.[10]

This is to acknowledge the importance of class oppression (which is here unquestionedly the result of other peoples' actions, and which falls into the category of deprivation of access to the means of life and labour), only to put it aside as being a diminution of the conditions for liberty, not of liberty itself. But this distinction is meaningful only when liberty has already been defined so narrowly. Only when the impediments whose absence comprises negative liberty are defined so as to leave out lack of access to the means of life and the means of labour, does the distinction hold: only then does access become a condition of liberty rather than a part of liberty. Berlin apparently intends[11] to omit such lack of access from the list of impediments. To the extent that he does so, we are back with the same difficulty as before: his negative liberty does not include access to the means of life and the means of labour, in spite of the fact that lack of access does diminish negative liberty, that is, does diminish the area in which a man cannot be interfered with.

To omit lack of access from the category of coercive impediments to liberty, and so to remove such class-imposed denials from the department of liberty into the department of justice or equality, seems to me an unfortunate reversion towards the extreme liberalism of Herbert Spencer. On the narrowness of the proper concept of liberty they have much in common. Consider Berlin's defence of the distinction between freedom and the conditions of freedom: 'This is not a mere pedantic distinction, for if it is ignored, the meaning and value of freedom of choice is apt to be downgraded. In their zeal to create social and economic conditions in which alone freedom is of genuine value, men tend to forget freedom itself; and if it is remembered, it is liable to be pushed aside to make room for those other values with which the reformers or revolutionaries have become preoccupied' (p. liv). This is precisely Spencer's, and Milton Friedman's, complaint.[12]

[9] He makes this point about 'the Egyptian peasant' on p. 124, and about the English workmen of T. H. Green's time in the Introduction (p. xlix, n. 1).

[10] p. 125. In the Introduction to *Four Essays* he seems to acknowledge what the text of *Two Concepts* does not: that such class deprivation is indeed a deprivation of *liberty*, not merely of the conditions of liberty: e.g. p. xlv (unrestricted *laissez-faire* led to 'violations of "negative liberty"'); and pp. xlvii–xlviii (new ways in which liberty 'has been curtailed' in the twentieth century by discriminatory economic and social policies 'which have blocked and diminished human freedom'). Yet he has not altered the original text on this point, and he even re-emphasizes, a few pages later in the Introduction (pp. liii–liv), the importance of distinguishing between liberty and the conditions of liberty.

[11] I say 'apparently' because the passages cited in the previous note leave this uncertain.

[12] See Essay VII, second paragraph.

Berlin does not, of course, accept what Spencer and Friedman have treated as the obverse of this complaint, namely, that full market freedom is to be valued above all other values. He is unsparing in his criticism of *laissez-faire* as having been destructive of 'conditions for both positive, and at least a minimum degree of negative liberty', and he holds that the case for state intervention to secure those conditions 'is overwhelmingly strong'. He adds: 'The case for social legislation or planning, for the welfare state and socialism, can be constructed with as much validity from considerations of the claims of negative liberty as from those of its positive brother . . .' (p. xlvi). This is a far cry from Spencer. But is it self-consistent?

A case for welfare-state intervention can indeed be constructed from the claims of negative liberty, but only, surely, if one drops the distinction between liberty and the conditions of liberty. For the point about welfare-state intervention is to open some doors (as well as to compensate for some others being closed). It is not merely to provide some conditions for freedom of choice, it is to broaden the area of choice for those who previously had few doors open to them.

The same may be said about socialism. That a case could be made for socialism on grounds of negative liberty seems strange at first sight. But it is quite possible, provided that one does not, as Berlin appears to do (p. 130, n. 1) dismiss as 'logically absurd' the possibility of calculating a net gain or loss of liberty for a whole society as a result of a change in the society's arrangements. Socialism, by definition (since it requires social, not individual, ownership of capital) removes from the arena of negative liberty the main individual activities celebrated as 'free enterprise'. But it increases the aggregate negative liberty, if the gain in liberty by those who had had doors closed to them more than offsets the loss of liberty by those (relatively few) who had been in a position to take full advantage of market freedoms. This calculation, however, cannot be allowed by Berlin, since it depends on the possibility of measuring changes in aggregate impediments, including lack of access to the means of life and labour (which he has ruled out as impediments). It thus appears very difficult to square Berlin's narrow concept of negative liberty with his claims for its usefulness. We are back again with the difficulty noticed already, now in a sharpened form: his concept of negative liberty is too narrow to serve the minimum purposes he wants it to serve.

Why is it so narrow? Why is the distinction between liberty and the conditions for liberty so important for Berlin? Why is he so uncomfortably close to Herbert Spencer on this? I think it is because, like Spencer, he is working with a concept of liberty which is mechanical and inertial. It goes back through Bentham to Hobbes, and beyond him to Galileo, from whom Hobbes borrowed the concept of inertial motion: bodies, including people, go on moving until they are stopped by the impact of other bodies. This concept can properly be imported from mechanics to politics if, and only if, one postulates, as Hobbes did, that every man's motion is opposed and hindered by every other man's. That postulate in turn makes good sense if, and only if, one is assuming an atomized market society in which everyone is put on his own to compete with everyone for everything.

This seems to me to be a fundamental limitation of Berlin's concept of negative liberty: it requires the postulate of universally opposed motions, which requires the postulate of an atomized market society. Berlin clearly does not want to treat men simply as bodies of matter in opposed motion,[13] but he has adopted a concept of liberty which stems from that market concept of man. Liberty, even negative liberty, if we are to keep that term, surely needs a less mechanical and more human dimension. If I am right about this, the division Berlin makes between negative and positive liberty is faulty from the negative side.

Indeed Berlin himself finds it impossibly narrow to work with. When he comes to consider how the amount of negative liberty can be estimated, he lists five factors on which its extent depends, including '(a) how many possibilities are open to me', and '(b) how easy or difficult each of these possibilities is to actualize' (p. 130, n. 1). The (b) seems to admit by the back door those factors which he had pushed out as mere 'conditions' of liberty. The need for so many epicycles casts some doubt on the central thesis, although he re-emphasizes the thesis in the Introduction: 'The fundamental sense of freedom is freedom from chains, from imprisonment, from enslavement by others. The rest is extension of this sense, or else metaphor . . . Freedom, at least in its political sense, is co-terminous with the absence of bullying or domination' (p. lvi). It is a long step from absence of bullying or domination or chains or enslavement, to the number of possibilities open and the ease of actualizing them. It is a step which carries negative liberty much of the way towards positive liberty.

2. *Positive Liberty*

If Berlin's negative liberty is merely the absence of direct political and social-conformist interferences with any individual's actions (and of direct invasion of one individual by others), his positive liberty is not so narrowly conceived. It requires absence of other impediments as well. For what other than absence of all humanly imposed impedi-

[13] Although he comes close to that in one passage: 'I cannot remove all the obstacles in my path that stem from the conduct of my fellows. . . . despite . . . heroic attempts to transcend or dissolve the conflicts and resistance of others, if I do not wish to be deceived, I shall recognize the fact that total harmony with others is incompatible with self-identity . . .' (pp. xliii–xliv).

ments to men's powers is the positive liberty Berlin describes so effectively?

The 'positive' sense of the word 'liberty' derives from the wish on the part of the individual to be his own master. I wish my life and decisions to depend on myself, not on external forces of whatever kind. I wish to be the instrument of my own, not of other men's, acts of will. I wish to be a subject, not an object; to be moved by reasons, by conscious purposes which are my own, not by causes which affect me, as it were, from outside. I wish to be somebody, not nobody; a doer—deciding, not being decided for, self-directed and not acted upon by external nature or by other men as if I were a thing, or an animal, or a slave incapable of playing a human role, that is, of conceiving goals and policies of my own and realizing them. This is at least part of what I mean when I say that I am rational, and that it is my reason that distinguishes me as a human being from the rest of the world. I wish, above all, to be conscious of myself as a thinking, willing, active being, bearing responsibility for my choices and able to explain them by references to my own ideas and purposes. I feel free to the degree that I believe this to be true, and enslaved to the degree that I am made to realize that it is not (p. 131).

There could scarcely be a more eloquent statement: positive liberty is liberty to act as a fully *human* being. A man's positive liberty is virtually the same as what I have called a man's power in the developmental sense. It depends on the absence of impediments over and above simple coercion (understood as direct political and social interference with what any individual might wish to do, plus direct invasion of one individual by other individuals), whereas Berlin's negative liberty is defined simply as the absence of such coercion.

This distinction, which might be thought to contain the crucial difference between his two concepts of liberty, is not investigated by Berlin. Instead, after referring to the two concepts as seeming to be, on the face of it, 'at no great logical distance from each other—no more than negative and positive ways of saying much the same thing', he goes on to show that in fact they 'developed in divergent directions not always by logically reputable steps until, in the end, they came into direct conflict with each other' (pp. 131–2).

He shows, most tellingly, how in the hands of Idealists, and of any extreme rationalists, this notion of positive liberty can lead, and has led, by apparently logical stages, to monstrous denials of liberty. Liberty as self-mastery becomes mastery of a 'higher' or 'real' self over a lower, desirous, animal self. Then the 'real' self is identified with some social whole of which the individual is a part, and this organic whole is then taken to embody all the real or higher selves or wills of all the individuals. So, in imposing its organic will on individuals, the society, or those who act in its name, is said to achieve a higher liberty for all its members. This is the Idealist road (or slippery slope) which ends in coercion: the individual is forced to be free.

Or, as he shows, the same result can be reached by the enlightened rationalism, whether idealist or materialist, which starts from a secular 'the truth shall make you free'. Freedom is then the (rational) recognition of necessity. It requires a state governed by laws which all men would rationally accept if they were fully rational. But at present most men are not, whether from having been stunted by prevailing social institutions (as the Enlightenment optimists, including Marx, would have it), or from some other cause. So it is in most men's own (rational) interest that others—those who have attained full rationality or have understood the true forces of history—should impose on them the institutions which will bring them (as far as they can be brought) to full rationality and, therefore, full freedom. Either way, coercion is the only means to the fullest freedom: Sarastro at least, Procrustes if necessary.

This is a brilliant analysis. There is no doubt that the concept of positive liberty *has* been taken to these conclusions and, so perverted, *has* been used to deny the very freedom for human self-development that it began by invoking. Nor is it to be doubted that the transformation has generally proceeded by the way of the postulate that most men have been so stunted or debased by the social institutions in which they have had to live that they are themselves not capable of changing them, and that such change must therefore be primarily the work of a select group, whether it be an intelligentsia advising a benevolent monarch (as the eighteenth-century *philosophes* saw it) or a politically aware vanguard party (as Lenin would have it). The terrible thing about this is that the postulate is often correct. In many societies individuals *are* stunted by the social institutions in which they have had to live; they cannot be fully human, or fully free, until those institutions have been changed; and in some circumstances the institutions may be unchangeable except by revolutionary coercion, coercion not only of those who upheld the old order but also, in some measure and for some time, of those whose support and effort are needed to install a new order.

No one, I think, who observes the transfers of political power that have been the means to revolutionary social changes in so many countries in Asia and Africa in our time and in Eastern Europe in earlier decades of this century, and, for that matter, the revolutionary changes in England and France in the seventeenth and eighteenth centuries which ushered in the liberal state itself, would deny that a degree of coercion exceeding that permitted by any liberal theory has often been a necessary (though certainly not a sufficient) condition of any advance towards both positive and negative liberty. The degree of coercion needed can be seen to vary with several circumstances: the willingness and ability of the old regime to resist, and (whether or not the transfer of political power was violent) all the circumstances in which the post-revolutionary 'vanguard' has to operate. This is not to say that the amount of coercion actually used in any case has been no more than was needed, or that it has not sometimes perverted the end. Nor is it to say that the justification offered for the coercion has always been positive liberty. But in our century it often has been. And the temptation for a vanguard to go the whole way to the perverted doctrine, the doctrine that only they can know, and that it is sufficient for them to know, is clearly very strong: the classic case is Stalin's Russia.

But I would argue that the perverted doctrine is not only not a necessary refuge of such a vanguard, but that it is, increasingly clearly in our time, apt to be a self-defeating refuge. What I have in mind is the lesson that may be read from the fate of the many new African states which came into being as a result of movements of national independence directed by vanguards. The only ones where the original vanguard has survived seem to be the ones where the vanguard did not embrace the perverted doctrine, but made it its business to develop a grass-roots democratic participation. We cannot, on such evidence, assert as a general rule that reliance on the perverted doctrine is always self-defeating. But we may at least assert that reliance on such a doctrine is not a necessary feature of even a revolutionary regime which is for a time necessarily illiberal.

However, it remains true that resort to the perverted doctrine has been common in our century, so common that Berlin may well regard the likelihood of a theory of positive liberty degenerating into a wholesale denial of liberty as the chief predicament of liberty in our time. Nevertheless, it can be argued that the predicament is due not to the logic of positive liberty, nor to the assumptions of the Idealist and rationalist theorists who have pushed positive liberty, in thought, to positions which have supported such repulsive extremes. I want now to argue that it is due rather to a specific failure of liberal theory, and of those who hold power in the societies which justify themselves by liberal theory, to take account of the concrete circumstances which the growing demand for fuller human realization has encountered and will encounter.

No doubt, since the way in to the predicament was partly the work of political theorists, a way out will not be found without more and different theorizing. Berlin's claim for the importance of political philosophy (pp. 118–20) should surely be allowed to that extent. But if the way out is to depend on political philosophers, it must be political philosophers of a less abstract and remote sort than those whose logic Berlin has so strikingly exposed. My plea is certainly not to abandon logic or philosophy, which have never been more needed than now. It is rather that we can no longer rely on the sort of logic which, even though it starts, as Berlin's does, from solid historical observation of the lengths to which certain philosophic positions have in fact been taken in political practice, is content to analyse those positions on their own terms, that is, to analyse them at their own abstract level. They need to be brought a little further down to earth. They need to be judged in terms of the actual impediments to liberty in concrete historical situations. And these, if my analysis of the implications of the maximizing of men's powers has any merit, are more specific than those Berlin has considered.

To argue that the predicament is not due to the logic of positive liberty we may begin by noticing how Berlin has fused three different things in his concept of positive liberty. We first meet positive liberty as the right to participate in the sovereign authority. Positive liberty 'is involved in the answer to the question "What, or who, is the source of control or interference that can determine someone to do, or be, this rather than that?"' (p. 122); or in the answer to the question '"By whom am I ruled?" or "Who is to say what I am, and what I am not, to be or do?"' (p. 130). It is the right 'to participate in the process by which my life is to be controlled' (p. 131).

But when Berlin comes to expound the idea of positive liberty more fully, he starts from something quite different: the desire of the individual to be his own master, to be self-directed, to be moved by his own conscious purposes, to act and decide rather than be acted upon and decided for by others. This idea of positive liberty, as set out in the eloquent passage quoted above,[14] is clearly the basic one. But it is surely different from participation in the controlling authority. Berlin acknowledges at one point that they are not identical, but generally treats them as indistinguishable or equivalent; they merge into a single notion of positive liberty, in sharp contrast to negative liberty: 'The desire to be governed by myself, *or at any rate to participate* in the process by which my life is to be controlled, may be as deep a wish as that of a free area for action, and perhaps historically older. But it is not a desire for the same thing' (p. 131, emphasis added).

Then there is still the other concept of positive liberty that we have already noticed: the one reached by Idealists and metaphysical rationalists who, starting from liberty as self-mastery or freedom of the 'rational' self, end with liberty as coercion by the fully rational selves of everyone else.

We thus have three different concepts merged into the one concept of positive liberty. For convenience I shall designate them numerically as PL^1, PL^2, and PL^3.

PL^1, which is basic, is individual self-direction or—the term is

[14] From *Two Concepts*, p. 131.

unfortunate, since it contains the seed of the Idealists' transformation into PL^2—self-mastery. It is the ability to live in accordance with one's own conscious purposes, to act and decide for oneself rather than to be acted upon and decided for by others.

PL^2 is the Idealist or metaphysical rationalist transformation of PL^1: liberty is coercion, by the fully rational or by those who have attained self-mastery, of all the rest; coercion, by those who say they know the truth, of all those who do not (yet) know it.

PL^3 is the democratic concept of liberty as a share in the controlling authority.

The central problem about positive liberty is the relation between PL^1 and PL^2—how and why does the former change into the latter? But before we look at this, we should notice that Berlin's main division of liberty into 'negative' and 'positive' depends partly on his using *one* of the senses of positive liberty, namely PL^3, when drawing the contrast between negative liberty (NL) and positive liberty as a whole.

The distinction between NL and PL^3 is indeed sharp and clear. Berlin is certainly right in saying that positive liberty in the sense of having a share in the sovereign power (PL^3) is something logically and historically distinct from negative liberty. An individual's negative liberty, the area within which he is free from interference by anybody else including the state, can be curtailed as much (or more) by a popular (or populist) sovereign as by an autocrat or an oligarchy. Democracy as the sovereignty of the people or the sovereignty of the majority does not guarantee the negative liberty of the individual. That is not to say that democracy (PL^3) is necessarily hostile to NL; it may even be helpful to it. For as Berlin also notes, democracy or self-government 'may, on the whole, provide a better guarantee of the preservation of civil liberties than other regimes, and has been defended as such by libertarians' (p. 130). PL^3, then, while it is compatible with NL and may even be held to be a prerequisite of it, is clearly not the same as NL.

This plain distinction between negative liberty and one of the senses of positive liberty (PL^3) cannot, I think, justifiably be carried over and made into a general distinction between negative and positive liberty. For PL^3 is not the same as PL^1.[15] It should be said at once that Berlin does not rest his whole case for the division between negative

[15] Their relation is that PL^3 is a prerequisite of PL^1 in two respects. First, without PL^3, the man who cannot participate in the making of political decisions is governed by rules made entirely by others, i.e. is directed entirely from outside himself, which is inconsistent with PL^1. Second, no political movement to enlarge men's powers (PL^1) is likely to succeed nowadays unless it is strongly and effectively democratic (PL^3).

and positive liberty on the distinction between NL and PL^3.[16] Much of his case rests rather on the clear incompatibility of NL and PL^2. But that can only be held to justify the over-all division of liberty into NL and PL if PL^1 is assimilated to PL^2. I do not find any case argued for a clear distinction between NL and PL^1: the case that is argued is that PL^1 tends to become PL^2 (which is incompatible with NL).

The central theoretical problem, therefore, is the relation of PL^1 to PL^2. PL^2 is obviously the villain of the piece. It is incompatible with or destructive of all the others. It is clearly incompatible with negative liberty, and with any genuine democracy (genuine PL^3), and with PL^1, of which it is a debasement. The falsity of the logic by which PL^2 is reached from PL^1 has, as Berlin remarks, often been exposed, yet the doctrine keeps reappearing in different guises, with results fatal to negative liberty, to the basic notion of positive liberty, and to any genuine democracy. Perhaps the exposure has been conducted too much in abstract logical terms.

The main problem is, why and in what circumstances does PL^1 change into PL^2? We have to notice that PL^2 is important only when it moves out of the philosopher's study into the forum and the market-place, only when it becomes an ideology or a creed sustaining and justifying those 'great, disciplined, authoritarian structures', as Berlin calls them, which are so destructive of negative liberty. So we should not expect the change to PL^2 to be explicable entirely in terms of the inherent logic of the original theory. Yet the change must begin in the minds of theorists.

Does it begin there because of something inherent in PL^1? Berlin suggests that it does. Of the two ways in which he finds PL^1 commonly transformed into PL^2, one he treats as logically immanent in PL^1, and the other as likely to be induced by PL^1. To take the second of these first: when (at p. 133) he points to the fallacious derivation of PL^2 from PL^1 by way of the notion of self-mastery, he is not, of course, implying that PL^2 is logically immanent in PL^1, but he does urge (p. 134) that 'the "positive" conception of freedom as self-mastery, with its suggestion of a man divided against himself', lends itself more easily to that fallacious reasoning than does the negative concept of freedom.

The other way in which he finds PL^1 transformed into PL^2 he sees

[16] Though he does state or imply several times that that is the fundamental distinction: 'The answer to the question "Who governs me?" is logically distinct from the question "How far does government interfere with me?" It is in this difference that the great contrast between the two concepts of negative and positive liberty, in the end, consists' (p. 130). His restatements of the difference between positive and negative liberty in the Introduction to *Four Essays on Liberty* also cast it in terms of the difference between those two questions, i.e. between NL and PL^3, e.g. at pp. xliii, xliv, xlvii.

as the result of something immanent in PL^1. The rationalist transformation of a Kantian PL^1 into a modern totalitarian PL^2 is attributed to the rationalist assumption that there is a 'single true solution' (p. 152), or, more fully, to a set of four rationalist assumptions:

> first, that all men have one true purpose, and one only, that of rational self-direction; second, that the ends of all rational beings must of necessity fit into a single universal, harmonious pattern, which some men may be able to discern more clearly than others; third, that all conflict, and consequently all tragedy, is due solely to the clash of reason with the irrational or the insufficiently rational—the immature and underdeveloped elements in life—whether individual or communal, and that such clashes are, in principle, avoidable, and for wholly rational beings impossible; finally, that when all men have been made rational, they will obey the rational laws of their own natures, which are one and the same in them all, and so be at once wholly law-abiding and wholly free (p. 154).

It will not be disputed that any theory containing these assumptions is bound to end up as a doctrine of PL^2. But it must be disputed that all these assumptions are inherent in any concept of positive liberty. The first assumption may be allowed as essential to PL^1, if the *rational* element of 'rational self-direction' is given the sense Berlin gives it in his definitive statement of positive liberty, that is, the faculty (which distinguishes the human being) of being 'moved by reasons, by conscious purposes' (p. 131). So interpreted, 'rational self-direction' includes the pursuit of whatever purposes a man may consciously form; it covers the whole of what I have called a man's developmental power. There is perhaps no logical fault in attributing to the doctrine of positive liberty the assumption that something as broad as this is 'the one and only true purpose of man' but it can be dangerously misleading, for already it suggests a monism which in fact is not there. The real monism is contained in the last three assumptions. They are indeed at the heart of PL^2. But they do not follow from the first assumption. For in them, 'rational' no longer means simply the pursuit of (multifarious) conscious purposes, but means conformity to a preordained cosmic order.

My point is that the last three assumptions are not needed in any concept of positive liberty, and are indeed inconsistent with PL^1. It is *not* necessary for an advocate of positive liberty to assert or assume that there is a single universal harmonious pattern into which the ends of all rational beings must fit. For there is a great deal of difference between (i) believing that there is such a pattern (which fully rational men can know, and which they should impose on others), and (ii) believing that if the chief impediments to men's developmental powers were removed, if, that is to say, they were allowed equal freedom, there would emerge not a pattern but a proliferation of many ways and styles of life which could not be prescribed and which would not necessarily conflict.

It is only the second of these beliefs that is essential to the concept of positive liberty. Certainly, the stipulation that the ways of life would not necessarily conflict is a necessary stipulation if a society of positive liberty is to be worth striving for. But it is not the same as the postulate of a preordained harmonious pattern. I have suggested earlier[17] how such a society of non-conflicting but non-prescribed ends can be envisaged. The requirements for its realization are steep but not, I think, impossible—the ending of scarcity and of class conflict. It is, if I understand him rightly, because Berlin thinks these requirements *are* impossible that he rejects the possibility of a non-conflicting but non-prescribed society. At any rate he is emphatic in his belief that there will always in any society be irreconcilable conflicts of ends or values: 'the human condition is such that men cannot always avoid choices . . . they cannot avoid choice for one central reason . . . namely that ends collide; that one cannot have everything . . . The need to choose, to sacrifice some ultimate values to others, turns out to be a permanent characteristic of the human predicament' (p. li). 'That we cannot have everything is a necessary, not a contingent, truth' (p. 170).

It is difficult to see how it can be so categorically asserted that some ultimate values will always have to be sacrificed to others. What are these values or ends which may clash and some of which always will clash? We are given many examples: negative liberty *v.* security, status, prosperity, power, virtue, rewards in the next world, or justice, equality, or fraternity (p. 161); negative liberty *v.* equality, or justice, or happiness, or security, or public order (p. 170); negative liberty *v.* positive liberty, in such forms as individual freedom *v.* democracy, artistic achievement *v.* equality, spontaneity *v.* efficiency, and so on (pp. xlix–l). What is most noticeable about all these lists is that in every case the conflict is between negative liberty and some other value. And this perhaps explains why conflict of values is taken to be perpetually inevitable. For when negative liberty is defined so narrowly as we have seen it to be, that is, when absence of the crucial impediments (of lack of access to the means of life and labour) is not counted as part of liberty but relegated to being 'conditions for liberty', then one may well count on perennial conflict between negative liberty and some of the other values.

If negative liberty were defined more broadly, as I have argued it should be, it would not be in necessary conflict with those other values; and to the extent that it was actually achieved the area of unavoidable conflict would diminish. It is true that the conflicts Berlin speaks of are

[17] In Essay III, at pp. 74–5.

not conflicts of material interests. They are neither class conflicts nor collisions between the ends of narrowly self-interested appetitive individuals. They are conflicts between values, opposite ones of which can be, and have frequently been, maintained by men (and groups) of equally good will. That is what makes their perpetual presence plausible. But how many of those conflicts would remain endemic in a society without class conflict and without scarcity? They are endemic in a class-divided society, and particularly in a class-divided market society which lives on the postulate of infinite desirousness. In such a society it is indeed a necessary, not a contingent, truth 'that we cannot have everything'. But we do not have to go to the opposite extreme of a brainwashed utopia to envisage a society where diverse, genuinely human (not artificially contrived) desires can be simultaneously fulfilled.

If such a society is at all possible, the conflict of values need not be perpetual. If the conflict is not necessarily perpetual, the repressive monism which Berlin so rightly deplores is not needed to support a society of genuine positive liberty. In short, the monism which is the essence of PL^2 is not entailed in PL^1.

If the transformation of PL^1 into PL^2 does not flow from the logic of PL^1, what does it flow from? I suggest that the change to PL^2, where it occurs, may be better seen as the result of the theoretical and practical handling of certain implications of PL^1, specifically, of the role of impediments. PL^1 is, as we have noticed, virtually the same as what I have called men's developmental powers. The attempt to achieve or maximize PL^1 must therefore be an attempt to remove or minimize the impediments to each man's developmental power. Among those impediments are some men's lack of access to the means of life and labour. Failure to see this and to follow it up appears to be the cause, directly or indirectly, of the emergence of PL^2.

In looking at this possible causal relation, we may, to begin with, distinguish between conservative and radical forms of PL^2. 'Conservative' is used here in a broad sense to mean those doctrines which would maintain something like the existing class structure of power and property: doctrines ranging from Hegel's to the conservative property liberalism to T. H. Green, and including various élitist theories; and 'radical' to mean those which reject, and would like to encompass the destruction of, the existing class structure. Conservative PL^2 then appears as a direct, and radical PL^2 as an indirect, result of a failure of traditional liberal theory and practice to see and deal with the problem of impediments. Let us see how each of these forms of PL^2 may be said to come from this single failure.

Conservative PL^2 on the whole, Idealist and otherwise, may be said to neglect, as impediments to men's powers, lack of access to the means of life and labour. Failing to take them into account, its thinking consequently remains on a somewhat abstract plane. Its exponents see no future for PL^1 except in rule by a fully rational élite—themselves or their pupils, which rule, since it makes no effort to remove those impediments, ends in an authoritarian PL^2.

Of the Idealist theorists, T. H. Green came closest to casting the ideal of positive liberty, or full realization of powers, in terms of reducing impediments, and to recognizing the importance of these particular impediments.[18] Yet even the 'mild liberalism', as Berlin calls it, of Green's version of 'Objective Reason' puts his theory in the PL^2 category. Why? Because, I think, although Green was emphatic that the poverty and lack of access to land or capital which characterized the 'proletariate' (Green's word) of his own day were drastic impediments to the realization of men's powers,[19] he did not see (indeed he denied, with some warmth but no grasp of political economy) that these impediments were an inevitable part of the property system which as a liberal he fully supported, i.e. the capitalist market economy with the right of unlimited individual appropriation. He would not admit the inherency in capitalism of either the transfer of powers or the deficiency of powers coming from lack of control of one's labour and life. He did not see that his goal of positive liberty was unattainable along with the negative liberty he also demanded, the negative liberty of the classical liberals, central to which was freedom from interference with the operations of the capitalist market economy and with the right of unlimited appropriation. He did not see that this negative liberty, because it was available only to the few, hindered the possibility of positive freedom (PL^1) being achieved by the many. In Green's case this resulted in no more than a mild conservative liberalism: it did not push him very far into PL^2.

The full transition to a *conservative* PL^2 is more apt to come from those who pay less attention than Green did to the importance of the impediments imposed by an existing property structure. In so far as they do not see that the removal of those impediments is a *sine qua non* of the achievement of positive liberty (PL^1), and in as much as they believe that it must, in the nature of the universe, be possible to achieve PL^1, they are pushed into the position of holding that it can be done and should be done by an authoritarian élite using whatever coercive means are necessary (PL^2).

The transition to PL^2 in *radical* adherents of PL^1 comes not from any failure of theirs to see the importance of the impediments to PL^1 inherent in an existing class structure, but on the contrary from their seeing this and finding, or assuming, that all non-authoritarian ways to

[18] *Lectures on the Principles of Political Obligation*, sects. 220 ff.

[19] Ibid., sects. 222, 226.

the removal of those impediments are blocked, whether in theory, in practice, or in both, because of their opponents' failure to see or to acknowledge the impediments. This is not to say that radical theorists and leaders who start from a PL^1 position and make that sort of analysis are always pushed into PL^2. Marx himself surely was not: the end he sought was always the leap from the realm of necessity to the realm of freedom which would enable the utmost flowering of human diversity. Nor do I think Lenin could properly be described as an exponent of PL^2: he did indeed demand vanguard rule for a revolutionary transition, but vanguard rule, as I have pointed out, does not require PL^2 for its justification. The transformation of radical PL^1 into PL^2, which comes with Stalinism, comes, it appears, only after long-continued and intensive refusal of the beneficiaries of unequal institutions, on a world-wide scale, to permit any moves to alter the institutions in the direction of more nearly equal powers. In any case, the radical transition to PL^2 does appear to be a result not of anything inherent in PL^1 but of a failure somewhere in the prevailing system to deal with the problem of impediments.

It thus seems that in both the conservative and radical cases the transition to PL^2 is not to be ascribed to any logical process the seeds of which are in PL^1, and that PL^1 is not equally likely to be turned into PL^2 in all circumstances. The circumstances in which PL^1 sours into PL^2 can be narrowed down first by noticing that the whole concept of positive liberty is a modern one. Authoritarianism in the name of some higher reason or higher purpose is of course as old as Plato, but not until the modern world was such authoritarianism called liberty. The reason is not far to seek: it is that individual liberty of any kind was not a central value of political theory in ancient or medieval civilizations. Berlin has made this point about negative liberty (p. 129); we have only to add that until negative liberty became highly prized it would have been meaningless for any theorist to put his case for the dominance of the rational will, or the unfolding of man's full nature, in terms of the attainment of (positive) liberty.

We may say, then, that the concept of positive liberty arose and could only arise after the ideal of individual liberty had taken pretty firm hold. And that is to say that the concept of positive liberty is a product of bourgeois society. So, therefore, is any transformation of PL^1 into PL^2. And in fact PL^2, in both the conservative and radical forms we have distinguished, has emerged in and from bourgeois societies. Conservative PL^2, we may now say, emerges among theorists who accept bourgeois values but who fail to see that the chief impediments to both NL and PL^1 are the same; and radical PL^2 among theorists who reject bourgeois values as incompatible with PL^1 and find the way to PL^1 blocked by the holders of political power. The two kinds of PL^2 are results, direct and indirect, of the failure of liberal-individualist theorists and defenders of an established capitalist society to see what impediments to PL^1 are inherent in that society, and hence their failure to recommend, or permit to be taken, the action required to remove those impediments. Conservative PL^2 is a direct result of this failure; radical PL^2 is an indirect result of it.

It is not easy to narrow still further the circumstances in which these transformations of PL^1 into PL^2 take place. It might be suggested that the likelihood of the transformation varies inversely with the sensitivity of the intellectuals to the society's shortcomings; or that it varies directly with the structural or historical accidents which encourage or permit a high degree of intransigence in the ruling class. But for our present purposes, which are simply to try to identify the theoretical failures which lead to PL^2, and so to indicate how they may be averted, the analysis sketched here is perhaps sufficient.

I conclude that the emergence of PL^2 is less a result of any inherent predisposition of PL^1 towards Idealist fallacies, or of any fatal assumption (such as Berlin finds inherent in the extreme rationalist treatment of positive liberty) that there is a final and singular solution to all ethical problems, than it is the result of a specific failure of theorists to isolate the impediments to PL^1 inherent in liberal societies hitherto, and a concomitant failure of those who wield political power in liberal societies to take the action required to realize PL^1. In the circumstances of the late twentieth century, with democratic currents running as strongly as they are, the result of this double failure is all too apt to be either a conservative garrison state or a communist totalitarianism.

If this analysis is at all valid, if both of these denials of liberty and humanity are results not of any inherent fault in the notion of positive liberty but of specific defects in seeing and acting on what it requires in the given kind of society, then we should not, as Berlin advises us, jettison positive liberty. It contains, after all, the noblest strivings possible to any individualist theory. And to give it up—that is, to try to root it out of the liberal-democratic tradition of the West—would not, in our twentieth-century circumstances, give us any more security for genuine negative liberty. It might well give us less. For negative liberty is no longer, as Mill tried to make it and as Berlin would still like to see it, the shield of individuality: it has become the cloak for un-individualist, corporate, imperial, 'free enterprise'. The same, unfortunately, can be said about much of the current political theory of pluralism,[20] so that the reformulation of negative liberty as pluralism cannot be relied upon either. Yet the dangers of the concept of positive liberty are vividly clear. Is there any other way out?

[20] See the critiques of pluralism in the works cited in note 2 of Essay IV.

3. *An Alternative Division of Liberty*

I have argued that Berlin's division of liberty into positive and negative fails to serve the purpose for which it was designed, namely, to rescue liberty from the hands of all those who use the word in order to deny the substance. His division, I have suggested, empties too much out of negative liberty—understood as absence of interference with potential choices—by counting as interference only direct physical obstruction. Chains, enslavement, direct physical domination, are counted in. But domination by withholding the means of life or the means of labour is not: it is put outside the province of liberty altogether.

Because it is put outside the province of liberty, it does not figure in the definition of positive liberty either. But positive liberty, in its basic sense of ability to form and follow one's own conscious purposes, requires even more clearly than negative liberty that there be no indirect domination by withholding the means of life and labour. Berlin's formulation of positive liberty neglects this, so his positive liberty has nowhere to go except into the clouds. It becomes an abstraction, emptied of any content: it has not even the narrow but concrete content which his negative liberty has—'no chains'. So he finds it natural or even necessary, that positive liberty should be converted into metaphysical rationalism, and so end up as a denial of liberty. It *is* natural that a concept of positive liberty so emptied of content should end up that way. But there is no reason why it must be so emptied.

Could an alternative division of liberty better serve the purpose of protecting individual liberty against its perversion? Let us start, as Berlin does, with liberty as absence of interference or domination. And let us acknowledge that liberty is entirely a matter of each individual's liberty. But let us also acknowledge that, since each individual's liberty may diminish or destroy another's, the only sensible way to measure individual liberty is to measure the aggregate net liberty of all the individuals in a given society. That this is so is most apparent when the place of law is considered.

'Every law', said Bentham, 'is an infraction of liberty.'[21] Quite so. But equally so, if there were no laws to protect individuals against direct invasion by others, there would be no liberty (in Berlin's sense), i.e. no area in which anyone was secure from interference or domination. So, if one starts with no laws, each law preventing some type of invasion increases the aggregate liberty.[22] There must be interference

[21] Quoted, with approval, by Berlin, p. 148.

[22] Berlin seems to allow this when he adds, to the quotation from Bentham cited in the previous note: 'even if such "infraction" leads to an increase in the sum of

to protect me from interference: interference by the state to protect me from interference by other individuals. This is clear enough in the case of laws preventing direct invasion of one individual by others. And if one counts as deprivations of an individual's liberty the indirect interference imposed by withholding from him the means of life or means of labour, then state interference to prevent such indirect invasion must also be held to increase aggregate liberty.

It certainly does not follow from this that every law, every state interference, is designed to increase aggregate liberty. For the state has usually been also an engine of domination of one class over others. Its laws of property, whether designed to maintain slavery or serfdom or capitalist enterprise, have ensured an order of domination. Their purpose has been to enable some to extract benefit for themselves from others. The central distinction, then, between laws, is whether they increase or decrease net aggregate individual liberty.

And the central point about liberty is whether the liberties which are allowed or guaranteed by a society increase or decrease the net aggregate liberty, by preventing or permitting the extraction of benefit by some from others. The measure of liberty is the absence of extractive power.[23] For it can be assumed that the reason others wish to dominate me is, in the last analysis, to get something out of me, to extract some of my power for their benefit. And the reason the state wishes to interfere with me (beyond the amount of interference required to secure me from private interference) is to permit those whom it chiefly represents to get something out of me.

It seems, therefore, that Berlin's negative liberty might well be redefined as *immunity from the extractive power of others* (*including the state*). This might be described, for want of a simpler term, as *counter-extractive liberty*. This concept has the advantage of staying closer to reality than 'negative' liberty. It moves away from the mechanical image of negative liberty as 'a field (ideally) without obstacles, a vacuum in which nothing obstructs me' (p. 144). It acknowledges that obstructions are necessary to protect the field.

As to positive liberty, that is, the genuine positive liberty I have designated PL^1, the difference between it and counter-extractive liberty is even less than the original difference between negative and positive, which was 'no more than negative and positive ways of saying much the same thing' (pp. 131–2). For when the impediments to negative liberty are spelled out, they turn out to be much the same as the impediments to positive liberty.

liberty' (p. 148). Yet he also appears to consider such summing 'logically absurd' (p. 130, n.).

[23] As defined in Essay III, at p. 42.

There is, however, still a difference of emphasis between counter-extractive liberty and positive liberty: the former is a prerequisite of the latter. So it may still be analytically helpful to keep a division between two kinds of liberty. But the division will be better marked if we change the name of positive liberty to *developmental liberty*. As we have already seen, Berlin's positive liberty (PL^1) is virtually the same as what I have called a man's developmental power. 'Developmental liberty' covers PL^1, and excludes PL^2. It also provides no toe-hold for the metaphysical rationalism which so easily moves from the abstractness of Berlin's original positive liberty to his debased positive liberty.

The advantage I see in a redivision of liberty, from negative/positive to counter-extractive/developmental, is that it better serves the libertarian purpose of warning people off the kind of debased liberty which negates liberty. For if people thought in terms of 'counter-extractive' and 'developmental' liberty, rather than continuing to think in terms of 'negative' and 'positive' liberty, it would be clearer that the latter requires the former, and it would be less easy for any theorist or leader or movement to pull positive liberty away from its moorings.

ESSAY VI

A Political Theory of Property

MANY of the threads of the preceding essays converge on the concept of property. The weakness of the 'traditional' liberal-democratic theory has been traced to its retention of the concept of man as infinite consumer and infinite appropriator: that concept of man is clearly inextricable from a concept of property. Alternatively, the failure of the traditional theory of Mill and Green has been traced to their failure to recognize that the individual property right on which they insisted meant a denial to most men of equitable access to the means of life and the means of labour, without which access men could not hope to realize their human potential: here again the concept of property is crucial.

The shortcomings of what I have called revisionist liberalism[1] could be restated in much the same terms. So could the deficiencies of those twentieth-century political theories which have in their various ways reduced democracy to a market phenomenon.[2] And so could the illogic of extreme neo-liberals.[3]

The central importance of access to the means of life and the means of labour has been seen in other contexts as well. Denial or limitation of access is a means of maintaining class-divided societies, with a class domination which thwarts the humanity of the subordinate and perverts that of the dominant class; this is a condition which neither any amount of 'consumers' sovereignty', nor the fairest system of distributive justice, can offset or remedy.[4] And one main constituent of liberty itself, both 'negative' and 'positive', is, I have argued, this same access to the means of life and labour.[5] The extent and distribution of that access is set by the institution of property.

Again, the dangerous flaw in liberal-democratic theory has been presented as the conflict within it between developmental power and extractive power.[6] Progress towards the democratic goal of maximizing men's developmental powers has been seen to be impeded by the market society's retention of individual and corporate extractive powers. And extractive powers, which are the obverse of access, are maintained by an institution of property. Property in capital, which is

[1] Cf. Essay IV, sections 2 and 3.
[2] Cf. Essay IV, section 1; and Essay X.
[3] Cf. Essay VII. [4] Cf. Essay IV. [5] Cf. Essay V.
[6] As defined in Essay III.

the accumulation of extractive power, has become the measure of man. I have argued that genuine democracy, and genuine liberty, both require the absence of extractive powers. But this does not mean the absence of any institution of property. A society in which extractive powers were absent would of course also need an institution of property, if only to prevent a recurrence of types of property which support extractive powers.[7] But it would clearly need to be a very different institution of property.

So all roads lead to property. The retrieval of a genuine democratic theory, the attainment of an adequate theory of liberty, and the realization of both in practice, all require a fresh look at the theory and practice of property. How need that theory and practice change, to yield a genuinely democratic and genuinely liberal society? And what are the chances of their so changing? This will depend partly on the relation we find between the theory and the practice of property. We cannot undertake here a whole social history of property. But we can perhaps sufficiently point to an interdependence between the theory and practice to allow us to presume that an inquiry which focuses on the theory may take us to the heart of the matter.

Briefly it may be said that the theory and practice, or the concept and the institution, of property are interdependent, in that both change over time and the changes are related. As an institution, property—and any particular system of property—is a man-made device which establishes certain relations between people. Like all such devices, its maintenance requires at least the acquiescence of the bulk of the people, and the positive support of any leading classes. Such support requires a belief that the institution serves some purpose or fills some need. That belief requires, in turn, that there be a theory which both explains and justifies the institution in terms of the purpose served or the need filled. As needs change new theories are developed, and the institution itself is changed by political action. Changes in the theory and in the institution may come in either order; or they may come bit by bit, each reinforcing the other by such small stages that one cannot assign priority to either. But the general pattern seems to be, first, a change in perceived needs or wants which the institution could serve, then a change in the concept and theory of what the institution is and could be, then political action (ranging from legislation and judicial and administrative action to revolution) to change the institution. Some support for this generalization is offered in the following sections of this essay.

[7] It might be argued that in an ultimately ideal non-extractive society, from which the possessive ethos had disappeared, no institution of property would be needed. But short of that, and certainly in a transition period of indefinite duration, some institution of property would be needed.

When the theory of property is examined, historically and logically, it turns out to be more flexible than the classical liberals or their twentieth-century followers have allowed for. The concept of property has changed more than once, and in more than one way, in the past few centuries. It changed in discernible ways with the rise of modern capitalism, and it is changing again now with the maturation of capitalism. The more fully we can understand these changes and the reasons for them, the more able we shall be to see the necessary and the possible directions of future change.

It may even be that the break-through of consciousness of which I spoke at the end of Essay III, which would release us from the false image of man as infinite consumer and infinite appropriator, will come through a further transformatiom of the notion of property, induced by changes now already visible in the institution of property itself and in the needs which it serves.

I want now to argue

(1) that the concept of property which now prevails in Western societies is largely an invention of the seventeenth and eighteenth centuries, and is fully appropriate only to an autonomous capitalist market society: this is the concept of property as (a) identical with private property—an individual (or corporate) right to exclude others from the use or benefit of something; (b) a right in or to material things rather than a right to a revenue (and even, in common usage, as the things themselves rather than the rights); and (c) having as its main function to provide an incentive to labour, as well as (or rather than) being an instrument for the exercise of human capacities;

(2) that this concept of property has already begun to change, noticeably first in respect of (b): property is increasingly being seen again as a right to a revenue; and that for most people this must now be a right to *earn* an income, which is a right of access to the means of labour;

(3) that any society which claims to be democratic (i.e. to enable individuals equally to use and develop their human capacities) will have to acknowledge that individual property must increasingly consist in the individual right not to be excluded from access to the means of labour, now mainly corporately or socially owned: so that a democratic society must broaden the concept again from property as an individual right to exclude others, by adding property as an individual right not to be excluded by others; and

(4) that the concept of property as a right of access to the means of labour (in the narrow sense of labour devoted to material production) will in turn become obsolete, as and to the extent that technological change makes current labour less necessary; that, if the concept (and the institution) of property is to be compatible with any real democracy

(including any real liberal democracy), it will have to change *from* access to the means of labour *to* access to the means of a fully human life, and will therefore have to become (a) a right to a share in political power to control the uses of the amassed capital and the natural resources of the society, and (b), beyond that, a right to a kind of society, a set of power relations throughout the society, essential to a fully human life.

1. *Modern Property a Product of Capitalist Society*

I have mentioned three characteristics of the prevalent concept of property which I have said can be shown to be products of capitalist society: (a) that property means private property, a right to exclude others; (b) that property is a right in or to material things rather than a right to a revenue (and even, in common usage, that property is the things rather than the right); and (c) that the main function of property is to provide an incentive to labour. We may now consider each of these in turn.

(a) *Property as private property*

Property, nowadays, in the general understanding, at all levels from the usage of social and political theorists to that of the ordinary newspaper writer and reader, is usually equated with private property—the right of an individual (or a corporate entity) to exclude others from some use or benefit of something. So much is this the case that the very notion of 'common property' is sometimes treated as if it were a contradiction in terms. 'State property' is of course recognized as an existing fact, but this is a right of a corporate entity—the state or the government or one of its agencies—to exclude others, not (as common property is, as we shall see) an individual right not to be excluded.[8]

At first sight, the identification of property with private property may seem entailed in the very idea of property, for the idea of property is undoubtedly the idea of an enforceable claim of a person to some use or benefit of something. It will not be disputed that the very idea of property, as something over and above mere momentary physical possession or occupancy, is the idea of an enforceable claim, extending

[8] The distinction between *private property*, *state property*, and *common property*, is set out more fully in my introductory essay to a forthcoming volume of readings on *Property* (Chicago and New York, 1973). I have used some passages, without significant change, in this essay and in that (and also in this and in the concluding essay in that volume) whenever that seemed the most economical procedure.

over time, to the use or benefit of something. Property is a claim which the individual can count on having enforced in his favour by society or the state, by custom or convention or law.

But it does not follow from this that an individual's property is confined to his right to exclude others. An enforceable claim of an individual to some use or benefit of something equally includes his right *not to be excluded from* the use or benefit of something which society or the state has proclaimed to be for common use. Society or the state may declare that some things—for example, common lands, public parks, city streets, highways—are for common use. The right to use them is then a property of individuals, in that each member of the society[9] has an enforceable claim to use them. It need not be an unlimited claim. The state may, for instance, ration the use of public lands, or it may limit the kinds of uses anyone may make of the streets or of common waters (just as it now limits the uses anyone may make of his private property); but the right to use the common things, however limited, is a right of individuals.

The fact that we need some such term as *common* property, to distinguish such rights from the exclusive individual rights which are private property, may easily lead to our thinking that such common rights are not individual rights. But they are. They are the property of individuals, not of the state. The state indeed creates and enforces the right which each individual has in the things the state declares to be for common use. But so does the state create and enforce the exclusive rights which are private property. In neither case does the fact that the state creates the right make it the property of the state. In both cases what is created is a right of individuals. The state *creates* the rights, the individuals *have* the rights. Common property is created by the guarantee to each individual that he will not be excluded from the use or benefit of something; private property is created by the guarantee that an individual[10] can exclude others from the use or benefit of something. Both kinds of property, being guarantees to individual persons, are individual rights. It therefore does not follow, from the fact that all property is enforceable claims of (natural or artificial) individuals, that property is logically confined to private property (the right to exclude others).

The now common notion that it is so confined goes back no further than the seventeenth century, where it can be seen to be the product of the new relations of the emergent capitalist society. It is true that from

[9] The society may be as small as a medieval village or as large as a nation-state (or even larger, as when international law recognizes e.g. rights to use the high seas).

[10] Including the artifical individuals created by the state as corporate bodies, which corporate bodies may include, as they do in the case of state property, the state itself or its agents.

the beginning of argument about property—which argument is as old as political theory itself—the argument was mainly about private property. This is not surprising, since it is only the existence of private property that makes property a contentious moral issue. In any case, the earliest extant theorizing about property was done in societies which did have private property. But those societies were also familiar with common property. So, while the argument was mainly about private property, the theorists did not equate it with property. Aristotle could talk about two systems of property, one where all things were held in common and one where all things were held privately, and about mixed systems where land was common but produce was private and where produce was common but land was private: all these he saw as systems of property.

From then on, whether the debate was about the relative merits of private versus common property, or about how private property could be justified or what limits should be put on it, it was private property that bulked largest in the debate. It was attacked by Plato as incompatible with the good life for the ruling class; defended by Aristotle as essential for the full use of human faculties and as making for a more efficient use of resources; denigrated by earliest Christianity; defended by St. Augustine as a punishment and partial remedy for original sin; attacked by some heretical movements in medieval (and Reformation) Europe; justified by St. Thomas Aquinas as in accordance with natural law, and by later medieval and Reformation writers by the doctrine of stewardship. In all that early controversy, stretching down through the sixteenth century, what was chiefly in question was an exclusive, though a limited or conditional, individual right in land and goods.

But in that early period the theorists, and the law, were not unacquainted with the idea of common property. Common property was, by one writer or another, advocated as an ideal, attributed to the primitive condition of mankind, held to be suitable only to man before the Fall, and recognized as existing alongside private property in such forms as public parks, temples, markets, streets, and common lands. Indeed Jean Bodin, the first of the great early modern political theorists, in making a strong case at the end of the sixteenth century for modern private property, argued that in any state there must also be some common property, without which there could be no sense of community and hence no viable state: part of his case for private property was that without it there could be no appreciation of common property.

It is only when we enter the modern world of the full capitalist market society, in the seventeenth century, that the idea of common property drops virtually out of sight. So David Hume, who saw the protection of property as the chief business of government, could define property as an individual's right to use to the exclusion of others.[11] That common property dropped out of sight can be seen as a reflection of the changing facts. From the sixteenth and seventeenth centuries on, more and more of the land and resources in settled countries was becoming private property, and private property was becoming an individual right unlimited in amount, unconditional on the performance of social functions, and freely transferable, as it substantially remains to the present day. Modern private property is indeed subject to certain limits on the uses to which one can put it: the law commonly forbids using one's land or buildings to create a nuisance, using any of one's goods to endanger lives, and so on. But the modern right, in comparison with the feudal right which preceded it, may be called an absolute right in two senses: it is a right to dispose of, or alienate,[12] as well as to use; and it is a right which is not conditional on the owner's performance of any social function.

This of course was exactly the kind of property right needed to let the capitalist market economy operate. If the market was to operate fully and freely, if it was to do the whole job of allocating labour and resources among possible uses, then all labour and resources had to become, or be convertible into, this kind of property. The market had to be allowed to allocate labour and resources not only between the alternative uses that could be said to be determined by the effective demands of consumers, but also (and overridingly) between the alternatives of more for accumulation of capital and more (or more

[11] Cf. Hume's definition, note 15.

[12] The right to alienate one's property in land, though inconsistent with the feudal principle of personal tenure, was indeed won in the thirteenth century, long before the emergence of modern capitalism: the Statute of *Quia Emptores* (1290) gave that right to tenants in fee-simple. But at the same time the landowners were equally interested in the right to tie up their property: they 'did not wish to be deprived of the power of making family settlements, which would be secure, not only against voluntary alienation by their heirs, but also against the involuntary alienation which followed upon a conviction for treason or felony' (Sir William Holdsworth: *Essay in Law and History* (Oxford, 1946), p. 105). The right to *prevent* future alienation was established by the statute *De Donis Conditionalibus* in 1285, and was widely exercised, so that thenceforth much of the land was not alienable. In the subsequent centuries various ways around this inalienability were tried, but it was not till the end of the seventeenth century that the courts were able 'to confirm the legality of the expedients devised for circumventing the statute *De Donis*, to pronounce illegal all attempts to create an unbarrable entail, and finally to evolve the rule against perpetuities' (Ibid., p. 107). To say that alienability is one of the features that distinguishes modern from medieval property is not to say that it was absent from still earlier societies. Alienability was generally recognized in classical Greece and Rome, whose economies were more market-based than those of feudal societies. All market societies require alienability of property in some degree; the full market society requires it in the highest degree.

immediate) satisfaction of the demand for consumption goods. As the capitalist market economy found its feet and grew, it was expected to, and did, take on most of this work of allocation. As it did so, it was natural that the very concept of property should be reduced to that of *private* property—an exclusive, alienable, 'absolute' individual or corporate right in things.

(b) *Property as a right to (or even as) material things, rather than as a right to a revenue*

In pre-capitalist England, property had generally been seen as a right to a revenue (whether in the form of services or produce or money) rather than as a right to specific material things, and had not been seen as the material things themselves.[13] This reflected the real situation: until the emergence of the capitalist economy, property had in fact mainly been a right to a revenue rather than a right to a thing. In the first place the great bulk of property was then property in land, and a man's property in a piece of land was generally limited to certain uses of it and was often not freely disposable. Different people might have different rights in the same piece of land, and many of those rights were not fully disposable by the current owner of them either by sale or bequest.[14] The property he had was obviously some right in the land, and usually the right to a revenue from the land, not the land itself. And in the second place, another substantial segment of property consisted of those rights to a revenue which were provided by such things as corporate charters, monopolies granted by the state, tax-farming rights, and the incumbency of various political and ecclesiastical offices. Clearly here too the property was the right to a revenue, not a right to any specific material thing.

The change in common usage, to treating property as the things themselves, came with the spread of the capitalist market economy, which brought the replacement of the old limited rights in land by virtually unlimited rights, and the replacement of the old privileged rights to commercial revenues by more marketable properties in

[13] Medieval English law did treat rights as 'things' (i.e. did treat present and future and partial rights in material things, chiefly land, as legal 'things'), but it did not treat things (in the modern sense of material things) as property. Somewhat as in Roman law, where *res* included *res corporales* and *res incorporales* ('things' which are not material things), so in English law there were *corporeal* and *incorporeal hereditaments*. These were property, but in each case the property was a right in the material thing, not the material thing itself: a *corporeal hereditament* was 'a *present* right to enjoy the possession of land either personally or through tenants', an *incorporeal hereditament* 'a future right to possession or a right to use for a special purpose land in possession of another, e.g. a right of way' (Topham's *Real Property* (3rd edn., London, 1921), pp. 7–8; cf. C. Reinold Noyes: *The Institution of Property* (New York, 1936), pp. 267–8).

[14] See note 12.

actual capital, however accumulated. As rights in land became more absolute, and parcels of land became more freely marketable commodities, it became natural to think of the land itself as the property. And as aggregations of commercial and industrial capital, operating in increasingly free markets and themselves freely marketable, overtook in bulk the older kinds of movable wealth based on charters and monopolies, the capital itself, whether in money or in the form of actual plant, could easily be thought of as the property. The more freely and pervasively the market operated, the more this was so. It appeared to be the things themselves, the actual parcels of land and portions of commercial capital, not just rights in them, that were exchanged in the market. In fact the difference was not that things rather than rights in things were exchanged, but that previously unsalable or not always salable rights in things were now salable; or, to put it differently, that limited and not always salable rights *in* things (land, and trading privileges that were in effect capital) were being replaced by virtually unlimited and salable rights *to* things (land and actual capital).

As property became increasingly salable absolute rights to things, the distinction between the right and the thing was easily blurred. It was the more easily blurred because, with these changes, the state became more and more an engine for guaranteeing the full right of the individual to the disposal as well as use of things. The state's protection of the right could be so much taken for granted that one did not have to look behind the thing to the right. The thing itself became, in common parlance, the property.

This usage, which is still today the commonplace one, has on the whole been avoided by legal and political writers, who have fairly steadily seen that property is a right not a thing, although it can occasionally be found in theorists as early as the eighteenth century.[15]

[15] Hume, for instance, although generally quite clearly stating that property is a right in something, or 'such a relation betwixt a person and an object as permits him, but forbids any other, the free use and possession of it, without violating the laws of justice and moral equity' (*Treatise of Human Nature*, Book II, Part I, section X, Green and Grose edition, Vol. II, p. 105), did at least once slip into the other usage: 'A man's property is some object related to him' (ibid., Book III, Part II, section II; Vol. II, p. 264). Bentham in 1789 noted, disapprovingly, the common usage: 'It is to be observed, that in common speech, in the phrase *the object of a man's property*, the words *the object of* are commonly left out; and by an ellipsis, which, violent as it is, is now become more familiar than the phrase at length, they have made that part of it which consists of the words *a man's property* perform the office of the whole' (*Introduction to the Principles of Morals and Legislation*, chap. XVI, section 26, footnote (Harrison edn., p. 337, n. 1)). The common usage is now recognized by legal writers (e.g. J. C. Vaines: *Personal Property* (3rd edn., London, 1962), p. 3), perforce, since the common usage had crept into the courts (cf. Noyes: *The Institution of Property*, pp. 356–7).

But what the political theorists generally did do, from the seventeenth century on, was to treat property as rights in material things rather than as rights to revenues. The reason for this is presumably the same as the reason for the common misusage: with the rise of the capitalist market economy, the bulk of actual property shifted *from* often non-transferable rights to a revenue from land, monopolies, charters, and offices, *to* transferable rights in freehold land, salable leases, physical plant, and money, which is a claim at will on any of those material things. It is in this sense that the change from property as rights to revenues, to property as rights in material things, can be seen as the product of the rise of capitalist market relations.

(c) *Property as the incentive to necessary labour*

The idea that the main function of the institution of property is to be an incentive to the labour required by a society, is also new in the seventeenth century. Before then, property was held to be needed (and justified) mainly for other reasons: e.g. to enable men to express their human essence (Aristotle), or to counteract their sinful nature (Augustine). Reasoning from such bases did justify some exclusive individual property, but only for the fully rational (or fully human) individuals, not for slaves or serfs.

What required a new case for exclusive individual property in the seventeenth century, that is, for turning virtually *all* property into *exclusive* private property, was the change in fact and in ideology that came with the rise of capitalist relations. The change in fact was that all men were being brought to the valuation of the market, and were being made free to contract in the market. The change in ideology was that all men were now asserted to be capable of a fully human life (clearly, by the Levellers; grudgingly and ambiguously by Locke). Given the assertion of the natural equal humanity of all men, it became logically necessary to assert a property right open to everyone. But it was impossible to derive, from human needs alone, an exclusive individual right, open to everyone, in land and capital. For it was assumed that land and capital always necessarily would be, as they always had been, held by less than all men, and on that assumption need alone could not confer on everyone an exclusive right.

So, if the new kind of property required by the capitalist market society, i.e. property as an exclusive, alienable right to all kinds of material things including land and capital, was to be thought to be justified, the right would have to be based on something more universal than the old feudal or customary class differentials in supposed needs and capacities.

The universal basis was found in 'labour'. Every man had a property in his own labour. And from the postulate that a man's labour was peculiarly, exclusively his own, all that was needed followed. The postulate reinforced the concept of property as exclusion. As his labour was his own, so was that land with which he had mixed his labour, and that capital which he had accumulated by means of applying his labour. This was the principle that Locke made central to the liberal concept of property.

The labour justification of individual property was carried down unquestioned in the liberal theory. Even Bentham, scorning natural rights and claiming to have replaced them by utility, rested the property right on labour. Security of enjoyment of the fruits of one's labour was the reason for property: without a property in the fruits and in the means of labour no one would have an incentive to labour, and utility could not be maximized. Mill and Green also held to the labour justification. 'The institution of property', Mill wrote, 'when limited to its essential elements, consists in the recognition, in each person, of a right to the exclusive disposal of what he or she have produced by their own exertions, or received either by gift or by fair agreement, without force or fraud, from those who produced it. The foundation of the whole is the right of producers to what they themselves have produced.'[16] Similarly Green: 'The rationale of property, in short, requires that everyone who will conform to the positive condition of possessing it, viz. labour, and the negative condition, viz. respect for it as possessed by others, should, so far as social arrangements can make him so, be a possessor of property himself, and of such property as will at least enable him to develope a sense of responsibility, as distinct from mere property in the immediate necessaries of life.'[17] So the derivation of property in things from the property in one's labour stamped property as an exclusive right from the beginning of the liberal tradition.

It provided a justification of precisely the kind of property that was required by a full capitalist market society. A man's own labour, as well as capital and land, was made so much a private exclusive property as to be alienable, i.e. marketable. The concept of property as nothing but an exclusive, alienable, individual right not only in material things but even in one's own productive capacities was thus a creation of capitalist society: it was only needed, and only brought forth, when the formal equality of the market superseded the formal inequality of pre-capitalist society.

Thus we may say that the now dominant concept of property is, in its three leading characteristics, a creation of the capitalist market society. It was the needs of that society, as of no previous society, that produced (a) the identification of property with private, exclusive

[16] J. S. Mill: *Principles of Political Economy*, Book II, Chapter 2, section 1.
[17] T. H. Green: *Lectures on the Principles of Political Obligation*, section 221.

property, (b) the concept of property as a right to material things rather than a right to a revenue, and (c) the justification of such property in terms of labour.

2. *Mid-Twentieth-Century Changes in the Concept of Property*

The concept of property just outlined, which became dominant with the full development of capitalism in the nineteenth and twentieth centuries, is already undergoing changes. The most general change is that property is again being seen as a right to a revenue or an income, rather than as rights in specific material things. The change is evident in all sectors of advanced capitalist societies: the changed view is common to investors, beneficiaries of the welfare state, independent enterprisers, and wage and salary earners.

Investors, to the extent that they are pure *rentiers*, have of course always seen their property as a right to a revenue. But with the rise of the modern corporation, and the predominance of corporate property, more individual investors of all sorts become *rentiers* and become aware that that is what they are. Their property consists less of their ownership of some part of the corporation's physical plant and stock of materials and products than of their right to a revenue from the ability of the corporation to manoeuvre profitably in a very imperfect market. True, an investor may see his property as a right to expected capital gains rather than to expected dividends, but this is still a right to a revenue (a more sophisticated one, less subject perhaps to reduction by the income tax). Moreover, with the spread of affluence and of security-consciousness, increasing numbers of people have some property in the form of rights in pension funds or annuities, if not of rights to a revenue from stocks or bonds. This of course has not turned the whole population into *rentiers*, but it is making members of all classes more revenue-conscious than many of them were before.

The rise of the welfare state has created new forms of property and distributed them widely—all of them being rights to a revenue. The old-age pensioner, the unemployed, and the unemployable, may have as his sole property the right to such a revenue as his condition entitles him to receive from the state. Where in addition the state provides such things as family allowances and various free or subsidized services, almost everyone has some property in such rights to a revenue.

But while almost everyone may get some of his income from the welfare state, and increasing numbers get some of theirs (at least indirectly) as investors, most people still have to work for most of their income. Their main property is their right to *earn* an income, whether as self-employed persons or as wage or salary earners. Whichever way they earn their income, they are coming to see their main property as the right to do so, and to see that this depends on factors outside their control.

Those who may still be counted as independent enterprisers—the self-employed, from taxi operators to doctors—find that their property in their enterprises increasingly depends on governmental licences to ply their trade or exercise their profession: their property is an expectation of a revenue dependent on their conformity to increasingly stringent regulations laid down by the state or its agents 'in the public interest'.[18]

However, the bulk of those whose main income is from their work is now made up of wage and salary earners. And they are increasingly coming to see their property as the right to a job, the right to be employed. Since they are by definition employed by others, that right amounts to a right of access to the means of labour which they do not own. What is new is not the fact, but the increasing perception of it.

That an individual's access to the means of labour is his most important property has been true for most men in most societies. For wherever a society's flow of income requires the current labour of most of its members, and wherever most individuals' incomes depend on their contributing their labour, most men's property in the means of life depends on their access to the means of labour. In a simple society most might have access by communal or tribal rights, or, where there was private property in land but still plenty of land, most might have access by owning, that is, having some exclusive right in, the land or materials which were their necessary means of labour. In a capitalist society, where most do not own their own means of labour, their right to the means of life is reduced to their right of access to means of labour owned by others.

It was all very well for Locke and subsequent liberal theorists to suggest that a man's labour was his most important property: the fact was that the value of a man's labour was zero if he had no access to land or capital. The value of the property in one's labour depended on one's access to the means of labour owned by others. It has been so ever since the predominance of the capitalist market system. It still is so. One's main property is still, for most men, one's right of access to the means of labour. This, as I have said, is not new.

What is new in mid-twentieth century is that this fact is being more widely recognized. It was seen in the nineteenth century only by a

[18] The proliferation of the regulatory powers of the state, and the extent to which this has replaced the older forms of property by a 'new property' in government licences (and government largess), is strikingly documented by Professor Charles Reich: 'The New Property', *Yale Law Journal*, Vol. 73 (April 1964). A shorter version of his paper, with the same title, is printed in *The Public Interest*, no. 3 (Spring 1966). A substantial part of the longer article is reprinted in my volume on *Property* referred to in note 8 above.

handful of radicals and socialists: it is now seen by a large part of the non-socialist organized labour movement, which thinks of the worker's main property as his right to the job. This is a considerable transformation of the concept of property. And it can have explosive consequences. For to see as one's property a right to earn an income through employment is to see (or to come close to seeing) as one's property a right of access to some of the existent means of labour, that is, to some of the accumulated productive resources of the whole society (natural resources plus the productive resources created by past labour), no matter by whom they are owned.

3. *An Impending Change in the Concept of Property*

It can now be forecast that the concept of property as solely private property, the right to exclude others from some use or benefit of something, which is already a concept of an individual right to a revenue, will have to be broadened to include property as an individual right not to be excluded from the use or benefit of the accumulated productive resources of the whole society.

The forecast is made on two grounds: (a) that property as an exclusive alienable 'absolute' right is no longer as much needed in the quasi-market society of the late twentieth century as it was in the earlier, relatively uncontrolled, full market society; and (b) that democratic pressures on those governments which uphold capitalist property rights are becoming strong enough that any such government which claims also to be furthering a democratic society (i.e. to be enabling individuals equally to use and develop their human capacities), will have to acknowledge that property as a right of access must be increasingly an individual right not to be excluded from access.

(a) *The change from market to quasi-market society*

We noticed above that property as exclusive, alienable, 'absolute', individual, or corporate rights in things was required by the full market society because and in so far as the market was expected to do the whole work of allocation of natural resources and capital and labour among possible uses. In such an autonomous market society there is very little room for common property, since common property by definition withholds from the play of the market those resources in which there is common property and so interferes with total market allocation of resources (and of labour, since the more common property there is, the less dependent on employment, i.e. the less compelled to enter his labour in the market, is each individual who lacks material productive resources of his own).

There is of course still a place in capitalist market society for some state property, such as transportation and communications facilities that are necessary for, but not profitable to, private enterprise. But such state property is sharply distinct from common property, as we have seen above. State property may assist, but common property hinders, market allocation.

As long as the market was expected to do the whole job of allocation, then, the concept of property that was needed was the concept of private, exclusive, alienable right. But now, even in the most capitalist countries, the market is no longer expected to do the whole work of allocation. We have moved from market society to quasi-market society. In all capitalist countries, the society as a whole, or the most influential sections of it, operating through the instrumentality of the welfare state and the warfare state—in any case, the regulatory state—is doing more and more of the work of allocation. Property as exclusive, alienable, 'absolute', individual, or corporate rights in things therefore becomes less necessary.

This does not mean that this kind of property is any less desired by the corporations and individuals who still have it in any quantity. But it does mean that as this kind of property becomes less demonstrably necessary to the work of allocation, it becomes harder to defend this kind as the very essence of property. Again, no one would suggest that the removal or reduction of the necessity of this kind of property would by itself result in the disappearance or weakening of this as the very image of property: positive social pressures would also be required.

(b) *Democratic pressures on governments*

Democratic pressures for more equitable and more secure access to the means of labour and the means of life are clearly increasing. They are, I think, now reaching such a strength that governments which still uphold the exclusive property rights of a capitalist society, and which claim also, as they all do, that they are promoting a fully democratic society—one in which all individuals are enabled equally to use and develop their human capacities—will have to acknowledge that property can no longer be considered to consist solely of private property—an individual right to exclude others from some use or benefit of something—but must be stretched to cover the opposite kind of individual property—an individual right not to be excluded from the use or benefit of something. This means the creation, by law, either of more common property or of more guaranteed access to the means of labour and the means of life which remain privately owned, i.e. a diminution of the extent to which private property, especially in productive resources, is a right to exclude.

The pressure comes from several directions. There is the already mentioned insistence by many sectors of organized labour on 'the right to the job', an insistence which the modern state and its agencies have found themselves in a weak position to resist. There is the markedly increasing public awareness of the menaces of air and water and earth pollution, which are seen as a denial of a human right to a decent environment, a denial directly attributable to the hitherto accepted idea of the sanctity of private (including corporate) property. Air and water, which hitherto had scarcely been regarded as property at all, are now being thought of as common property—a right to clean air and water is coming to be regarded as a property from which nobody should be excluded.

So the identification of property with exclusive private property, which we have seen has no standing in logic, is coming to have less standing in fact. It is no longer as much needed, and no longer as welcomed, as it was in the earlier days of the capitalist market society.

The pressures against it can only be strengthened by the logic of the situation. Private property as an institution has always needed a moral justification. The justification of private property (which became the justification of all property, as capitalism took hold and reduced common property to insignificance) has always ultimately gone back either to the individual right to life at a more than animal level (and hence a right to the means of such a life), or to the right to one's own body, hence to one's own labour, hence to the fruits of one's own labour, and hence also to the means of one's labour.

Sometimes the case is made on a ground that appears to be different from either of these, namely, that individual exclusive property is essential to individual freedom both economic and political—freedom from coerced labour and from arbitrary government. This is the case that Jefferson made much of. He argued convincingly that property in the means of one's own labour was not only rightful in itself but was also an indispensable safeguard of individual liberty. With one's own small property one could not be made subservient. And small property was the great guarantee against government tyranny as well as against economic oppression. It was to secure individual liberty, and all the virtues that can flourish only with sturdy independence, that Jefferson wanted America to remain a country of small proprietors.

This justification of property rests, in the last analysis, on the right to life at a more than animal level: freedom from coerced labour and from arbitrary government are held to be part of what is meant by a fully human life. At the same time this justification is an assertion of the right to the means of labour: the whole point is that by working on his own land or other productive resources a man can be independent and uncoerced. However, while the Jeffersonian argument is a branch of the case resting on the right of life, it is important enough to be treated separately: its emphasis on property as a prerequisite of freedom adds something important to the narrow Utilitarian case for property as a prerequisite of a flow of the consumable material means of life. So we have three principles on which individual property is based: the right to the material means of life, the right to a free life, and the right to the (current and accumulated) fruits of one's labour.

It can easily be seen that, in the circumstances of mature capitalism, all three principles require that the concept of property be broadened—that it no longer be confined to the individual right to exclude others, but be extended to include each individual's right not to be excluded from the use or benefit of things, and productive powers, that can be said to have been created by the joint efforts of the whole society. (i) A right to the means of life must either be a direct right, irrespective of work, to a share in the society's current output of goods and services, which is a right not to be excluded from its flow of benefits; or a right to earn an income, which requires that one should not be excluded from the use of the accumulated means of labour. (ii) A right to the fruits of one's labour requires that one should be able to labour, that is, requires access to the means of labour, or non-exclusion from the accumulated means of labour. (iii) A right to a free life can no longer be secured, as it could in Jefferson's day, by each man having his own small property in his means of labour: it can only be secured by guarantees of access on equal terms to the means of labour that are now mainly corporately or socially owned.

Thus the rationale of property, in any of its three justifications, requires the recognition of property as the right not to be excluded—either the right not to be excluded from a share in the society's whole material output, or the right not to be excluded from access to the accumulated means of labour. Of these, the latter has been up to now much the most important. But this is likely to change.

4. *Beyond Property as Access to the Means of Labour*

We can now forecast that the concept of property as essentially access to the means of labour will in turn become inadequate, as and to the extent that technological advances make current human labour less necessary; and that, if property is to be consistent with any real democracy, the concept of property will have to be broadened again to include the right to a share in political power, and, even beyond that, a right to a kind of society or set of power relations which will enable the individual to live a fully human life. This is to take to a higher level the concept of property as the prerequisite of a free life.

(a) *Property as political power*

The importance to each individual of access to the means of labour will clearly diminish if and in so far as the amount of current human labour required to produce an acceptable flow of the means of life for all diminishes. For as less labour is needed, the requirement to work is less needed. The right to *earn* an income becomes less a prerequisite or co-requisite of the right *to* an income.

Already, for technical economic reasons as well as from social and political pressures, the most advanced capitalist countries are beginning to move in the direction of providing a 'guaranteed annual income' or setting up a 'negative income tax'. The effect of such measures is to give everyone an income (though it may at first be a small one) unrelated to work. If the amount of such income should become substantial, the right to *earn* an income would clearly decline in importance as a form of property. It is too early to say for certain whether, or when, future increases in the productivity of modern societies will so diminish the amount of socially required human labour that income can be detached entirely from labour expended. But we can say that, to the extent that this happens, property as a valuable individual right will again change its nature.

The change in that case will be more striking than any of the changes we have seen so far. It will be a change from property as a right of access to the means of labour, to property as a right to the means of a fully human life. This seems to move us back through the centuries, to bring us back again to the idea that property in the means of life (a 'good' life) is the main form of property, as it was for the earliest theorists, e.g. Aristotle, before emphasis shifted to property in land and capital (the means of producing the means of life).

So it does, but the outcome is not the same. For, in the assumed circumstances of greatly increased productivity, the crucial question will no longer be how to provide a sufficient flow of the material means of life: it will be a question of getting the quality and kinds of things wanted for a full life, and, beyond that, of the quality of life itself. And both of these matters will require a property in the control of the mass of productive resources. If one envisages the extreme of an automated society in which nobody has to labour in order to produce the material means of life, the property in the massed productive resources of the whole society becomes of utmost importance. The property that would then be most important to the individual would no longer be the right of access to the means of labour; it would be instead, the right to a share in the control of the massed productive resources. That right would presumably have to be exercised politically. Political power then becomes the most important kind of property. Property, as an individual right, becomes essentially the individual's share in political power.

This becomes *the* important form of property, not only because it is the individual's guarantee of sharing equitably in the flow of consumables, in some part of which he will of course still need a property in the sense of an exclusive right. It becomes important also because only by sharing the control can he be assured of the means of the good or commodious or free life, which would then be seen to consist of more than a flow of consumables.

Property has always been seen as instrumental of life, and justified as instrumental to a fully human life. In the circumstances of material plenty which we now envisage, the relative importance, for a fully human life, of a merely sufficient flow of consumables will diminish, and the importance of all the means of a life of action and enjoyment of one's human capacities will increase.

(b) *Property as a right to a kind of society*

If property is to remain justified as instrumental to a full life, it will have to become the right not to be excluded from the means of such a life. Property will, in such circumstances, increasingly have to become a right to a set of social relations, a right to a kind of society. It will have to include not only a right to a share in political power as instrumental in determining the kind of society, but a right to that kind of society which is instrumental to a full and free life.

The idea that individual property extends to, and that a crucially important part of it is, a right to a set of power relations that permits a full life of enjoyment and development of one's human capacities, may seem fanciful. How can such a right be reduced to a set of enforceable claims of the individual (failing which, it would not meet an essential criterion of the idea of property)? It could not easily so be reduced merely by amendments to the existing laws of property. The claims that will have to be made enforceable are much broader than those which 'property' has comprised in the liberal society up to now.

There is, in principle, no reason why such broader claims could not be made enforceable, as certain rights to life and liberty are now. But I am suggesting that the broader claims will not be firmly anchored unless they are seen as property. For, in the liberal ethos which prevails in our liberal-democratic societies, property has more prestige than has almost anything else. And if the new claims are not brought under the head of property, the narrow idea of property will be used, with all the prestige of property, to combat them. In short, the now foreseeable and justifiable demands of the members of at least the most technically advanced societies cannot now be met without a new concept of property.

What makes this urgent is the fact that the conquest of scarcity is now not only foreseeable but actually foreseen. In the conditions of material scarcity that have always prevailed up to now,[19] property has been a matter of a right to a *material* revenue. With the conquest of scarcity that is now foreseen, property must become rather a right to an *immaterial* revenue, a revenue of enjoyment of the quality of life. Such a revenue cannot be reckoned in material quantities. The right to such a revenue can only be reckoned as a right to participation in a satisfying set of social relations.

If we achieve this concept of property we shall have reached again, but now on a more effective level, and for more people, that broader idea of property that prevailed in the period just before the individual was at once released and submerged by the capitalist market—the idea that a man has a property not just in the material means of life, but in his life itself, in the realization of all his active potentialities. It is worth emphasizing here that in the seventeenth century the word 'property' was used in a far wider sense than it has had ever since then. Political writers in the seventeenth century spoke of a man's property as including not only his rights in material things and revenues, but also in his life, his person, his faculties, his liberty, his conjugal affection, his honour, etc.; and material property might be ranked lower than some of the others, as it was specifically by Hobbes.[20]

The fact that property once had such a wider meaning opens up the possibility, which our narrower concept has not allowed, that property may once again be seen as more than rights in material things and revenues. The seventeenth-century broad concept of property may strike us as very odd, even quaint and unrealistic. But it seems odd only because we have become accustomed to a narrow concept which was all that was needed by and suited to a market society in which maximization of material wealth became the overriding value. Now that we have the possibility, and as I have argued the democratic need, to downgrade

[19] To say that scarcity has always prevailed up to now and that its conquest is now foreseeable is not to say that it has all been the result of hitherto inadequate technology, or that its conquest will be automatically accomplished by technological advances. Much of the scarcity in capitalist societies is created by the very requirements of the system of capitalist production, which (i) generates ever-increasing consumer demands, in relation to which there is scarcity by definition (cf. Essay II, section 4), and which (ii) distributes the whole social output in such a way that the poor are subject to real scarcity. But whether the scarcity is real or artificial, it is scarcity.

[20] 'Of things held in propriety, those that are dearest to a man are his own life, & limbs; and in the next degree, (in most men,) those that concern conjugall affection; and after them riches and means of living' (*Leviathan*, Chapter 30, pp. 382–3, Pelican edition). Locke, when he defined property in the broad sense, also put life and liberty ahead of 'estate', and 'person' ahead of 'goods' (*Second Treatise of Government*, sections 87, 123, 173). On seventeenth-century usage generally, see my *Political Theory of Possessive Individualism*, index entry 'Property'.

material maximization, the broader concept of property becomes the more realistic.

Property can and should become again a right to life and liberty; and it can now, in the measure that we conquer scarcity, become a right to a fuller and freer life, for more people, than was attainable (though it was dreamed of) in the seventeenth century. And the right to live fully cannot be less than the right to share in the determination of the power relations that prevail in the society. Property then, we may say, needs to become a right to participate in a system of power relations which will enable the individual to live a fully human life.

It may *need* to become so, but *can* it become so? My argument has been that both the concept and the actual institution of property need to be broadened in this way if they are to be consistent with the needs and the possibility of a society fully democratic and fully free. I have indicated ways in which the concept, and even the institution, are beginning to change in that direction. Whether or how far those changes will proceed depends on both the degree of democratic pressure on governments and the extent of consciousness of what the issues are, and each of these depends partly on the other. The seriousness of the obstacles should not be underestimated.[21] But nor should the possibility of their being overcome: not by goodwill, nor by any improbable conversion of ruling élites to a new morality; nor necessarily by traumatic revolutionary action; but by a conjuncture, such as was sketched at the end of Essay III, of partial breakdowns of the political order and partial break-throughs of public consciousness.

The former, it may now be seen, may well come through failures of the system to respond adequately to growing demands for access to the means of labour, that is, by failure to put such new limitations on exclusive property rights as are needed to meet those demands. The latter might come naturally enough as a growing, even a fairly sudden, realization that a new property in the quality of life and liberty is now within reach. And each of these changes would reinforce the other.

[21] I have referred to some of the operational difficulties in other essays, e.g. in the concluding pages of Essay II and Essay III; and have discussed related logical problems in Essay III and Essay V (at p. 112).

PART TWO

Related Papers on the Twentieth-Century Predicament

ESSAY VII

Elegant Tombstones: A Note on Friedman's Freedom

ACADEMIC political scientists who want their students to think about the problem of liberty in the modern state are properly anxious to have them confront at first hand various contemporary theoretical positions on the relation between freedom and capitalism. The range of positions is wide: at one extreme freedom is held to be incompatible with capitalism; at the other freedom is held to be impossible except in a capitalist society; in between, all sorts of necessary or possible relations are asserted. Different concepts of freedom are involved in some of these positions, similar concepts in others; and different models of capitalism (and of socialism) are sometimes being used. It is clearly important to sort them out. But there is some difficulty in finding adequate theoretical expositions of the second extreme position, which might be called the pure market theory of liberalism. There are very few of them. Probably the most effective, and the one most often cast in this role, is Milton Friedman's *Capitalism and Freedom* (Chicago, 1962), which is now apt to be treated by political scientists as the classic defence of free-market liberalism. As such it deserves more notice from the political theorists' standpoint than it got on publication, when its technical arguments about the possibility of returning to *laissez-faire* attracted most attention. Whether or not *Capitalism and Freedom* is now properly treated as the classic defence of the pure market theory of liberalism, it is at least a classic example of the difficulty of moving from the level of controversy about *laissez-faire* to the level of fundamental concepts of freedom and the market.

The first thing that strikes the political scientist about *Capitalism and Freedom* is the uncanny resemblance between Friedman's approach and Herbert Spencer's. Eighty years ago Spencer opened his *The Man versus the State* by drawing attention to a reversal which he believed had taken place recently in the meaning of liberalism: it had, he said, originally meant individual market freedom as opposed to state coercion, but it had come to mean more state coercion in the supposed interest of individual welfare. Spencer assigned a reason: earlier liberalism had in fact abolished grievances or mitigated evils suffered by the many, and so had contributed to their welfare; the welfare of the many then easily came to be taken by liberals not as a by-product of the real end, the relaxation of restraints, but as the end itself. Spencer regretted this, without offering any evidence that market freedom ever was more basic, or more desired, than the maximization of wealth or of individual welfare. Professor Friedman does the same. *Capitalism and Freedom* opens by drawing attention to the same reversal of meaning, and rejecting it out of hand. 'Freedom of the individual, or perhaps of the family' is for him the liberal's 'ultimate goal in judging social arrangements' (p. 12). His case is that 'a free private enterprise exchange economy', or 'competitive capitalism' (p. 13), is both a direct component of freedom, and a necessary though not a sufficient condition of political freedom, which he defines as 'the absence of coercion of a man by his fellow men' (p. 15).

To maximize this freedom, he argues, governments should be allowed to handle only those matters 'which cannot be handled through the market at all, or can be handled only at so great a cost that the use of political channels may be preferable' (p. 25). This would mean government moving out of almost all its welfare and regulatory functions. Controls on, or support of, any prices, wages, interest rates, rents, exports, imports, and amounts produced, would all have to go; so would present social security programmes, housing subsidy programmes, and the like. The functions properly left to governments because the market cannot perform them at all, or perform them well, are summarized:

> A government which maintained law and order, defined property rights, served as a means whereby we could modify property rights and other rules of the economic game, adjudicated disputes about the interpretation of the rules, enforced contracts, promoted competition, provided a monetary framework, engaged in activities to counter technical monopolies and to overcome neighborhood effects widely regarded as sufficiently important to justify government intervention, and which supplemented private charity and the private family in protecting the irresponsible, whether madman or child—such a government would clearly have important functions to perform. The consistent liberal is not an anarchist (p. 34).

No one ever thought that *laissez-faire* was anarchism; Spencer would scarcely have objected to this list of allowable government functions. But what is this economic game which is supposed to maximize individual freedom? The argument is that competitive capitalism can resolve 'the basic problem of social organization', which is 'how to co-ordinate the economic activities of large numbers of people' (p. 12), by voluntary co-operation of individuals as opposed to central direction by state coercion.

In addition to arguing that competitive capitalism is a system of economic freedom and so an important component of freedom broadly understood, Professor Friedman argues that capitalism is a necessary condition of political freedom (and that socialism is incompatible with political freedom). And although he is more concerned with freedom than with equity, he does argue also that the capitalist principle of distribution of the whole product is not only preferable to a socialist principle but is in fact accepted by socialists.

This essay deals with (I) an error which vitiates Friedman's demonstration that competitive capitalism co-ordinates men's economic activities without coercion; (II) the inadequacy of his arguments that capitalism is a necessary condition of political freedom and that socialism is inconsistent with political freedom; and (III) the fallacy of his case for the ethical adequacy of the capitalist principle of distribution.

I

Professor Friedman's demonstration that the capitalist market economy can co-ordinate economic activities without coercion rests on an elementary conceptual error. His argument runs as follows. He shows first that in a simple market model, where each individual or household controls resources enabling it to produce goods and services either directly for itself or for exchange, there will be production for exchange because of the increased product made possible by specialization. But 'since the household always has the alternative of producing directly for itself, it need not enter into any exchange unless it benefits from it. Hence no exchange will take place unless both parties do benefit from it. Co-operation is thereby achieved without coercion' (p. 13). So far, so good. It is indeed clear that in this simple exchange model, assuming rational maximizing behaviour by all hands, every exchange will benefit both parties, and hence that no coercion is involved in the decision to produce for exchange or in any act of exchange.

Professor Friedman then moves on to our actual complex economy, or rather to his own curious model of it:

> As in [the] simple model, so in the complex enterprise and money-exchange economy, co-operation is strictly individual and voluntary *provided*: (a) that enterprises are private, so that the ultimate contracting parties are individuals and (b) that individuals are effectively free to enter or not to enter into any particular exchange, so that every transaction is strictly voluntary (p. 14).

One cannot take exception to proviso (a): it is clearly required in the model to produce a co-operation that is 'strictly individual'. One might, of course, suggest that a model containing this stipulation is far from corresponding to our actual complex economy, since in the latter the ultimate contracting parties who have the most effect on the market are not individuals but corporations, and moreover, corporations which in one way or another manage to opt out of the fully competitive market. This criticism, however, would not be accepted by all economists as self-evident: some would say that the question who has most effect on the market is still an open question (or is a wrongly posed question). More investigation and analysis of this aspect of the economy would be valuable. But political scientists need not await its results before passing judgement on Friedman's position, nor should they be tempted to concentrate their attention on proviso (a). If they do so they are apt to miss the fault in proviso (b), which is more fundamental, and of a different kind. It is not a question of the correspondence of the model to the actual; it is a matter of the inadequacy of the proviso to produce the model.

Proviso (b) is 'that individuals are effectively free to enter or not to enter into any particular exchange', and it is held that with this proviso 'every transaction is strictly voluntary.' A moment's thought will show that this is not so. The proviso that is required to make every transaction strictly voluntary is *not* freedom not to enter into any *particular* exchange, but freedom not to enter into any exchange *at all*. This, and only this, was the proviso that proved the simple model to be voluntary and non-coercive; and nothing less than this would prove the complex model to be voluntary and non-coercive. But Professor Friedman is clearly claiming that freedom not to enter into any *particular* exchange is enough: 'The consumer is protected from coercion by the seller because of the presence of other sellers with whom he can deal... The employee is protected from coercion by the employer because of other employers for whom he can work...' (pp. 14–15).

One almost despairs of logic, and of the use of models. It is easy to see what Professor Friedman has done, but it is less easy to excuse it. He has moved from the simple economy of exchange between independent producers, to the capitalist economy, without mentioning the most important thing that distinguishes them. He mentions money instead of barter, and 'enterprises which are intermediaries between individuals in their capacities as suppliers of services and as purchasers of goods' (pp. 13–14), as if money and merchants were what distinguished a capitalist economy from an economy of independent producers. What distinguishes the capitalist economy from the simple exchange economy is the separation of labour and capital, that is, the existence of a labour force without its own sufficient capital and therefore without a choice as to whether to put its labour in the market or not. Professor Friedman would agree that where there is no choice there is coercion. His attempted demonstration that capitalism co-ordinates without coercion therefore fails.

Since all his specific arguments against the welfare and regulatory state depend on his case that the market economy is not coercive, the reader may spare himself the pains (or, if an economist, the pleasure) of attending to the careful and persuasive reasoning by which he seeks to establish the minimum to which coercion could be reduced by reducing or discarding each of the main regulatory and welfare activities of the state. None of this takes into account the coercion involved in the separation of capital from labour, or the possible mitigation of this coercion by the regulatory and welfare state. Yet it is because this coercion can in principle be reduced by the regulatory and welfare state, and thereby the amount of effective individual liberty be increased, that liberals have been justified in pressing, in the name of liberty, for infringements on the pure operation of competitive capitalism.

II

While the bulk of *Capitalism and Freedom* is concerned with the regulatory and welfare state, Friedman's deepest concern is with socialism. He undertakes to demonstrate that socialism is inconsistent with political freedom. He argues this in two ways: (1) that competitive capitalism, which is of course negated by socialism, is a necessary (although not a sufficient) condition of political freedom; (2) that a socialist society is so constructed that it cannot guarantee political freedom. Let us look at the two arguments in turn.

1. The argument that competitive capitalism is necessary to political freedom is itself conducted on two levels, neither of which shows a necessary relation.

(a) The first, on which Friedman properly does not place very much weight, is a historical correlation. No society that has had a large measure of political freedom 'has not also used something comparable to a free market to organize the bulk of economic activity' (p. 9). Professor Friedman rightly emphasizes 'how limited is the span of time and the part of the globe for which there has ever been anything like political freedom' (p. 9); he believes that the exceptions to the general rule of 'tyranny, servitude and misery' are so few that the relation between them and certain economic arrangements can easily be spotted. 'The nineteenth century and early twentieth century in the Western world stand out as striking exceptions to the general trend of historical development. Political freedom in this instance clearly came along with the free market and the development of capitalist institutions' (pp. 9–10). Thus, for Professor Friedman, 'history suggests . . . that capitalism is a necessary condition for political freedom' (p. 10).

The broad historical correlation is fairly clear, though in cutting off the period of substantial political freedom in the West at the 'early twentieth century' Friedman seems to be slipping into thinking of economic freedom and begging the question of the relation of political freedom to economic freedom. But granting the correlation between the emergence of capitalism and the emergence of political freedom, what it may suggest to the student of history is the converse of what it suggests to Professor Friedman: i.e. it may suggest that political freedom was a necessary condition for the development of capitalism. Capitalist institutions could not be fully established until political freedom (ensured by a competitive party system with effective civil liberties) had been won by those who wanted capitalism to have a clear run: a liberal state (political freedom) was needed to permit and facilitate a capitalist market society.

If this is the direction in which the causal relation runs, what follows (assuming the same relation to continue to hold) is that freedom, or rather specific kinds and degrees of freedom, will be or not be maintained according as those who have a stake in the maintenance of capitalism think them useful or necessary. In fact, there has been a complication in this relation. The liberal state which had, by the mid-nineteenth century in England, established the political freedoms needed to facilitate capitalism, was not democratic: that is, it had not extended political freedom to the bulk of the people. When, later, it did so, it began to abridge market freedom. The more extensive the political freedom, the less extensive the economic freedom became. At any rate, the historical correlation scarcely suggests that capitalism is a necessary condition for political freedom.

(b) Passing from historical correlation, which 'by itself can never be convincing', Professor Friedman looks for 'logical links between economic and political freedom' (pp. 11–12). The link he finds is that 'the kind of economic organization that provides economic freedom directly, namely, competitive capitalism, also promotes political freedom because it separates economic power from political power and in this way enables the one to offset the other' (p. 9). The point is developed a few pages later. The greater the concentration of coercive power in the same hands, the greater the threat to political freedom (defined as 'the absence of coercion of a man by his fellow men'). The market removes the organization of economic activity from the control of the political authority. It thus reduces the concentration of power and 'enables economic strength to be a check to political power rather than a reinforcement' (p. 15).

Granted the validity of these generalizations, they tell us only that the market *enables* economic power to offset rather than reinforce political power. They do not show any necessity or inherent probability that the market *leads to* the offsetting of political power by economic power. We may doubt that there is any such inherent probability. What can be shown is an inherent probability in the other direction, i.e. that the market leads to political power being used not to offset but to reinforce economic power. For the more completely the market takes over the organization of economic activity, that is, the more nearly the society approximates Friedman's ideal of a competitive capitalist market society, where the state establishes and enforces the individual right of appropriation and the rules of the market but does not interfere in the operation of the market, the more completely is political power being used to reinforce economic power.

Professor Friedman does not see this as any threat to political freedom because he does not see that the capitalist market necessarily gives coercive power to those who succeed in amassing capital. He knows that the coercion whose absence he equates with political freedom is not just the physical coercion of police and prisons, but extends to many forms of economic coercion, e.g. the power some men may have over others' terms of employment. He sees the coercion possible (he thinks probable) in a socialist society where the political authority can enforce certain terms of employment. He does not see the coercion in a capitalist society where the holders of capital can enforce certain terms of employment. He does not see this because of his error about freedom not to enter into any particular exchange being enough to prove the uncoercive nature of entering into exchange at all.

The placing of economic coercive power and political coercive power in the hands of different sets of people, as in the fully competitive capitalist economy, does not lead to the first checking the second but to the second reinforcing the first. It is only in the welfare-state variety of capitalism, which Friedman would like to have dismantled, that there is a certain amount of checking of economic power by political power.

The logical link between competitive capitalism and political freedom has not been established.

2. Professor Friedman argues also that a socialist society is so constructed that it cannot guarantee political freedom. He takes as the test of political freedom the freedom of individuals to propagandize openly for a radical change in the structure of society: in a socialist society the test is freedom to advocate the introduction of capitalism. He might have seemed to be on more realistic ground had he taken the test to be freedom to advocate different policies within the framework of socialism, e.g. a faster or slower rate of socialization, of industrialization, etc.: it is on these matters that the record of actual socialist states has been conspicuously unfree. However, since the denial of freedom of such advocacy has generally been on the ground that such courses would lead to or encourage the reintroduction of capitalism, such advocacy may all be subsumed under his test.

We may grant at once that in the present socialist states (by which is meant those dominated by communist parties) such freedom is not only not guaranteed but is actively denied. Professor Friedman does not ask us to grant this, since he is talking not about particular socialist states but about any possible socialist state, about the socialist state as such; nevertheless the actual ones are not far from his mind, and we shall have to refer to them again. His case that a socialist state as such cannot guarantee political freedom depends on what he puts in his model of the socialist state. He uses in fact two models. In one, the government is the sole employer and the sole source from which necessary instruments of effective political advocacy (paper, use of printing presses, halls) can be had. In the other, the second stipulation is dropped.

It is obvious that in either model a government which wished to prevent political advocacy could use its economic monopoly position to do so. But what Professor Friedman is trying to establish is something different, namely, that its economic monopoly position would render any socialist government, whatever its intentions, incapable of guaranteeing this political freedom. It may be granted that in the first model this would be so. It would be virtually impossible, for a government which desired to guarantee freedom of political advocacy, to provide paper, presses, halls, etc., to all comers in the quantities they thought necessary.

But in the second model this would not apply. The second model appears when Professor Friedman is urging a further argument, namely, that a government which desired to guarantee free political advocacy could not effectively make it possible because, in the absence of capitalism and hence of many and widely dispersed private fortunes, there would be no sufficient source of private funds with which to finance propaganda activities, and the government itself could not feasibly provide such funds. Here there is assumed to be a market in paper, presses, and halls: the trouble is merely shortage of funds which advocates can use in these markets.

This second argument need not detain us, resting as it does on the unhistorical assumption that radical minority movements are necessarily unable to operate without millionaire angels or comparably few sources of large funds. Nor, since the second argument assumes that paper, presses, and halls can be purchased or hired, need we challenge the assumption put in the first model, that these means of advocacy are unobtainable in the socialist state except by asking the government for them.

We have still to consider the effect of the other stipulation, which is made in both models: that the government is the sole employer. Accepting this as a proper stipulation for a socialist model, the question to be answered is: does the monopoly of employment itself render the government incapable (or even less capable than it otherwise would be) of safeguarding political freedom? Friedman expects us to answer yes, but the answer is surely no. A socialist government which wished to guarantee political freedom would not be prevented from doing so by its having a monopoly of employment. Nor need it even be tempted to curtail political freedom by virtue of that monopoly. A government monopoly of employment can only mean (as Friedman allows) that the government and all its agencies are, together, the only employers. A socialist government can, by devolution of the management of industries, provide effective alternative employment opportunities. True, a government which wished to curtail or deny the freedom of radical political advocacy could use its monopoly of employment to do so. But such a government has so many other ways of doing it that the presence or absence of this way is not decisive.

It is not the absence of a fully competitive labour market that may disable a socialist government from guaranteeing political freedom; it is the absence of a firm will to do so. Where there's a will there's a way, and, for all that Friedman has argued to the contrary, the way need have nothing to do with a fully competitive labour market. The real problem of political freedom in socialism has to do with the will, not the way. The real problem is whether a socialist state could ever have the will to guarantee political freedom. This depends on factors Friedman does not consider, and until they have been assessed, questions about means have an air of unreality, as has his complaint that Western socialists have not faced up to the question of means. We shall return to both of these matters after looking briefly at the factors which are likely to affect such a will to political freedom.

On the question of the will, we cannot say (nor indeed does Professor Friedman suggest) that a will to guarantee political freedom is impossible, or even improbable, in a socialist state. True, if one were to judge by existing socialist states controlled by communist parties, the improbability would be high. (We are speaking here of day-to-day political freedom, which is the question Friedman has set, and not with the will to achieve some higher level of freedom in an ultimately transformed society.) But if we are to consider, as Professor Friedman is doing, socialist states that might emerge in the West, we should notice the differences between the forces in the existing ones and those inherent in possible future Western ones.

There are some notable differences. First, the existing socialist states were virtually all established in underdeveloped societies, in which the bulk of the people did not have the work habits and other cultural attributes needed by a modern industrial state. They have had to change an illiterate, largely unpolitical, peasant population into a literate, politicized, industrially oriented people. While doing this they have had to raise productivity to levels which would afford a decent human minimum, and even meet a rising level of material expectations.

The pressures against political freedom that are set up by these factors are obvious. In the few instances, e.g. Czechoslovakia, where socialism did not start from such an underdeveloped base, it started under an external domination that produced equal though different pressures against political freedom. None of these pressures would be present in a socialist state which emerged independently in an already highly developed Western society.

Secondly, in the existing socialist states the effort to establish socialism has been made in the face of the hostility of the Western powers, whether manifested in their support of counter-revolution or in 'encirclement' or 'cold war'. The ways in which this fact has compounded the pressures against political freedom due to the underdeveloped base are obvious. Presumably the force of this hostility would be less in the case of future socialist takeovers in Western countries.

Thirdly, the existing socialist states were all born in revolution or civil war, with the inevitable aftermath that 'deviations' from the line established from time to time by the leadership (after however much or little consultation) tend to be treated as treason against the socialist revolution and the socialist state. We may at least entertain the possibility of a socialist takeover in an advanced Western nation without revolution or civil war (as Professor Friedman presumably does, or he would not be so concerned about the 'creeping socialism' of the welfare state). A socialist state established without civil war would not be subject to this third kind of pressure against political freedom.

Thus of the three forces that have made the pressures against political freedom generally predominate in socialist states so far, the first will be absent, the second reduced or absent, and the third possibly absent, in a future Western socialist state that emerged without external domination.

When these projections are borne in mind, Professor Friedman's complaint about Western socialists appears somewhat impertinent. He complains that 'none of the people who have been in favour of socialism and also in favour of freedom have really faced up to this issue [of means], or made even a respectable start at developing the institutional arrangements that would permit freedom under socialism' (p. 19). Perhaps the reason is that they think it more important, in the interests of freedom, to examine and even try to influence the circumstances in which socialism might arrive, than to begin planning institutional arrangements. Western socialists who believe in political freedom are, or should be, more concerned with seeking ways to minimize the cold war (so as to minimize the chances that the second of the projected forces against political freedom will be present in the socialist transformation they hope to achieve in their country), and seeking ways to minimize the likelihood of civil war (so as to minimize the third of the forces against political freedom), than with developing 'institutional arrangements that would permit freedom under socialism'.

But although, in a socialist state, the existence of a predominant will for political freedom may be more important than institutional arrangements, the latter should not be neglected. For even where there is, on the whole, a will to guarantee political freedom, there are likely always to be some pressures against it, so that it is desirable to have institutions which will make infringements difficult rather than easy. What institutional arrangements, beyond the obvious ones of constitutional guarantees of civil liberties and a legal system able to enforce them, are required? Let us accept Professor Friedman's statement of additional minimum institutional requirements. Advocates of radical change opposed to the government's policies must be able to obtain the indispensable means of advocacy—paper, presses, halls, etc. And they must be able to propagandize without endangering their means of livelihood.

As we have already seen, there is no difficulty inherent in socialism in meeting the first of these requirements, once it is granted (as Professor Friedman's second model grants) that the absence of a complete capitalist market economy does not entail the absence of markets in paper, presses, and halls.

The second requirement seems more difficult to meet. If the government (including all its agencies) is the sole employer, the standing danger that the monopoly of employment would be used to inhibit or prevent certain uses of political freedom is obvious. The difficulty is not entirely met by pointing out that a socialist state can have any amount of devolution of industry or management, so that there can be any number of employers, or by stipulating as an institutional arrangement that this devolution must be practised. For it is evident that if there is a ubiquitous single or dominant political party operating in all industries and all plants (and all trade unions), it can make this multiplicity of employment opportunities wholly ineffective, if or in so far as it wishes to do so. The problem is not the absence of a labour market but the possible presence of another institution, a ubiquitous party which puts other things ahead of political freedom.

The stipulation that would be required to safeguard political freedom from the dangers of employment monopoly is not merely that there be devolution of management, and hence employment alternatives (which could be considered an institutional arrangement), but also that there be no ubiquitous party or that, if there is, such a party should consistently put a very high value on political freedom (which stipulation can scarcely be set out as an institutional arrangement). We are back at the question of will rather than way, and of the circumstantial forces which are going to shape that will, for the presence or absence of such a party is clearly going to depend largely on the circumstances in which a socialist state is established.

There is, however, one factor (which might be institutionalized) which may, in any socialist state established in the West, reduce even the possibility of such intimidation through employment monopoly. This is the decreasing necessity, in highly developed societies whose economic systems are undergoing still further and rapid technological development, of relating income to employment. One need not be as sanguine as some exponents of the guaranteed income[1] to think it possible, even probable, that before any advanced Western nation chooses socialism it will have seen the logic of using its affluence and averting difficulties both political and economic by introducing a guaranteed minimum annual income to everyone regardless of employment. In this event, the technical problem that worries Professor Friedman—how to ensure that a threat to employment and hence to livelihood could not be used to deny political freedom—would no longer be a problem. A threat to employment would no longer be a threat to livelihood. It would indeed be a cost, but as Professor Friedman says, 'what is essential is that the cost of advocating unpopular causes be tolerable and not prohibitive' (p. 18).

But even without such a separation of employment from income, the technical problem of securing political freedom from being denied by the withholding of employment can be met by such devolution of management as would constitute a set of alternative employments *provided* that this is not offset by a ubiquitous party hostile to political freedom. If there is such a party, no institutional arrangements for safeguarding political freedom are reliable; if there is not, the institutional arrangements do not seem to be difficult.

III

We noticed (at the end of section I above) that Professor Friedman, in arguing that freedom would be increased if most of the regulatory and welfare activities of contemporary Western states were abandoned, did not take into account the coercion involved in the separation of capital from labour or the possible mitigation of this coercion by the regulatory and welfare state. But in Chapter 10, on the distribution of income, he does deal with a closely related problem. Here he sets out the ethical case for distribution according to product, as compared with 'another [principle] that seems ethically appealing, namely, equality of treatment' (p. 162). Distribution according to product he describes, accurately enough, as the principle 'To each according to what he and the instruments he owns produces' (pp. 161–2): to be strictly accurate

[1] Robert Theobald, ed.; *The Guaranteed Income* (New York, 1967).

this should read 'resources' or 'capital and land' instead of 'instruments,' but the sense is clear. This is offered as 'the ethical principle that would directly justify the distribution of income in a free market society' (p. 161). We can agree that this is the only principle that can be offered to justify it. We may also observe that this principle is not only different from the principle 'to each according to his work', but is also inconsistent with it (except on the fanciful assumption that ownership of resources is always directly proportional to work). Professor Friedman does not seem to see this. His case for the ethical principle of payment according to product is that it is unthinkingly accepted as a basic value judgement by almost everybody in our society; and his demonstration of this is that the severest internal critics of capitalism, i.e. the Marxists, have implicitly accepted it.

Of course they have not. There is a double confusion here, even if we accept Friedman's paraphrase of Marx. Marx did not argue quite, as Friedman puts it (p. 167), 'that labour was exploited . . . because labour produced the whole of the product but got only part of it'—the argument was rather that labour is exploited because labour produces the whole of the value that is added in any process of production but gets only part of it—but Friedman's paraphrase is close enough for his purpose. Certainly the implication of Marx's position is that labour (though not necessarily each individual labourer) is entitled to the whole of the value it creates. But in the first place, this is, at most, the principle 'to each according to his work', not 'to each according to what he and the instruments he owns produces' or 'to each according to his product'. In the second place, Marx accepted 'to each according to his work' only as a transitionally valid principle, to be replaced by the ultimately desirable principle 'to each according to his need'. Professor Friedman, unaccountably, only refers to this latter principle as 'Ruskinian' (p. 167).

Having so far misread Marx, Professor Friedman gives him a final fling.

> Of course, the Marxist argument is invalid on other grounds as well . . . [most] striking, there is an unstated change in the meaning of 'labor' in passing from the premise to conclusion. Marx recognized the role of capital in producing the product but regarded capital as embodied labor. Hence, written out in full, the premises of the Marxist syllogism would run: 'Present and past labor produce the whole of the product.' The logical conclusion is presumably 'Past labor is exploited,' and the inference for action is that past labor should get more of the product, though it is by no means clear how, unless it be in elegant tombstones (pp. 167–8).

This nonsense is unworthy of Professor Friedman's talents. The Marxist premisses are: present labour, and the accumulation of surplus value created by past labour and extracted from the past labourers, produce the whole value of the product. Present labour gets only a part of that part of the value which it creates, and gets no part of that part of the value which is transferred to the product from the accumulated surplus value created by past labour. The logical conclusion is presumably that present labour is exploited and past labour was exploited, and the inference for action is that a system which requires constant exploitation should be abandoned.

Ignorance of Marxism is no sin in an economist, though cleverness in scoring off a travesty of it may be thought a scholarly lapse. What is more disturbing is that Professor Friedman seems to be satisfied that this treatment of the ethical justification of different principles of distribution is sufficient. Given his own first postulate, perhaps it is. For in asserting at the beginning of the book that freedom of the individual, or perhaps of the family, is the liberal's 'ultimate goal in judging social arrangements', he has said in effect that the liberal is not required seriously to weigh the ethical claims of equality (or any other principle of distribution), let alone the claims of any principle of individual human development such as was given first place by liberals like Mill and Green, against the claims of freedom (which to Friedman of course means market freedom). The humanist liberal in the tradition of Mill and Green will quite properly reject Friedman's postulate. The logical liberal will reject his fallacious proof that the freedom of the capitalist market is individual economic freedom, his undemonstrated case that political freedom requires capitalism, and his fallacious defence of the ethical adequacy of capitalism. The logical humanist liberal will regret that the postulate and the fallacies make *Capitalism and Freedom* not a defence but an elegant tombstone of liberalism.

ESSAY VIII

Revolution and Ideology in the Late Twentieth Century

THE revolutions and the ideologies likely to be most important in the second half of the twentieth century are those of the underdeveloped countries. This proposition does not denigrate the obviously great continuing importance of the communist revolutions of the first half of the century or of the Marxist ideology. They will go on working themselves out. But the new revolutions, having altered the terms on which the senior revolutionary ideologies can continue to be influential, may be regarded as the critical new factor in the problems of revolution and ideology of the next several decades. The revolutionary and ideological currents in the underdeveloped countries, currents which are not formed entirely from either Marxist or liberal-democratic ideologies, are already having and will increasingly have an effect on the communist and Western structures of power and of ideas.

Problem and Terms Defined

I want first to show that the new revolutions depend to an unusual degree on ideology, that the new states built on these revolutions will continue that dependence, and that their ideologies are not likely to conform either to the communist or the Western pattern. I shall then offer some speculations on the possible effects of this fact on the Western ideology.

Throughout I use *ideology* in a neutral sense, neither implying, with Marx, an idealist philosophy and 'false consciousness', nor, with Mannheim, contrasting ideology and 'utopia'. I take ideology to be any more or less systematic set of ideas about man's place in nature, in society, and in history (i.e. in relation to particular societies), which can elicit the commitment of significant numbers of people to (or against) political change. This does not exclude a set of ideas essentially concerned with merely a class or a nation, if it relates the place and needs of that section of humanity to the place of man in general. Thus liberalism, conservatism, democracy (in various senses), Marxism, Populism, Nkrumaism, pan-Africanism, and various nationalisms are all ideologies. Ideologies contain, in varying proportions, elements of explanation (of fact and of history), justification (of demands), and faith or belief (in the ultimate truth or rightness of their case). They are informed by, but are less precise and systematic than, political theories or political philosophies. They are necessary to any effective political movement, hence to any revolution, for they perform the triple function of simplifying, demanding, and justifying.

By *revolution* I mean a political overturn more far-reaching than a *coup d'état* or 'palace revolution'. I take revolution to mean a transfer of state power by means involving the use or threat of organized unauthorized force, and the subsequent consolidation of that transferred power, with a view of bringing about a fundamental change in social, economic, and political institutions. How long a period of consolidation is to be included in the revolution itself is a matter of theoretical convenience; here it will be convenient to consider the revolution to extend for as long as ideological zeal is needed (and is forthcoming) to secure a sufficient basis for the new institutions.

My interest in the revolutions and ideologies of the underdeveloped countries arises from my concern with the prospects of liberal-democratic political theory. The present widely felt inadequacy of liberal-democratic justificatory theory is, I think, due to the possessive quality of its basic individualism. I have argued elsewhere[1] (a) that the philosophy of liberalism has been, from its origins in the seventeenth century, permeated by possessive individualism, which assumes that the individual is human *qua* proprietor of his own person, that the human essence is freedom from any but self-interested contractual relations with others, and that society is essentially a series of market relations between these free individuals; (b) that this individualism was ethically adequate for societies dominated and vitalized by competitive market relations; (c) that it becomes ethically inadequate once the natural rightness or inevitability of market relations is challenged or denied by substantial sections of the people (as it began to be in England and Europe from the middle of the nineteenth century); but (d) that possessive individualism cannot simply be discarded from the justificatory theory of liberal democracy because liberal democracy is still in our day coterminous with market-dominated societies, so that the assumptions of possessive individualism (though now ethically inadequate) are still factually accurate. The question about which I now speculate is whether the impact of the underdeveloped countries' revolutions and ideology may provide some basis for the requisite change in Western political theory or ideology.

[1] In my *Political Theory of Possessive Individualism.*

Importance of Ideology in the Revolutions of the Underdeveloped Countries

Compared to the classic revolutions of the seventeenth to nineteenth centuries, the revolutions of the underdeveloped countries in our time depend to a much higher degree on ideology. Two reasons are evident: (a) The new revolutions, in order to move toward their goal of bringing backward peoples rapidly into the modern world, must in most cases virtually create a nation. They must do in a few years what the classic European revolutions either did not have to do at all or were able to do with much less difficulty, that is, create a sense of primary loyality to a political nation, rather than to local, tribal, or feudal communities. The leaders of the new revolutions, themselves generally intellectuals,[2] politicized by training abroad, have had to bring a prepolitical people to a sense of nationality and national self-esteem, to create a political and national consciousness, and to infuse a hope and a faith that great things can be done by the new nation.[3] This is a task for ideology. And the leaders, being intellectuals, have been able to provide the ideology. They have generally proceeded by setting up the nation as the charismatic object, in place of the tribe, the kinship group, feudal or royal rulers, priests and magicians, in which the ordinary man hitherto had found the sacred quality.[4] But however the new ideology is brought into existence, its creation and spread are indispensable to the revolution.

(b) Just as the immediate aim of the revolution—the transfer of power from an outside imperial government to an indigenous national government—requires a high degree of ideology, so does the longer-term but equally necessary aim of rapid economic development. The classic Western revolutions of the seventeenth to nineteenth centuries came, generally speaking, when there was already an enterprising bourgeoisie ready and able to press ahead with economic development.

[2] 'The gestation, birth, and continuing life of the new states of Asia and Africa, through all their vicissitudes, are in large measure the work of intellectuals. In no state-formations in all of human history have intellectuals played such a role as they have in these events of the present century' (Edward Shils: 'The Intellectuals in the Political Development of New States', *World Politics* (April 1960)).

[3] 'Differences of caste, tribe, clan or religion must be integrated into the political process, and it is precisely because they loom so large as an obstacle to the creation of the modern nation-state that the leaders place great emphasis on the primacy of "the nation" and the elimination of traditional status differentiations . . . The first requirement is the implementation of the common ideal of universal participation in the nation' (Paul E. Sigmund, Jr. (ed.): *The Ideologies of the Developing Nations* (New York, 1963), p. 7).

[4] See Edward Shils: 'The Concentration and Dispersal of Charisma: Their Bearing on Economic Policy in Underdeveloped Countries', *World Politics* (October 1958), pp. 3–4.

In the new revolutions there is, generally speaking, no indigenous bourgeoisie and no indigenous accumulation of private capital. The desired economic development has therefore to be undertaken by state initiative, state accumulation and investment of capital, state planning and controls. The accumulation of capital, and the provision of incentives which will convert the ordinary people into a modern labour force, obviously require, and will require for a long time, heavy reliance on ideology.

In short, both of the practical objectives of the new revolutions—the change from colony to viable independent nation, and the promotion of rapid economic development—require and will continue to require a high degree of ideology. In the nature of the case, the ideology has to be developed by the political élite, who are at once the intelligentsia and the political leaders. They do not, of course, create ideologies out of nothing. Where they can, they find historical roots in the precolonial cultures and polities of their own lands. And they draw, of course, on the ideological traditions they find in the advanced countries, both Western and communist. What sort of ideologies have resulted?

Revolutionary Ideologies neither Communist nor Liberal-Democratic

One may say in general of the new ideologies that they are neither communist nor Western (using Western to mean pluralist, liberal-democratic, bourgeois-individualist). One may say also that it is not very useful to try to place them in a continuum stretching from communist to Western. They see themselves as outside that continuum. For them, the polar division of the world is not between communism and liberal capitalism but between the rich nations and the poor nations. They know where they stand now in that division, and they know where they want to move. In order to move, they will take from both the Marxist and the liberal-democratic traditions whatever seems to them to go to the root of their problems.

As a brief analysis will show, they have, on the whole, taken something from Marxism, while refusing to identify themselves with Soviet communism; they have rejected almost wholly the liberal individualist utilitarianism of the West, but have drawn heavily on its earlier democratic tradition, the tradition of Rousseau and Populism. Indeed, it is where Marxism and this original Western democratic ideology overlap that the leaders of the modern underdeveloped countries' revolutions find themselves ideologically most at home.

We may look first at what they have taken from, and what they have rejected in, the Western ideology. The clearest thing about the new ideologies is their rejection of the capitalist ethos. Whether or not they accept, or how much they accept of, the thesis of Lenin's *Imperialism*, they tend to have a strong moral aversion to the ethics of competitive individualism. This goes deeper than the natural reaction of an exploited colonial people to the ethos of their former exploiters and to any fear that they may still be exploited economically even after winning political independence. It goes back to their traditional culture, which saw no intrinsic value in wealth getting and gave no respect to the motive of individual gain.[5] These traditional roots might, of course, have been pulled up, just as the traditional reliance on the prepolitical local community is being uprooted. But there has been neither need nor inclination to try to do so, for it has seemed clear to the revolutionary leaders that the rapid national economic development they demanded could come only through social control of the economy; to have left it to private capitalist enterprise would have meant leaving it to foreigners, which would have negated the revolutionary goal of national independence.

Thus both the traditional ethos of the prepolitical society, and the political needs of the revolution, have operated against acceptance of the Western capitalist ethos. Added to this has been a strong moral egalitarianism, which may be explained partly in traditional terms and partly as revulsion against the dehumanizing contrast of poverty and wealth which they see in capitalism. All these forces may be expected to continue to operate against acceptance of the capitalist ethos.

At the same time that the economic ethos of capitalism has been rejected, so has the political ethos of liberal pluralism. And here too, traditional outlook has been reinforced by the requirements of a modernizing revolution. The local, community-centred society traditionally made its decisions by discussion between equals. The more primitive the society, the less do plural interests exist and demand recognition. In the underdeveloped societies generally there was little basis for pluralism, or for the Western system of competing political parties and pressure groups. Furthermore, the requirements of the struggle for independence generally favoured the emergence of a dominant single party or movement, and this has been carried into the post-independence structure in most cases as a single-party or single-party-dominance system.[6] The political leaders, as ideologists,

[5] The 'autonomous movement of the economic system is thought undesirable even if possible'. It 'is believed that no intrinsic value resides in the economic sphere—in the way in which the religious and political spheres possess the intrinsic value connected with sacred things. The only truly respected motives are those generated by authority, the exercise of that sovereignty, religious or political, which entails communion with the sacred' (Shils: *World Politics* (October 1958), p. 2).

[6] A recent study of new states in Africa shows that, of the independent states in which an indigenous majority participates in government (i.e. excluding the

find no difficulty in justifying one-party rule, both as fitting the indigenous traditional idea of democracy and as necessary for the task of making and consolidating the national revolution.

While the practical basis of the antipluralist ideology is the revolutionary need for unified command and unified popular support, the moral basis is found in a Rousseauian concept of a general will. This concept is the moral basis also of the economic side of the ideology—the rejection of competitive capitalist individualism. Just as Rousseau found the source of social ills, of moral depravity, of dehumanization and loss of human freedom, in the institution of inequality, and believed that the secular redemption of mankind could be got through a purified general will (which, to be operative, would require the institution of substanital economic equality and the absence of effective interest groups), so do the new ideologies. To them, the period of colonialism was the period of inequality forcibly or fraudulently imposed in place of an original equality. Inequality had destroyed the human dignity and freedom of the people. Dignity, freedom, and humanity could be restored by re-establishing equality. This required not only the political revolution but also a moral revolution—an assertion of the will of an undifferentiated people as the only legitimate source of power.

It is less important to stress the Rousseauian parallels than to notice that the essential assertion—the ultimate moral worth of the freedom and dignity of the individual, which can however only be realized by the operation of an undifferentiated popular or mass will—goes back to a preliberal democratic tradition. In England, the classic home of liberalism, democracy was feared, down to the middle of the nineteenth century and even later, by the most enlightened liberals, as being inconsistent with liberal society and the liberal state. If the ideology of democracy was then inchoate, it was strong enough to be dreaded. It is this earlier tradition of democracy that the new leaders have tapped. They have seen that, historically, it has as good a claim to the title democracy as has the now more familiar pluralist liberal democracy. This has given the leaders confidence that their regimes are in a genuine sense democratic. If they have deserted Rousseau in the matter of the representation of the general will, they have not deserted Robespierre; the party and its leaders are the bearers of the will of the people.

Republic of South Africa, Southern Rhodesia, etc.), all but four (Libya, Egypt, Sudanese Republic, and Ethiopia, in which no parties are permitted) have a single-party or single-party-dominance system. Single-party-dominance means that more than one party exists but one party has an overwhelming legislative majority and employs its legal, police, and political powers to restrict the competitive position of opposition parties and groups. M. L. Kilson: 'Authoritarian and Single-Party Tendencies in African Politics', *World Politics* (January 1963), pp. 262–3.

This egalitarian general-will ideology is likely to become firmly established. It feeds and is fed by the necessary nationalism of the underdeveloped countries' revolutions. And it is a highly valuable, if not indispensable, support to the position of the revolutionary leaders; it upholds their one-party or dominant-party state, and validates their authority as leaders of it. Without such authority they cannot hope to carry through the programme of economic development necessary to consolidate the revolution. They may therefore be expected to use all the resources of state and party to strengthen that ideology.

We may say, then, that the leaders of the underdeveloped countries' revolutions, rejecting the ideology of contemporary Western liberal democracy, have anchored themselves in the earlier Western ideology of preliberal democracy. Just as they have rejected alignment with either Western or communist power blocs, and have seen themselves as outside the capitalism-communism continuum, so in rejecting contemporary Western ideology they have swung not to communist ideology but to a position historically outside of both the dominant contemporary ideologies, a preliberal-democratic and pre-Marxist position.

It is in this light that the measure of their acceptance of Marxism may best be understood. Even the new nations whose ideology has come closest to Marxism, e.g. Sékou Touré's Guinea, can be seen to accept only those elements of Marxism that fit in with the pre-Marxian democratic position. Thus they gladly accept the basic moral position of Marx's humanism, which has its roots in the Rousseauian tradition. Although they may not be versed in the latest scholarly debates about the role of alienation in Marxism, they find immediately and deeply attractive the general thrust of Marx's analysis of the dehumanization of man by capitalism, and the Marxian belief that man can remake himself and can overcome his alienation, by concerted revolutionary action. But they do not accept as applicable to their countries or to the contemporary world the Marxian theory of class struggle as the motor of history, nor the theory of the state as essentially an instrument of class domination, both before the proletarian revolution and in the post-revolutionary dictatorship of the proletariat. Nor, consequently, are they interested in the withering away of the state. For they insist that their own countries are now classless societies, that the new national state (or the dominant party) consequently speaks for the whole of the people, and that its authority emanates directly from the whole of the people.

With this view of their own society as classless, they are able to accept what looks like the 'vanguard' theory of Lenin's but which is not quite the same. Lenin argued, as early as 1902 in *What Is To Be Done?* that a working class by itself, under capitalism, could not reach more than trade-union consciousness, that only a vanguard of dedicated intellectual Marxists could see through to reality, and that it must therefore be their task, by building round themselves a tightly organized party, to lead and control the revolution. The vanguard, rather than the proletarian mass, was made the effective agent of the revolution. In thus clearly separating the function of the vanguard from that of the proletarian mass, and asserting that the vanguard could make a revolution before there was a thoroughly class-conscious proletariat, Lenin made it easier for the later underdeveloped revolutions to speak in Marxist terms. The fact that they had no industrial proletariat did not now matter; they had an intellectual vanguard.[7] Yet the theory and practice of the vanguard in most of the underdeveloped countries' revolutions is not exactly Leninist. The role of the vanguard is not to end class domination but foreign domination. It is to seize and wield power not in the name of a not yet fully conscious proletariat, but in the name of an undifferentiated people who are never to become a proletariat because industrialization is not to be allowed to take place under capitalist auspices.

Thus, in the matter of the vanguard, as in their beliefs about the sources of their people's dehumanization and the way to overcome it, the new ideoloties have taken over less from Marxism or Leninism than from a pre-Marxist radical tradition, suitably reformulated to meet the needs of underdeveloped peoples in a highly developed world. The new ideologies may, in a sense, be said to have bypassed Marxism. For the conditions in which their revolutions are rooted are neither those envisaged by Marx nor those envisaged by Lenin. They have no industrial proletariat, and do not intend to have one. In the scales of Western economic history, they are peasants at most. Yet a colonial people may be called proletarian in a deeper sense. For, in the measure that the colony was fully subject to the purposes of the metropolitan economy, the people were held to their economic position not, as the pre-revolutionary Russian peasant, by feudal or pre-capitalist relations of production, but by capitalist relations of production, albeit imposed by an economic force from beyond their own borders. In this sense their revolutions might be called proletarian, for they have been made by peoples subjugated by capitalist relations of production in order to throw off those relations. But the classic Marxist and Leninist categories do not fit them exactly. An underdeveloped people caught up in capitalist relations is, so to speak, at once non-proletarian and more completely proletarian than the trade-union-conscious labour force of an advanced capitalist society. It is non-proletarian in that it has not the

[7] This point was made by Eduard Heiman, 'Marxism and the Underdeveloped Countries', *Social Research* (September 1952), who argued then that the addition of the vanguard theory had made Marxism readily transferable to the underdeveloped countries without distortion.

industrial worker's factory discipline and subordination to the machine (which Marx counted on to produce proletarian consciousness, and which Lenin counted on too, though with some impatience). It is more proletarian in that it, rather than the working classes of the advanced countries, has experienced the immiseration (*verelendung*) that Marx predicted for the latter, and in that virtually the whole people rather than just one class has been immiserized.

The attractiveness of Marxism to underdeveloped revolutionaries is no doubt due to this fact. Yet an underdeveloped people is not a Marxist proletariat even when they develop a consciousness of their common subjugation by capitalism, for their consciousness is not a class consciousness but a national consciousness. They intend, as the immediate aftermath of their taking power, not a dictatorship of the proletariat (or of a vanguard in the name of the proletariat) over a bourgeoisie, but the dictatorship of a general will,[8] or of a vanguard in the name of the general will, over a people undifferentiated by class (for once the imperial power has been driven out, there is no bourgeoisie remaining to be dominated).

Yet if the ideologies of the underdeveloped nations have bypassed Marxism and rooted themselves in an earlier radical democratic tradition, it should also be noticed that recent Soviet Marxism has been making an effort to catch up. The Soviet leaders have abandoned the nineteenth-century Marxist view that the world trend to communism must come through proletarian revolutions, and see it now as coming through colonial revolutions which, though they set up non-communist systems, may be encouraged to move into the Soviet orbit. 'It was no doubt with this prospect in view', Robert Tucker has written, 'that Soviet doctrine was amended by Khruschchev in 1956 to provide for a "peaceful" mode of "transition to socialism". In his report to the 20th Party Congress, he particularly singled out countries where capitalism is weak and relatively underdeveloped as the most likely places for the "peaceful" mode of transition.'[9]

One further factor must be taken into account in assessing the

[8] Cf. Sékou Touré's concept of 'democratic dictatorship'. He begins by defining dictatorship as the exercise of sovereign power, so that all conceivable governments are dictatorships. Democratic dictatorship is then defined as government based on the sovereignty of the people. 'A democratic state comes from the will of the people. Its program is therefore necessarily in conformance with the interests of the people. Likewise, its force, its authority, the powers it exercises, the discipline it imposes—in short, the dictatorship it exercises—arise exclusively from the interests, the requirements, and the principles of popular sovereignty' (*La Lutte du Parti Démocratique de Guinée pour l'Emancipation Africaine* (1959), as translated in Sigmund, op. cit., p. 163).

[9] Robert C. Tucker: 'Russia, the West and the World Order', *World Politics* (October 1959), p. 18.

probability of Marxist penetration of the new ideologies. Most of the new nations have, from the beginning, taken a stand on non-alignment with either the Soviet or the Western powers. Whatever aid they receive from either bloc, they have remained uncommitted. They are likely to remain so, partly because their ideology has a strong moralizing element—a disapproval of power politics as such; partly because they hope, by remaining neutralist (even though not acting as a neutralist third bloc) to diminish the chances of conflict between the two great power blocs (an open conflict between which would finish their chances of economic development); and perhaps fundamentally because they are beginning to have some confidence that *they* see the long-range problem of a peaceful world order more realistically than those who are still caught up in the cold war. Whatever the reasons for it, their deliberate non-alignment with either bloc entails some reserve about Soviet theoretical principles, and thus throws up a barrier to their acceptance of a full Marxist ideology. Indeed, to the extent that the third of the reasons suggested above is operative, they will be apt to regard Soviet ideology (as well as Western) as less realistic than their own.

I have argued that the ideologies of the underdeveloped countries' revolutions are, and are likely to remain, neither liberal-democratic nor communist; that while they may be said to have adapted elements both of Marxism and of liberal democracy, they may better be understood as having their roots in a pre-Marxist and pre-liberal notion of democracy. The new ideologies are not so much eclectic compilations of bits from the two competing ideologies of the advanced countries as they are growths from an earlier stem, with such grafts from the two modern plants as the original stem will take. Grafts are needed because the new soil is not entirely congenial to the old stem.

I have suggested also that the emergence of the new nations and the new ideologies has already had some effect on one of the two advanced ideologies—the Soviet theory has been adjusted to the fact and the prospects of the underdeveloped revolutions. Can Western ideology also be adjusted to them?

Possible Effects of the New Revolutions on Western Ideology

We may notice first that the requisite Western adjustment is not simply one that would make Western ideology more attractive to the underdeveloped countries. The notion of currying favour is as unnecessary as it is distasteful. What is needed is an ideology that would allow the West to maintain a position of world importance in a world one third communist, one third uncommitted, and one third Western (I assume that Western leaders will come to recognize that world dominance is no longer a feasible aim). I assume also that it is recognized by the leaders of both West and East (though not yet by the whole people or all the influential groups) that in the present and any future condition of nuclear armament no great power can maintain or improve its position in the world merely by a show of force. It follows that the West requires, beyond its military forces, a set of values or an ideology by which it can coexist with, while contesting with, the other two-thirds of the world. A viable Western ideology must be built on the recognition that the world is no longer a Western preserve. This is difficult but not impossible.

In the second place we may notice that the requisite adjustment of Western ideology does not involve altering or abandoning the values on which the West most prides itself. It would, however, be misleading to suggest that the Western adjustment would be simply related to means, not ends, as the Soviet theoretical adjustment has been. The Soviets have not given up any of their values. They are still communist, and still intend to further the 'transition to socialism' outside the Soviet bloc. They have merely dropped their insistence that class war and dictatorship of the proletariat are the only possible ways to achieve their ends. The Western adjustment would involve not only an alteration in the theory of means but some alteration in the theory of ends as well. For the Western ideology treats as ends not only the ethical values of liberal democracy but also the ethos of capitalist enterprise, or what I have called the values of possessive individualism. As stated above, possessive individualism regards the individual as human in his capacity as proprietor of his own person; the human essence is freedom from any but self-interested contractual relations with others; society consists of a series of market relations between these free individuals. I have argued that these assumptions have been built into the value system of liberal democracy, and they are no longer an adequate ethical basis for it. The point here is that a Western ideology that is to be internationally viable from now on will have to abandon this possessive individualism. The reasons may be reduced to two. First, it is, of all the Western values, precisely this possessive individualism which has been rejected by the uncommitted nations. Secondly, possessive individualism entails continual capitalist aggrandizement; a nation devoted to possessive individualism must be, in Harrington's phrase, 'a commonwealth for increase', and this is what the Western nations can no longer expect to be.

The real question, then, is whether possessive individualism is so built into the Western ideology that it cannot be dropped or decisively modified. This is too big a question to try to deal with here in all its aspects, but we can consider one specific aspect: is the fact of the underdeveloped countries' revolutions (added to the preceding fact of the communist revolutions) itself a new force making for Western abandonment of possessive individualism?

To consider this question we must notice that Western ideology is not simply (as I have so far by implication defined it) a compound of pluralist liberal democracy and possessive individualism, but that it has defined itself increasingly in the last two decades as a cold-war ideology. It has done so by embracing the assumption that there is between East and West not merely a long-term contest for world influence but an implacable and absolute hostility, such that Western nations must bend their whole effort to forcibly defeating, or not being forcibly defeated by, the East. This assumption has fused with the other two elements in Western ideology to produce a new compound. *The* Western value becomes 'the free way of life', a concept in which the values of liberal democracy, of possessive individualism, and of anti-communism, are merged. They are merged in such a way that, of the two original elements, one particularly, possessive individualism, draws much of its vitality from the hostility to communism.

To the extent that possessive individualism has been so fused with cold-war anti-communism, anything that produces a Western move away from the latter will also carry Western ideology away from the former. The emergence of the underdeveloped nations may alter the Western cold-war ideology in two ways.

First, in the measure that the world effect of the underdeveloped countries' revolutions is realistically assessed in the West, it must modify the cold-war attitude of the West. I assume that as neither East nor West can now hope to advance their power or influence by war, and as the two now have comparable technical and economic strengths (at least when rates of growth are taken into account), the future relative world strength of East and West depends mainly on who wins (or does not lose) the good will of the uncommitted parts of the world. On this assumption, a Western policy of peaceful coexistence with the East becomes the rational policy, for coexistence is the only policy the uncommitted nations can regard as rational for others as well as for themselves.

Second, the revolutions of the underdeveloped countries have already, as we have seen, led to substantial modification of the Soviet doctrine of class conflict. Soviet abandonment of the doctrine of the necessary class war and proletarian dictatorship should increase the possibility of peaceful coexistence between East and West. In both these ways the underdeveloped revolutions have set in motion forces tending to moderate the cold-war ideology and thus, on our earlier assumption, to carry Western ideology away from possessive individualism.

The possessive individualism of the Western ideology may be affected by the underdeveloped revolutions in a third way, operative even if cold-war attitudes are not greatly reduced. Even on cold-war assumptions, there is no ground for implacable hostility between the West and the underdeveloped new nations. Their ideology does not commit them to proletarian revolution or world revolution. Their goals are more modest. They seek only to realize an egalitarian humanism, and that only for their own countries. The West can coexist with these ideologies. The longer the West lives with them, and the more widely they are propagated, the more the ethical contrast between their egalitarian humanism and possessive individualism (which is already under wide attack by theologians, philosophers, and publicists in the West) will be borne in on the conscience of the West. In recognizing the merits of the new ideologies' humanism, the West would be going back to the roots of its own democratic tradition.

None of these prospects, it must be said, can be counted upon to reduce the possessive quality of our modern individualism to a point consistent with the requirements of twentieth-century liberal-democratic theory. But there is at least a possibility that Western recognition of the new world alignment of our time, in which the underdeveloped revolutions are playing the final decisive part, will be enough, coming as it does on top of the other new fact that individuals throughout the world are now equally insecure in face of the possibility of nuclear war,[10] to overcome the dominance of possessive individualism in Western ideology.

[10] The possible role of this new equality of insecurity in providing some part of a sufficient sense of equality to serve as an ethical base for a modern theory of liberal democracy is discussed in my *Political Theory of Possessive Individualism*, chap. VI, sect. 2.

ESSAY IX

Post-Liberal-Democracy?

I

It is quite generally thought to be commendable, but only marginally worthwhile, for a political theorist to devote any great attention to economic assumptions, much less to economic theory. My own university is now one of the last which has a joint department of political science and economics. The general separatist trend of political science is quite understandable. As political science becomes a more confident, more developed, and more extensive discipline, the natural tendency is for it to seek a greater measure of independence.

Along with the trend to separatism in political science has been a marked trend towards empirical, value-free analysis. The concern with values, which was central in the great theoretical writing on politics in the past, has been pushed out to the fringes of the subject as empirical work has proliferated.

I am going to suggest that both these trends are now rather dangerous, that they are a result of overconfidence in the strength of liberal democracy. I shall argue that political science is now more than ever in need both of rethinking its normative theory, and of doing so in full consciousness of the bearing of economic systems and economic assumptions on that theory. Political values have become more, not less, in need of central attention in political science, and economic assumptions more, not less, important in political theory.

The first of these contentions should not need much argument. In these days of uncertain coexistence, everyone in the liberal-democratic world who thinks about politics can see that political value systems, political ideologies, or call them what you will, are of great practical importance. There are, we may say, *vis-á-vis* coexistence two classes of people—believers in hostile coexistence and believers in peaceful coexistence. Believers in hostile coexistence see a battle of irreconcilable ideologies, and see a need to sharpen ours. Believers in peaceful coexistence see a present competition of hopefully reconcilable ideologies, ideologies which they hope are both changing in ways that could lead to their supersession by something containing the basic values of both. No one in his senses is outside one of these two groups. No one who has a rudimentary knowledge of the consequences of military technology believes that coexistence can be ended by all-out military action. It can only be ended by such internal development of one or both existing systems as would transform their relation into something not adequately described as coexistence.

We can take as given, then, the necessity for some kind of coexistence between two systems and two ideologies, until such time as the terms of existence are transformed. We can also take it as given that there has already been some change in the ideologies or the justifying theories of both liberal democracy and communism since their classic formulations, though whether the changes have been sufficient to take account of new facts is open to question. It follows that there is need for continued inquiry by liberal democrats into the rationale of the liberal-democratic society and state. We need to ask whether our theory is all that it might be, and, if not, on what lines we should proceed.

Although this conclusion seems to follow from a recognition of the facts of change, it is not a conclusion that has been generally drawn or widely acted upon by the theorists and publicists of politics in the liberal-democratic world. There has been some disposition among theorists not to let such practical matters as coexistence enter their consciousness at the level of their theoretical work. Others have admitted the facts but sought to conjure them away. It is not generally questioned that there have been some changes, in both practice and theory, in both the liberal-democratic and the communist worlds since the two systems first took shape. One reaction to this has been to claim that one or the other has changed out of all knowing, with the implication that the problems we have failed to solve are no longer real problems.

Thus there is a good deal of loose writing these days about something called 'post-capitalism'. The same publicists and theorists who use this term are apt to talk also about post-Marxism. The idea in both cases is the same: to suggest that the thing now hyphenated has in fact disappeared and has been replaced by something really quite different. If one cannot deny, in either case, that something superficially similar to the old thing is still around, one can perhaps exorcize its spirit by calling it 'post-'. Thus, as capitalism, old-style, has become increasingly difficult to justify in terms of any acceptable social ethic, it becomes highly advantageous to find that it has given way to something else. And as Marxism, old-style, continues to give trouble, it can perhaps more easily be dealt with by announcing its demise and replacement.

There is just a sufficient grain of truth in the alleged facts—the transformation of capitalism and of Marxism—to make the new concepts plausible. Capitalism has become a managed economy. It is managed partly by price-making firms and combinations of firms, themselves increasingly directed by the need to use administrative and other technological skills—to give full employment to accumulated administrative capital. And it is managed partly by the state, in pursuance of the goal of full employment of the labour force, a goal willingly shared and enforced by at least those capitalists who see that the stability of the whole system is a prerequisite of their profits and their power and that such stability does not permit a repetition of the great depression. A capitalism managed in those ways is not quite the same as the old model, which left everything to unmanaged competition between productive units none of which could by themselves make prices. I shall suggest, however, that this entitles us only to say that capitalism has developed, not that it has been replaced.

Marxism too has changed. Present Soviet Marxism, with its belief in the present and future possibilities of peaceful transition to socialism, is distinctly different from classical Marxism. Yet it can be argued that here, as in the case of capitalism, what we have is an adaptation of an established system to a change in the facts, an adaptation retaining the fundamental postulates of the original system.

My primary concern in this paper is neither with the economics of capitalism nor with the philosophy or sociology of Marxism, but with the politics of individualism. The three are, however, not unrelated. Perhaps we can come at the whole thing best by asking, with tongue not entirely in cheek, whether it is now proper to promote a concept of post-liberal-democracy. There are really two questions here. First, has liberal-democratic theory already changed so much, since its first formulation, as to merit a new name? In other words, have we *got* a post-liberal-democratic theory? I shall suggest that the answer is no. Secondly, is the theory as it now stands adequate in justifying the liberal-democratic state and society as they now are or as they might be improved, or do we need a still further changed theory, so changed as to merit a new name? In other words, do we *need* a post-liberal-democratic theory? I shall suggest that the answer is yes.

II

In seeking to assess the changes in liberal-democratic theory, what should we take as our benchmark? We need not go very far back in time to find the first formulation of what we now regard as liberal-democratic theory—probably no further back than J. S. Mill, although the formal democratic case was made along with the liberal case by Bentham earlier in the nineteenth century. Liberal theory proper—the theory of individual rights and limited government—goes back, of course, to the seventeenth century. But until the nineteenth century, liberal theory, like the liberal state, was not at all democratic; much of it was specifically anti-democratic. Liberal-democratic theory thus came as an uneasy compound of the classical liberal theory and the democratic principle of the equal entitlement of every man to a voice in choosing government and to some other satisfactions. It was an uneasy compound because the classical liberal theory was committed to the individual right to unlimited acquisition of property, to the capitalist market economy, and hence to inequality, and it was feared that these might be endangered by giving votes to the poor.

The central problem of liberal-democratic theory was to reconcile the claims of the free market economy with the claims of the whole mass of individuals to some kind of equality. It cannot be too often recalled that liberal democracy is strictly a capitalist phenomenon. Liberal-democratic institutions have appeared only in capitalist countries, and only after the free market and the liberal state have produced a working class conscious of its strength and insistent on a voice. The importance of the market, that is of the full capitalist market system in which labour itself is a marketable and normally marketed commodity, was well understood by the liberal theorists of the eighteenth and nineteenth centuries. So it is not surprising that economic assumptions, assumptions about the ultimate worth of different systems of relations between men in the process of producing material wealth, were never far below the surface of the classical liberal political theory, from, say, Locke to Bentham.

But there is a curious and interesting movement of these assumptions from the eighteenth century to the present. By the end of the eighteenth century, classical liberal theory had reached its mature form in Bentham's utilitarianism. Utility, defined as a quantity of pleasure minus pain, was taken as the sole criterion of individual and social good. The good of society was the maximization of the aggregate of individual utilities. And although Bentham was scornful of the natural rights postulates of earlier liberal theory, he put such a postulate into his system in another form; in aggregating individual utilities each individual was to count as one. The liberal state was then justified as the state most calculated to maximize utility. It could provide most efficiently what might be called the basic political utilities—security of life, freedom of individual movement, security of property. It would also maximize the material utilities of the whole society. Or rather, it would permit the market to maximize those utilities. With a liberal state guaranteeing a free market, everyone's natural desire to maximize his own utility, or at least not to starve, would bring everyone into productive relations which would maximize the aggregate utility of the society. Thus Benthamism, reinforcing and reinforced by the teachings of classical political economy, came close to justifying the liberal state on the main ground of its permitting the market to maximize material utilities. Bentham was clear that the market must be left to determine the allocation of the material product among the individuals who contributed to it by their labour or land or capital, although he saw that this would mean persistent inequality. He acknowledged, indeed, that there was a case for equality of wealth or income. This followed from the principle of diminishing utility—the principle that a second loaf of bread doesn't give a hungry man as much satisfaction as the first loaf, or more generally, that the more you have of anything the less the utility to you of any increment. Given this principle, and given that each individual's satisfaction was to count as one, it followed that the aggregate satisfaction or aggregate utility of the whole society would be greatest if everyone had equal amounts of wealth. But as soon as Bentham had thus demonstrated the case for equality he argued that it had to yield to the case for productivity. Without security for unequal property there would be no incentive to capital accumulation, and without capital accumulation there would be practically no productivity. Besides, without a large labour force whose incentive was fear of starvation, the market could not maximize productivity.

This was where classical liberal theory stood just before the demands of the common people for a political voice began to make themselves felt. Economic assumptions bulked very large in the liberal political theory; the liberal case was largely a material maximizing case.

With John Stuart Mill the emphasis became very different. He may be regarded as the first serious liberal-democratic theorist, in that he was the first liberal to take seriously, and to feel sensitively, the claims of the nascent democracy. He had some reservations, indeed, about a fully democratic franchise. He would not give the vote to those who were illiterate, nor to those who paid no direct taxes, but he was willing to have both literacy and direct taxes extended to the poor. And even those who were to have the vote were not all to have equal votes. The better educated, being more capable of political judgement, were to have more than one vote each. In these respects Mill's democracy was somewhat more qualified than Bentham's.

But in a more fundamental respect Mill must be counted more of a democrat. For he took people not as they were but as he thought them capable of becoming. He revolted against Bentham's material maximizing criterion of the social good. He could not agree that all pleasures were equal, nor that the market distributed them fairly. He held that men were capable of something better than the money-grubbing and starvation-avoiding existence to which Benthamism condemned them. He rejected the maximization of indifferent utilities as the criterion of social good, and put in its place the maximum *development* and use of human capacities—moral, intellectual, aesthetic, as well as material productive capacities.

This was, we may say, an act of democratic faith. It was a turn away from the market. It was a refusal to allow that the market should determine the value or worth of a man. It put other values higher than market values. Yet in the end, Mill found himself helpless, unable to reconcile his notion of values with the political economy which he still believed in. The world's work had to go on, and he could see no way in which it could be carried on except by competitive private enterprise. He saw clearly that the prevailing relation between wage-labour and capital was condemned by his own criterion of good, and he thought that it would before long become insupportable by the wage-labourers. His only way out was the hope that a network of co-partnerships in industry, or producers' co-operatives, might turn every worker into his own capitalist, and so enable the system of enterprise to operate without the degradation of wage-labour.

It is easy to see now that Mill, in spite of his ranking as an outstanding economist, did not grasp the essence of the capitalist market economy. It was his failure to do so that enabled him to reject the market morality. The founding father of liberal-democratic theory, we are compelled to say, was able to rise above the market morality only because he did not understand the market society.

The same must be said of the next outstanding figure in the English liberal-democratic tradition. T. H. Green, a philosopher with no pretensions as an economist, may be more readily forgiven for his economic *naïveté*. Like Mill he despised and rejected the market morality. He did so even more strongly than Mill, perhaps because he did not have Mill's problem of trying to be faithful to the utilitarian philosophy. Yet he held that the free development of individual personality required the right to accumulate unlimited property through the mechanism of the market, and even required the full right of inheritance. (This was a step backward from Mill, who wanted high inheritance taxes in order to iron out the inequalities produced by the working of the market.) Green recognized that the existence of a proletariat—his own word—was inconsistent with the rationale of private property, which required that everybody should have enough property, over and above a bare subsistence, to enable him to develop and perfect himself. But he had so little insight into the nature of capitalism that he could attribute the existence of a proletariat not to the nature of capitalist enterprise but to the continuing effect of an original forcible seizure of land in feudal times, and subsequent 'unrestricted landlordism'. By putting the blame on feudalism, and on the continuing rights of unproductive landowners, he exempted capitalism from any responsibility for the condition of the bulk of the people. To say the least, this shows rather less grasp of the essentials of the capitalist market economy than Mill had.

Mill and Green, between them, set the pattern of English liberal-democratic political theory from their time on. It is probably fair to say that there have been since then no new insights sufficient to carry liberal-democratic theory over the hurdles which they had failed to surmount. They had rebelled against the morality of the market, but their rebellion, even at the level of theory, had failed.

What has happened since then? While the liberal-democratic theorists have been, so to speak, coasting on Mill and Green, a new step was taken in liberal economic theory. The new step was the development of marginal utility theory. More sophisticated than the classical theory, and much better able to explain the price system, it had the additional effect of diverting attention from the question of the distribution of the social product between social classes, a question to which Adam Smith and Ricardo had paid some attention. The marginal utility theory, or neo-classical theory as it came to be called, contained some implied value judgements. It implied that the capitalist market system did maximize utility, and that it gave everyone—labourer, entrepreneur, capitalist, and landowner—exactly what his contribution was worth. The system tended to an equilibrium at which every factor of production—each lot of labour, of capital, of land, and of enterprise —got a reward equal to the marginal productivity of its contribution. This theory, first worked out in the 1870s and brought to definitive form by Marshall, still in its essentials holds the field. It has had to be modified in some respects, of course. Allowance has had to be made for monopolistic developments. And after Keynes demonstrated that the system did not automatically tend to equilibrium at maximum utility, but could find an equilibrium at any measure of underemployment of resources and labour, the theory had to be modified to admit the necessity of continual government action in order to keep the system up to the mark. But with these adjustments, the neo-classical theory can still be taken as providing a justification for a slightly modified system of capitalist enterprise. The modified market system can be held to be justified on the grounds that it maximizes utilities and that it distributes rewards according to marginal productivity. It is true that few modern economists do explicitly use their theory to justify anything. Most of them decline to draw value judgements from technical theory. Indeed, it is clearer to the economists than to the non-economists who have absorbed the elements of orthodox theory that the maximization of utility by the market can only be demonstrated by assuming a certain income distribution, and that the marginal productivity theory of distribution is not a demonstration of an ethically just distribution of wealth or income. It has, however, been easy for political theorists to overlook these limitations of economic theory.

I think it fair to say that liberal-democratic political theory, having failed to resolve the dilemma encountered by Mill and Green, has fallen back pretty heavily on this modified free enterprise theory for the main justification of the liberal-democratic state. It is true that current liberal-democratic theory still insists, very properly, on the central importance of certain individual freedoms—of speech and publication, of religion, of association. It still asserts the ultimate moral worth of the individual, and speaks of the self-development of the individual as the ultimate good. But it has persuaded itself that this good is to be achieved through the market, as modified of course by the welfare state. Its central value judgement is the value judgement it finds in the modified neo-classical economic theory, that the best society is the modified market society because it maximizes utilities and distributes them according to each man's deserts.

Seen in this light, current liberal-democratic theory appears to have taken two steps backward from the original liberal-democratic position formulated by Mill. The first step may be described as a reversion to the pre-democratic classical liberal emphasis on maximization of the material utility. Liberal-democratic theory has retreated back beyond John Stuart Mill to the value judgements of Bentham—to the indifferent weighing of the utilities of individuals, with their existing habits, tastes, and preferences taken as given, as the ultimate data.

The second step has carried the liberal-democratic theorists, along with the neo-classical economists, back even beyond the original classical economists. The classical economists were fighting against something as well as for something. They had refused to accept the values of the society they lived in, with its substantial element of *rentier* morality and of what was in their view wasteful expenditure. For them, the uses to which labour was put by the existing social order were not automatically justified by the fact of their existence. They distinguished between productive and unproductive labour and had some harsh things to say about the latter, and about the social and political arrangements that called it forth. In short, they were sizing up the existing scale of values and passing a critical judgement on it. The same cannot be said about the neo-classical economists. They concern themselves only with the scale of values that is actually registered in the market. The individual utilities on which their system is based are given by the preferences and tastes of individuals as they are. In maximizing utility or welfare, all wants are equal. Whatever is, is right.

This position has not been reached and held without some difficulty. The main difficulty was that the marginal utility theory relied for its explanation of relative prices on the principle of diminishing utility. The more you have of anything, the less your desire for still more of it. This seemed to entail (as Bentham had allowed that it did entail) that the richer you became the less satisfaction you could get from each additional lot of wealth. To admit this would be to recognize an order of urgency of wants in every man, ranging from the most basic necessities to pure frivolities. To recognize an order of urgency of wants would be to cast serious doubts on the ability of the market system, with all its inequalities of income, to maximize the aggregate utility of all members of the society, which ability is offered as the system's great justification.

The difficulty has been met by the simple device of refusing to admit that the satisfactions of an individual can be compared over time. A man who was poor yesterday and well-to-do today can indulge desires which he could not indulge before. He has new and different desires, and who is to say that the satisfaction he gets from indulging these is less than the satisfaction he got from meeting different wants when he was a different man? As soon as intertemporal comparisons of utility are ruled out, the socially dangerous implications of the principle of diminishing marginal utility are avoided. Utility can be said to be maximized no matter what the inequality of wealth or income.

Yet as Galbraith has pointed out, in discussing the marginal utility theorists from a somewhat different angle, they are here on very slippery ground. For they shut their eyes to the fact that the more affluent a society becomes the more the wants which are satisfied by the market have been created by the process of production itself. There is no reason, Galbraith argues, why we should attach the same urgency or the same moral value to wants created by the system as to wants original with the individual. Galbraith here seems to align himself with Rousseau, who insisted on the moral distinction between the original or natural desires and the artificial desires created by a competitive and unequal society.

The point I should like to emphasize is that one can only make a distinction between natural and artificial wants if one rejects the postulate that all men inherently desire to emulate others, or innately desire ever more. If you allow that postulate, and only if you allow it, there is no basis for the distinction. For if you allow it, then whatever new thing one man gets others will want, and the want will be just as genuine, will flow just as much from his inherent nature, as any apparently more natural or more basic wants.

The marginal utility theorists, then, are making the assumption of universal innate emulation, or innately insatiable wants. We may say that in doing so, they, and the liberal-democratic theorists in so far as they rely on the utility theorists, have gone not two steps but three steps backwards. They have gone back before even that arch-competitor of the seventeenth century, Thomas Hobbes. For even Hobbes started from the assumption that only some men naturally wanted ever more, while others would naturally be content with the level of satisfactions they had if the system did not force them to enter the competition for more in order to keep what they had. The system which compelled this was, as I have argued elsewhere, a system whose stipulated qualities can be found only in a capitalist market society. Hobbes saw that it was the society that made all men emulative, that thrust them all into the desire for 'precellence'. It was the social relations which created the desire. Our modern theorists, in having failed to see this, may be called pre-Hobbesian. We must not press this point too far. For Hobbes was to a considerable extent a prisoner of his own model of society; having constructed the model of a capitalist market society he treated it as a model of society as such. But at least when he did this it was an advance in thought. There is less excuse for doing it again three hundred years later.

The main lines of the changes I have pointed to in the development of liberal-democratic theory may now be summarized. The theory begins with a solid inheritance of classical liberal theory, which made it the great virtue of the liberal society and the liberal state that they maximized the aggregate utility of the whole membership of the society, or that they allowed the market to do so. Each individual was to count as one, and all utilities were as good as each other. With John Stuart Mill and Green this market morality is rejected. The goal is no longer the maximum material utility of men as they are, but the fullest development and enjoyment of men's faculties. This was a finer vision, and a democratic one. But they failed to deal with the inconsistency between this vision and the necessary requirements of the market economy, the essentials of which they did not fully see. Since then, I have suggested, liberal-democratic theory has followed the same lines and, having failed to master the central problem, has slipped back into increasing reliance on the old argument of maximum utility. It has done so a little shamefacedly, aware perhaps that this is scarcely up to the vision which Mill had offered of a free society whose aim was higher utilities, higher values. But it has done so. It has not noticeably rejected the marginal utility analysis which refuses to make intertemporal comparisons of utilities.

We began this inquiry into the changes in liberal-democratic theory with a question: has it changed enough to merit a new name? Is there now a post-liberal-democratic theory? The answer is evident. What we have now is not post-liberal-democratic theory, but recessive liberal theory. It would be nearer the mark to call it pre-democratic liberal theory.

We had also a second question: is the theory, as it now stands, at all adequate in justifying the liberal-democratic state and society as they now are or as they might be improved, or do we need a still further changed theory, so changed as to merit a new name. In other words, do we need a post-liberal-democratic theory? It will be apparent by now that I think we do need a post-liberal-democratic theory.

III

The extent of the need is to be measured not merely by the extent to which current theory is regarded as a step or two backward from the original liberal-democratic theory, but also by the extent to which the liberal-democratic society and state have themselves changed since the original theory was created to justify or demand them. If the society and state have changed significantly, in a direction different from the change in the theory, the distance to be made up is even greater. Or, more happily, the society and state may have changed in ways which tend to resolve in fact the difficulties that Mill and Green could not resolve in theory. The central difficulty was that the market economy, with its concentration of capital ownership, and its distribution of reward in accordance with the marginal productivity of each of the contributions to the product, maintained a massive inequality between owners and workers, an inequality which stood in the way of any extensive development and fulfilment of individual capacities. There was the further difficulty that the market society encouraged or demanded a money-grubbing, maximizing behaviour, which distorted the quality of life: the market might maximize utilities, but only by denying qualitative differences in utilities. Have the market society and the liberal state changed in ways that diminish or remove these difficulties?

We cannot here attempt a systematic answer to these questions. The most we can do is to notice one or two relevant trends. I will risk the generalization that the changes in the liberal-democratic *state*, since the introduction of the democratic franchise, have been less fundamental than the changes in the society and economy. By changes in the state I am thinking in the first place of changes in the ways governments are chosen and authorized. It is true that very considerable changes in the ways governments were chosen and authorized did come with the introduction of democratic franchise. As electorates increased in size, party organization became more important and party discipline stronger. Hence, the responsiveness of elected representatives to their constituencies diminished, as did the responsiveness of governments to elected representatives. But these are not changes in the liberal-democratic state, they are changes as between the pre-democratic liberal state and the liberal-democratic state. Apart from these there have been no great changes in the mechanism of choosing and authorizing governments, unless the proliferation and institutionalization of pressure groups as part of the standard method of determining government policy be so considered. When we turn to what governments do with their power there is a more noticeable change. But here we move into the area of changes in the society and economy. For it is these changes which have called forth the regulatory and welfare state.

When we look at changes in the society and the economy, two changes stand out: the decline of pure competition and the rise of the welfare state. The two changes may be summed up as a move away from a relatively unregulated free enterprise economy to a system more heavily managed and guided both by large private economic organizations and by the state.

These changes have become most striking in the last few decades. They are not confined to the last few decades, of course. But the cumulative effect of welfare measures, of monetary and fiscal policies designed to prevent depressions and maintain full employment, of control and direction of foreign trade and home production, and all the rest, has given our market economies quite a different look even since the 1930s. Equally important has been the change in scale of the productive units. The move has been from markets in which no producer or supplier could make prices, to markets in which prices are increasingly made by firms or groups of firms who can do so, and who are sometimes able to enlist governments or groups of governments in their arrangements.

This is familiar enough. And it throws us back to the question mentioned at the beginning of this paper: how much has capitalism changed? Are we in an era of post-capitalism? I do not think we are. The change is not as great as some would suggest. It all depends, of course, on how you prefer to define capitalism. If you define it as a system of free enterprise with no government interference, then of course our present heavily regulated system is not capitalism. But I find it very unhistorical to equate capitalism with *laissez-faire*. I think it preferable to define capitalism as the system in which production is carried on without authoritative allocation of work or rewards, but by contractual relations between free individuals (each possessing some resource be it only his own labour-power) who calculate their most profitable courses of action and employ their resources as that calculation dictates.

Such a system permits a great deal of state interference without its essential nature being altered. The state may, as states commonly do, interfere by way of differential taxes and subsidies, control of competition and of monopoly, control of land use and labour use, and all kinds of regulation conferring advantages or disadvantages on some kinds of production or some categories of producers. What the state does thereby is to alter the terms of the equations which each man makes when he is calculating his most profitable course of action. Some of the data for the calculation are changed, but this need not affect the mainspring of the system, which is that men do act as their calculation of net gain dictates. As long as prices still move in response to these calculated decisions, and as long as prices still elicit the production of goods and determine their allocation, we may say that the essential nature of the system has not changed.

One may grant that the regulatory role of the modern state, and the transfer payments involved in the welfare state, are not a contradiction of capitalism, but may still argue that capitalism has been transformed into something else by its other most obvious novelty. This is the rise of the modern corporation to a point where a few firms, whose behaviour is less competitive than (to use Schumpeter's fine word) 'corespective', can make prices and dominate markets, and whose decisions are said to be determined less by desire to maximize profits than to build empires and to grow. The appearance of this phenomenon does indeed cast doubts on the justifying theory implicit in neo-classical economics, for in these conditions there is no reason to believe that the corporations' price-making decision will maximize production or utilities. But it does not alter the basic nature of the system. The driving force is after all still maximization of profit, for it is only by accumulating profit that the corporation can continue to grow and to build empires. The only thing that is different is the time-span over which maximum profit is reckoned.

Our present managed economy, managed both by the state and by the price-making corporation, is not, in my view, to be regarded as a transcendence of capitalism. It is still capitalism. But it has made nonsense of the justifying theory that capitalism maximizes social utility. And so, to the extent that modern liberal-democratic theory has reverted to the maximizing justification, that theory is further out of step than it was in the days of more nearly pure competition.

On the extent to which the welfare state has diminished the old inequality of opportunity and increased the chances for fuller development of individual personality, there will be differences of opinion. Improvements in the general level of health and literacy should, other things being equal, improve the quality of life for the great mass of individuals. But other things are not equal. For the very system of production which has afforded the welfare state has brought other changes. It has, necessarily, organized the work process in such a way that, for most people, their productive labour cannot be itself regarded as a fulfilment or development of their capacities. Fulfilment and development of individual capacities become, therefore, increasingly a matter of the development and satisfaction of wants for all kinds of material and, in the broadest sense, aesthetic or psychic goods.

But here again the system has changed things. For the market system, based on and demanding competition and emulation, creates the wants which it satisfies. The tastes and wants which people learn to satisfy as they rise above bare subsistence are, as we have seen, tastes and wants created by the productive system itself. And as the system increasingly moves away from a pattern of widespread competition between many producers (when it was still possible to think of it in terms of consumer sovereignty) to a pattern of competition for power between fewer and larger corporate units and groupings, which are increasingly able to control prices and products, the tendency of the system to create the wants which it satisfies will become stronger. There is no reason to expect that the wants and tastes which it satisfies will reflect or permit that full development of the individual personality which is the liberal-democratic criterion of the good society.

On balance, then, the changes in the liberal-democratic society seem to have made the justifying theory less, rather than more, adequate. When the changes in the society are taken in conjunction with the changes in the theory, the theory seems less fitted to the society than was the case at the beginning of the liberal-democratic period. One of the changes in the society has gone in the opposite direction from the change in theory. That is, while the theory since Mill has come to rely more heavily on the maximizing of utilities justification, the society has moved towards a more managed system whose claim to maximize utilities can no longer be granted. The other main change in the society has not made up for this, has not provided a way out of the central difficulty of the original liberal-democratic theory. That is to say, the change to the welfare state and the managed market cannot be counted on to provide an improvement in the quality of life as judged by the liberal-democratic criterion. We can only count on the manufacture and control of tastes.

All this by itself would be enough to indicate that we do need a new theory, sufficiently different from what we have now to merit the description 'post-liberal-democratic'. But there is a further reason why such a theory is needed, and this may suggest the direction in which a new theory is to be sought.

IV

There has been in the last fifty years, and most strikingly in the last twenty, a change of tastes and wants quite different from the one we have noticed within liberal-democratic societies. The change I am thinking of is not a change in our tastes, but a change, on the world scale, of the taste of the aggregate of those who count, of those whose power can have reactions on us. Fifty years ago the world was almost the preserve of the Western liberal-democratic capitalist societies. Their economies were triumphant, and so were their theories. Since then, two-thirds of the world has rejected the liberal-democratic market society, both in practice and in theory. From Lenin to Nkruma and Sékou Touré, the value system of the West has been spurned, either in the name of Marxism or in the name of a Rousseauian populist general-will theory. It is true that all three ideologies assert much the same ultimate value—the development and realization of the creative capacities of the individual. It is the mediate principle of liberal democracy that the other two ideologies reject—the mediate principle that the ultimate human values can be achieved by, and only by, free enterprise in both political and economic life, only by the free party system and the capitalist market system. In the other two-thirds of the world the leaders, with willing enough followers and even positively willing followers, have concluded that for their countries at least it would be impossible to move towards the ultimate humanistic goals by liberal-democratic methods. They have perhaps seen more clearly than we have the dilemma of liberal-democratic theory, and the doubtful adequacy of liberal-democratic society even in the most advanced conditions.

It is time we reflected, more seriously than we have generally done, on their reading of our society. It is time we gave some thought as to whether it is any longer possible for us to move towards our goal within the pattern of the market society. The system of managed capitalism into which we are headed will have to compete steadily from now on with non-capitalist systems. The competition will be in the degree of satisfaction each provides for its members. At present we are well above the other systems in the extremely important psychic satisfaction of individual liberty. But it is possible that our curve is going down, and probable that theirs will come up.

We need a revolution in democratic consciousness if we are to avoid being caught up ourselves in the backwash of the revolutions in the rest of the world. We need to give up the myth of maximization. We need to inquire soberly whether competitive, maximizing behaviour is any longer rational for us, in any ethical or expedient sense, or whether the very high level of material productivity that we now command can be made to subserve the original liberal-democratic vision. We should be considering whether we have been asking the wrong question all this time, in asking, as we have done, how to hold on to the liberty we have got—the liberty of possessive individualists—while moving a little towards more equality. Perhaps we should be asking, instead, whether meaningful liberty can much longer be had without a much greater measure of equality than we have hitherto thought liberty required.

We should not shrink from either the populist teaching of Rousseau or the radical teaching of Marx. Neither will suit us, but we may have more to learn from them than we think. It may even be—if the economists present will permit me an intertemporal comparison of utilities—that the utility of Marxism as a means of understanding the world is increasing over time.

ESSAY X

Market Concepts in Political Theory

IF this paper were not too slight it might have been given a sub-title: a note on cultural lag in political science. For one of the things I want to suggest is that political scientists, whether out of envy or pure admiration for their economist colleagues, have in recent decades increasingly taken over an equilibrium-market concept from economics without realizing that they have been taking cast-off clothing. The epithet is perhaps unfair. But it does seem that just when economics has been moving away from its concept of the economy as a pure price system and turning to a notion of the economy as a system of power, carried on by power blocs rather than by maximizing individuals, political theory has been taking over the concept of the equilibrating price system and working it into a general theory of the political process. As economics adopts power concepts in a search for realism, political science adopts market concepts in a search for theoretical elegance. In this curious double process of transvestism I do not think political science has been the gainer. Economists may object that they have not abandoned marginal equilibrium analysis, and I would not insist that they have. Certainly they have not abandoned the search for elegance, and if their elegance is getting a little lumpier they are to be applauded for their greater realism. But the political scientists' use of market concepts is clear enough to be a matter of some concern.

The attractiveness of the economists' equilibrium concept to political theorists is understandable. Apart from the elegance and precision of economic models, and of the general and special theories that economists have developed from the concept of equilibrium, the main attraction of economics is the determinateness of its general theory. The economist has been able to show how the results of countless separate decisions by individual producers and consumers could be a determinate system. Taking for granted a society in which there was division of productive labour and exchange of products and of labour, it had only to be assumed (1) that every individual rationally tried to maximize his gains (or minimize his real costs), and (2) that there was a freely competitive market for the resources, materials, and energies needed to produce things, and for the things produced. It followed that competition would determine prices for everything and that prices would determine what would be produced, offered, and purchased. Large numbers of independent decisions issued in prices, while the prices determined the decisions in the sense that every decision had to be that which, given the prevailing prices, was calculated to maximize the gain of the person deciding. Each person, taken separately, was ruled by market values, while the market values were the product of all the separate decisions. The whole thing was a determinate system which tended to equilibrium, in that prices tended to be just what would induce buyers to buy what was produced and producers to produce what would be bought.

The essentials of this system had been set out by the classical economists. When marginal utility analysis was introduced, the notion of equilibrium became more refined. Its greater refinement was made possible by the fact that the marginal utility theorists, unlike the classical economists, abstracted from class and other social determinants of effective demand, and treated the consumers' wills as autonomous and independent. So the kind of economic theory available in the late nineteenth and the twentieth century, resting on completely atomized individual demands or utilities or preference schedules, seemed to provide the kind of apparatus needed to deal with the democratic political process.

The attractiveness, to political science, of a theory which produced a determinate system out of a multitude of conflicting individual wills which could be taken to be autonomous and undetermined is evident. Any general theory of the process of liberal-democratic government faces the same problem the economists appeared to have solved. If it is to be a general theory it must be in some degree determinate, yet if it is to be a liberal theory it must assume that the system is moved by separate individual wills which are not themselves determined.

Moreover, the economic theory appeared to show (if interpersonal comparisons of utility were allowed) that the equilibrium towards which the system tended must produce the maximum utility for the whole membership of the system. This demonstration in fact requires some further assumptions about the utility of certain distributions of property, as Bentham for instance saw, but after the victory of marginal utility, enchantment with equilibrium (among the political theorists at least) allowed this point to be obscured. I shall return to the question of the justificatory role of theory; here I merely remark that an economic theory which justifies as it explains is all the more attractive to the political scientist who already sees the democratic process as the analogue of the price system.

A final reason for the attractiveness of the market concept may well have been that a notion of equilibrium, in a much looser sense, had been familiar in political thinking ever since Machiavelli, or even since Aristotle. They had seen the main practical problem as one of maintaining stability, and had sought the solution in a rough balance of classes.

The idea of balance as the secret of political stability, carried into the formative period of modern liberal ideas by the English republicans and the American federalists, thus had a respectable intellectual position. It was not, of course, entirely satisfactory for a democratic theory, since it assumed that the main problem was class division: the equilibrium it proposed was between two or three classes whose opposition was assumed to be fundamental, permanent, and overriding. With the arrival of democratic franchise and equalitarian ideas, the notion of class equilibrium became disagreeable. But by then the concept of equilibrium could be rescued by pressing into service the newer and more precise economic concept of equilibrium, which, abstracting from class, postulated atomized individual demands. The transfer of the economic concept into political science thus seemed quite feasible by the twentieth century, at least in the most advanced countries. We had 'one man, one vote', we had a set of politicians arrayed in parties competing for votes, and we had an extensive supplementary apparatus of interest groups collecting, organizing, and focusing individual wills so as to make scattered wills into effective demands on legislatures and governments.

In these circumstances, the equilibrium-market model has been irresistible. The democratic political system is typically presented (especially by American political science, rather less so by English, and noticeably less so by European, for a reason that is perhaps already apparent, or will be so in a moment) as a mechanism whose function is to reconcile or balance or hold in adjustment a multitude of diverse and conflicting individual interests. The central mechanism is the party system, which is seen as an entrepreneurial system. It is said to tend to produce equilibrium in two ways. First, it continually combines a very diverse lot of demands, each of which is shared by different numbers of individuals, and no natural or spontaneous grouping of which would command the support of a majority, into a few groupings one of which can command the support of a majority and can therefore produce an effective government. The system thus enables political decisions to be made and enforced in a continuous, stable way. Second, because of the competition between parties for votes and between voters for governmental action favourable to themselves, the system tends to produce just that set of decisions (or, that allocation of political goods) which the citizens are willing to pay for in expenditure of political energy and other resources.

Thus by casting politicians and parties in the role of entrepreneurs in a profit-seeking economy (and voters in the role of consumers), one can get a political model which appears to explain how governments do carry out the social functions expected of them although the motives of the politicians who run the government are unrelated to these functions. Just as the entrepreneur is in business to make profit, not to perform a social function, but is compelled by the operation of the competitive market to perform social functions in order to make a profit, so the politician can be assumed to be in politics for the power, prestige, or other satisfactions he can expect, and yet be shown to be compelled to perform social functions by the operation of the competitive party and interest group system.

The main assumptions needed for this model are (1) that both politicians and voters behave rationally, that is, seek to maximize benefits to themselves; (2) that there is free competition between parties, with all that this implies by way of freedom of speech and association; and, of course, (3) that the party with the most (effective) votes will be the government until the next election, which must be at or within a fixed period of time. This set of assumptions provides a rough working model of the democratic process, a model which can easily be expanded to include the role of interest groups.[1]

The analogy between such a political system and the price system is, of course, not exact. The political system, besides equilibrating the supply and demand for political goods, has to produce and sustain a government. That is, it has recurrently to confer on identifiable persons the power to make (and the responsibility for making) the laws and orders by which political goods are distributed. This function is not paralleled anywhere in the economic market model. But it can be reduced to insignificance in the political model by treating governments in office as mainly inert recipients of pressures from interest groups. When the output of laws and orders is treated as a result of the input of pressures, it matters little what persons are in office as the government. The government, as the mechanism through which decisions are made, becomes in effect as impersonal or anonymous as the market in the economic model. One wonders whether it is because the political system can by this assumption be most nearly assimilated to the price system that the assumption has become so fashionable.

The rough theory of the democratic process that can be built in this way can be refined considerably by introducing marginal analysis. With the greater clarity that such analysis can give, some interesting propositions can be established.[2] It can be shown, for instance, that the

[1] A theory which depends on the organization of individual wills into parties and pressure groups may seem to be rather a power-bloc theory than (as I have classified it) an atomized equilibrium theory. But while the desire of organizers to maintain their own power is not overlooked in the market theory of the political system, the assumption usually is (as it must be in order to make the system tolerably democratic) that parties and groups respond to the shifting autonomous wills of individuals who have highly pluralistic demand schedules.

[2] The two propositions that follow are adapted from Anthony Downs's brilliant exercise in marginal analysis, *An Economic Theory of Democracy* (New York, 1957), chaps. VIII and XII.

tendency of the two-party system is to discourage rational voting, up to an indefinite limit. (Politicians in such a model can normally expect to increase their chances of gaining office by discouraging voters from choosing rationally, for example, by offering ambiguous programmes. The only limit is a degree of voters' irrationality that would destroy the democratic system, which party politicians have a stake in. But in each party's calculation, this limit will not appear to be approached by any action the party takes in the direction of greater ambiguity, that is, of greater irrationality imposed on voters. Hence the tendency of the system is to discourage rational behaviour indefinitely.)

Another proposition that can be reached from the model is that, although the rules of a democratic system are designed to distribute political power equally, such equality cannot result if all men act rationally. (The rational voter, to make his demand effective, must acquire a lot of information. The cost, in time, energy, and money, of acquiring it must, by a rational voter, be weighed against the expected benefit to him, which benefit must be discounted in view of the very small amount of influence one vote has. The amount, and the cost, of the information needed for a rational decision necessarily varies between individuals, because the division of labour in modern society gives direct access to such information to only a few in each policy area. To those furthest removed from the sources of information the rational decision will be not to pay the cost of informing themselves, but to let some interested agency pay the cost, and accept biased information from it. Hence if all men act rationally their influence on policy must be very unequal.)

This kind of analysis is fascinating, and useful within limits. It cannot be carried as far as marginal analysis in economics because there is nothing in the political system as precise and measurable as price in the economic system. Perhaps its chief value is to show that with realistic assumptions about knowledge and uncertainty the market concept of democracy becomes self-contradictory. To the extent that politicians are rational, voters cannot be so; to the extent that voters are rational they cannot have the equal effective demand that democratic theory asserts; if all men are rational there cannot be a rational democracy.

But any equilibrium analysis of the political process in democracy, however rough or refined, has more serious limitations. The most noticeable limitation is that it is applicable not to democratic states in general, but only to the special case of expanding and prosperous (or optimistic) capitalist democracies. (This I think is why this kind of analysis is most developed in the United States but is still an imported academic luxury in Europe, where it has spread since the war at roughly the square root of the speed of coca-cola.) That the equilibrium analysis is applicable at all only in the special case can be readily seen. The analysis rests on the extreme pluralist assumption that the politically important demands of each individual are diverse and are shared with varied and shifting combinations of other individuals, none of which combinations can be expected to be a numerical majority of the electorate. This position is most nearly approached in a prosperous and expanding capitalist society: where the economy provides or promises a share of affluence to everybody, class interest will not outrank all the other divisions of interest. But in any other case the model is not appropriate.

In capitalist societies not expanding at a rate sufficient to meet expectations, political life is usually dominated by class parties, if such societies manage to keep a democratic system working at all. Class interests are then more important than the variegated other interests whose predominance is assumed in the equilibrium theory. To the extent that men think it rational to act politically as members of a class, the operation of the party system becomes very different from that of the market model. The extent to which men will so act is of course a matter of empirical judgement. But in the western nations of our century, where democratic franchise and competitive parties coincide with mass expectation of material betterment, the extent of class politics seems to vary inversely as the supposed expansiveness of the economy. Post-war and cold war prosperity has moved most of the western nations some distance away from class politics, but it would be optimistic to assume that this was now the normal and permanent condition of the established democracies.

When democracy, or the prospect of democracy, in the emergent independent nations of Africa and Asia is brought into consideration, the inadequacy of the market concept of the democratic process becomes even more apparent. The function of the political system in such countries is not the achievement of equilibrium in a pluralistic society but the authorization of a government strong enough to work a transformation from colony to viable nation. A one-party or quasi-party system appears to be more appropriate here than the competitive party model. The party which has the edge just before, or at the moment of, national independence is apt to accumulate authority rather rapidly. And while its authority may be exercised somewhat dictatorially, it should not be written off as undemocratic. For the plentitude of its authority may well be a necessary condition of fulfilling national democratic aspirations. Tribal divisions, class divisions, and religious divisions within the national community may seriously complicate the problem of maintaining a unified authority able to transform a backward country into an advanced one fit for national independence. But once a people, through the political leaders of all its significant parties, has committed itself to the proposition that it is a backward country, and that it should advance, the need to support a party which has a chance of advancing it is apt to override the divisive interests which flourish in a more secure society.

It may be said, of course, that this sort of regime is a transition to democracy rather than a viable kind of democracy. But while there are grounds for supposing that such regimes may allow more freedom of association as they feel more secure, it would be arrogant for western theorists to assume that such nations will wish to move towards the highly pluralistic society that is postulated in the equilibrium theory. The new nations which hope to keep a position between the Western and communist worlds have several patterns of society to choose from, ranging from the most unified to the most pluralistic. There is no reason to suppose that they will strive exclusively for the most pluralistic. If they do not, their political systems cannot be fitted into the equilibrum theory, not even by setting up a special adolescent section of the equilibrium theory. And any theory of the democratic process that does not find room for such political systems can scarcely now claim to be a general theory.[3]

The inadequacy of the equilibrium theory for any but the special case of expanding and prosperous Western democracies is perhaps sufficiently obvious. It remains to point out that, even in those countries, the appropriateness of the pluralistic equilibrium model is open to considerable doubt on historical grounds. The competitive party system, as a way of choosing and authorizing governments, was not developed to take care of a pluralistic universe of individual wants. It began as a means of settling sectional differences within the English ruling class, when democracy was not yet thought of. Later, when a democratic franchise could no longer be withheld, the party system was extended with a view to taming the democracy which was so much feared. The main purpose of the party system, as it began to function with the democratic franchise, less than a century ago, was to moderate class conflict. The system has on the whole been remarkably successful in doing this. And it seems probable that even in the most prosperous and least class-conscious countries the party system still has this underlying function. To the extent that that is so, the system is not adequately

[3] Whether or not a general theory of the democratic process should be expected to cover communist systems, one-party or otherwise, is a matter of the definition of democracy. Since even in a one-party communist state there is necessarily some measure of intra-party democracy, and something approximating to a system of interest groups operating in or on the party and the government, a case can be made for trying to bring such political systems within a general theory of the democratic process. But they cannot readily be assimilated to the equilibrium model. For they have issued from revolutionary rejection of its individualist assumptions, and their viability depends on the re-education of the mass of the citizens away from competitive individualist behaviour and outlook.

described by the pluralistic market theory. The equilibrium theory, then, even for the advanced Western societies to which it seems most appropriate, is so unhistorical as to be dangerously misleading.

The trouble with the equilibrium theory of democracy, we may conclude, is that, like the economists' marginal utility theory, it leaves out of account the historical determinants of effective demand. It treats class interests in advanced countries, and national aspirations in advancing countries, as just one among many kinds of political pressure. In doing so it averts its thoughts from the most serious problems of democracy. Equilibrium is a nice tune for whistling in the dark.

I have spoken so far of the use of a market concept to explain the mechanism of democracy rather than to justify democratic ends. If we look now at the justificatory theory, we find a somewhat different situation. The difference can be stated, perhaps over-emphatically, as follows: whereas the mechanical theorists see a market relation where it does not exist, or does not predominate, the ethical theorists commonly fail to see a market relation where it does exist, that is, in the ethical assumptions of the liberal tradition.

Market assumptions, I would argue, entered the premises of liberal-democratic thought at its origin in the seventeenth century. Market assumptions were a vital part of the ethical individualism which was at the root of the English liberal tradition. My own view, which I can only indicate here,[4] is that market assumptions are still in the premisses of twentieth-century liberal-democratic theory to an extent not now warranted and not always realized. The market assumption is not now warranted, I think, not because we do not now live in a market society (for we do live in one), but because the rightness or justice of a market society is not now as nearly universally accepted within the society as it was from the seventeenth to the nineteenth centuries.

The market assumption which seems to me to lie unrealized within modern liberal-democratic ethical theory is the assumption which was explicit in much of the earlier individualist theory (from Hobbes to Bentham), namely, that the individual personality (which is the supreme value in the liberal tradition) consists of capacities which the individual *owns*, and for which he owes nothing to society. Man is the proprietor of his own person. He is what he owns. The human essence is freedom to do what one wills with one's own, a freedom properly limited only by such rules as are needed to secure the same freedom for others. On these assumptions, the best society (indeed the only possible good society) is one in which all social relations between individuals are transformed into market relations, in which men are

[4] It is developed in my *The Political Theory of Possessive Individualism: Hobbes to Locke*.

related to each other as possessors of their own capacities (and of what they have acquired by the exercise of their capacities).

The clearest model of such a society was set up by Hobbes, who found that 'the value or worth of a man is, as of all other things, his price, that is to say, so much as would be given for the use of his power',[5] who saw all human attributes as commodities, to be contracted for and exchanged at values set (and rightly set) by the impersonal operation of a market in power, and who reduced justice to the performance of contract. In proposing this model of society Hobbes was a little ahead of his time, but the model was approximated more and more closely with the spread of industrial capitalism. We have moved a little away from it again in the twentieth century, with the spread of humane welfare concepts. But even now our society is, in my opinion, closer to the market model than to any other.

It may seem inconsistent to assert that contemporary Western society is substantially market society while denying, as I have denied, that its political system is a market-like system. But the two positions are consistent. The market model of society, as just described, does not entail a freely competitive political system, and certainly not a democratic political system; it may even require a class monopoly of political power, as was appreciated by most theorists from the seventeenth to the nineteenth century.

I am arguing, then, that while our society is substantially a market society, it is no longer automatically justified by its fundamental assumption. In the period when the liberal tradition was being formed, the assumption that society was a series of market relations between individuals was an adequate basis not only for describing the society but also for justifying it. For at that time almost all the politically articulate, seeing themselves as proprietors of their own capacities, accepted the rightness of the market society. Those who might have had doubts about its rightness were confronted with its inevitability. The laws of the market became the laws of nature. Their justice was not easily questioned. And since the relations expressed by those laws prevailed in the social as well as the economic order, the justice of a market society was similarly demonstrable. This was the position until about the middle of the nineteenth century. But with the emergence of a politically conscious working class both the justice and the inevitability of market society were challenged. So the justification of market society, in terms of the freedom it gave the individual as proprietor of his own person, ceased to be morally adequate. The old foundation of liberal morality was undermined.

The question not sufficiently asked since then is whether the justification of the liberal-democratic state has not continued to rest on

[5] *Leviathan*, chap. X.

the old justification of the market society. In so far as possessive market concepts got into the liberal postulates about the nature of man and society, into its moral postulates about the human essence, and were thence carried into the postulates of liberal-democratic theory, the theory cannot be expected to be adequate in the twentieth century.

The justification of liberal democracy still rests, and must rest, on the ultimate value of the free self-developing individual. But in so far as freedom is still seen as possession, as freedom from any but market relations with others, it can scarcely serve as the ultimate value of modern democracy.

The two arguments of this paper can now be quickly summarized: political theorists have paid too much attention to the superficial analogy between the market and the political process at the operative level, and not enough attention to the market concept at the deeper level of the postulates about the nature of society and the nature of human freedom. In an age when the operations of the market are no longer assumed automatically to be good, and indeed are no longer assumed to be automatic, political science is still in full pursuit of the good old model.

ESSAY XI

The Deceptive Task of Political Theory

THE remarks which follow do no more than raise a question which might if pursued help to explain the paradox that an age in which fundamental political issues crowd upon us has yet produced no Hobbes or Bentham, no Locke or Hume. The question with which I begin, and with the implications of which the paper is largely concerned, is whether the well-known distinction Marx made between 'classical' and 'vulgar' political economy has any parallel in political theory and can illuminate in any way the position of modern political thought.

It will be well to start by looking at the real point of the distinction Marx made in political economy: there was more than name-calling in the epithet 'vulgar'. The distinction (*Capital*, vol. I, trans. Moore and Aveling, pp. xxii-xxiv, 52 n. 2) was briefly this. Classical political economy, stretching from Petty to Ricardo, 'investigated the real relations of production in bourgeois society'; it was, within its limits (the limits of the bourgeois horizon), genuinely scientific, seeking to establish laws of value and laws of distribution of the social product. It recognized increasingly (notably in the case of Ricardo) the difference and even antagonism of class interests. It knew that the state was needed to maintain coercively the institutions of property which made possible this economy with its class distribution of productive effort and of the whole product.

'Vulgar economy' (McCulloch, J. S. Mill, *et seq.*) is described as dealing with appearances only, ruminating on the materials provided by scientific economy in search of 'plausible explanations of the most obtrusive phenomena, for bourgeois daily use'. It replaced genuine scientific inquiry with either 'the bad conscience and the evil intent of apologetic', or (among those 'who still claimed some scientific standing and aspired to be something more than mere sophists') 'a shallow syncretism of which John Stuart Mill is the best representative', which 'tried to harmonize the Political Economy of capital with the claims, no longer to be ignored, of the proletariat'.

The change, then, is from disinterested inquiry to apologetics or syncretism. The change came, according to Marx, after 1830 and more especially after 1848. The reason assigned for the change was the emergence of a class-conscious proletariat coinciding with the final establishment of bourgeois political power. It was not simply that this put the bourgeoisie on the defensive intellectually; it was more that the actual change in society made it impossible for bourgeois thinkers either to stay honestly and clearly within the old assumptions or to abandon them. 'In so far as Political Economy remains within [the bourgeois horizon], in so far, i.e., as the capitalist regime is looked upon as the absolutely final form of social production, instead of as a passing historical phase of its evolution, Political Economy can remain a science only so long as the class-struggle is latent or manifests itself only in isolated or sporadic phenomena.' With Ricardo, 'the science of bourgeois economy had reached the limits beyond which it could not pass.'

We may disregard here Marx's scorn for 'the miserable McCulloch' and his contempt for the 'hired prizefighters'. The important point is contained in his assertion that political economy could remain a science, while staying within the limits of the assumption that capitalist relations were the ultimate form of social relations, only as long as the class antagonism in those relations was latent or only sporadically manifested. Political economy could, that is to say, recognize an element of class antagonism in the system and still regard the economy as a determinate system suitable for scientific analysis, as long as it could regard the antagonisms as fixed or equilibrated and incapable of altering the whole system. In the second place, political economy could be impartial, i.e. untroubled about the moral values of the system it was examining, as long as the system appeared to be absolutely given by the very nature of things. In these circumstances, and only in these, could analysis proceed unmoved either by a need to justify or to denounce. (It was in fact usually assumed that the system carried its own moral justification because it was shown to be a reflection of a rational natural order; but the point here is that, on the assumption that it was the final and irreplaceable form of economic society, moral judgement had no place.)

Hence, the effect of 1830 and 1848, of Sismondi and Proudhon, of Thompson and Hodgskin, was to make it impossible for political economy to regard classes as part of a system in equilibrium. The political economists could therefore neither continue on the evidence to regard the prevailing economy as the final form, nor continue to treat it impartially in the sense just described. In other words the economy could no longer be handled scientifically as a permanent and determinate system. Yet while political economy could not go any further on the assumption that capitalist relations were the final form of social relations, at the same time the economists could not abandon that assumption without abandoning their whole conception of the world. That they could not do, either because they were so immersed in it, or because to have done so would have been, by this time, to have ranged themselves morally against the system they knew and were strongly attached to. So the material of classical political economy (the economic relations of production and distribution of a capitalist society) had from then on to be dealt with in a less scientific way: economics became apologetics or a search for terms of accommodation between the old theory and the new facts which could not be fitted into it. Or else the economists had to abandon inquiry into that material and take to more superficial inquiry: if classes destroyed the vision of equilibrium, it was classes that had to go and equilibrium be kept.

Hence the move to the syncretism of J. S. Mill, and subsequently (it may be added) to marginal utility, which avoided the range of problems classical theory had been concerned with and served to prevent the basic processes of creation and social distribution of wealth being seen at all, thus creating an intellectual atmosphere unreceptive to anti-capitalist analysis.

Is there in this any insight applicable to the development of modern political theory? In so far as the change from classical to vulgar political economy was a change from scientific inquiry to justification (apologetics), no parallel change in political theory might be expected, for political theory in the great tradition has always been justificatory. Looked at more closely, however, this difference between political economy and political theory is not absolute, not a difference in the nature of two kinds of thought, but conditional on the way in which each, during any phase of its development, is related to the society in which and for which it is written.

This point is of some importance. Classical political economy was at the same time a scientific explanation, and a justification, of a certain economic and social system. The explanation of 'the system of natural liberty' was itself a vindication of it, in the circumstances; to explain the system was to demonstrate its superiority to the previous system in liberating man by increasing his ability to dominate his natural environment. As long as there was no realistically conceivable successor to that system, scientific explanation was justification. Only when a possible successor appeared was there a logical divorce between explanation and justification. There is, therefore, on this score, no absolute difference which would render a parallel development in political theory out of the question.

Another obstacle to parallel development appears to confront us. In order to have vulgar political economy there had to be something to vulgarize. There had to be a body of scientific theory of which something plausible could be made for apologetic purposes, or which was capable of being transformed into theory more superficial but inheriting the scientific mantle of the classical theory. Was there any such corpus of political theory by the middle of the nineteenth century? I think that the whole liberal tradition from Locke (or Hobbes) through to Bentham and James Mill can be so regarded. True, almost all these theorists were plainly and consciously justifying or advocating some political system, some kind or limits of political obligation. Yet a political theory may be scientific at the same time as justificatory. The great question political theorists seek to answer may be put in either of two ways: what sort of state ought men to obey? or, what sort of state is most congruous with the nature of man, most in conformity with man's needs and capacities? A political theory may be called scientific in so far as it seeks to deduce the desirable or right kind and degree of political obligation from the nature of man, and in so far as its view of the nature of man is based on inquiry as scientific as is possible within the prevailing limits of knowledge and vision.

The great tradition from Hobbes through Locke, Hume, Burke, and Bentham, does meet these standards. It makes up a corpus of classical theory, an essentially utilitarian theory of political obligation based on postulates of human nature which, within the limits of the then bourgeois vision, were profound. The limit of bourgeois vision with respect to political theory lay, not in the assumption of classical political economy (that capitalist production is the final form), but in the assumption that bourgeois human nature is the final form (or, more usually, the universal form except for some supposed primitive age) of human nature. The central assumption of this 'classical' political theory was eminently suitable to the bourgeois society and state; the theory was therefore honestly and solidly scientific about the material it was dealing with. Within the limits of its vision it studied the real relations of political society.

If this view of the English tradition of political theory in the seventeenth and eighteenth centuries be allowed, the possibility of 'classical' political theory being vulgarized is clear enough, and it is open to us to inquire whether it can properly be said to have been vulgarized, and whether its characteristics were conducive to its vulgarization when the circumstances changed. I shall suggest that both of these questions are to be answered in the affirmative, and that the usual view of the development from the seventeenth to the twentieth century points in that direction and, with a slight shift of emphasis, gives that result.

It is a commonplace that the chief characteristic of the liberal tradition from Hobbes to Bentham was its individualism, and the development from John Stuart Mill through Idealism and Pluralism to the neo-Idealism of Barker and Lindsay is often interpreted as a series of attempts to correct the defects of this individualism. The tendency of this interpretation is to attribute the defects mainly to the extreme Benthamite variety of individualism, or even to that caricature of Benthamite *laissez-faire* which Professor Lionel Robbins has lately exposed.[1] It is perhaps more illuminating to say that the same individualist assumption goes right back to Hobbes and Locke, that it was the strength of the liberal theory in the seventeenth and eighteenth centuries (when it corresponded with the social reality), and became the defect of that theory about mid-nineteenth century (when it ceased to do so).

It will be convenient to call the assumption 'possessive individualism'. It amounts roughly to this. (1) Man, the individual, is seen as absolute natural proprietor of his own capacities, owing nothing to society for them. Man's essence is freedom to use his capacities in search of satisfactions. This freedom is limited properly only by some principle of utility or utilitarian natural law which forbids harming others. Freedom therefore is restricted to, and comes to be identified with, domination over things, not domination over men. The clearest form of domination over things is the relation of ownership or possession. Freedom is therefore possession. Everyone is free, for everyone possesses at least his own capacities. (2) Society is seen, not (as it had been) as a system of relations of domination and subordination between men and classes held together by reciprocal rights and duties, but as a lot of free equal individuals related to each other through their possessions, that is, related as owners of their own capacities and of what they have produced and accumulated by the use of their capacities. The relation of exchange (the market relation) is seen as the fundamental relation of society. Finally (3) political society is seen as a rational device for the protection of property, including capacities; even life and liberty are considered as possessions, rather than as social rights with correlative duties.

All this is to be found in Locke; indeed Hobbes went even further than Locke in making man a commodity with an exchange value, but he saw too clearly that domination over things was domination over men, and vice versa, which is perhaps why he is not to be counted entirely in the liberal tradition. Possessive individualism was the predominant assumption of English political thinking from Locke until, say, James Mill. This was the period of the solid establishment of capitalism, when the whole society was recast in market relations, a greatly enlarged working class was created in dependence on the sale of its labour, production was enormously expanded, and unlimited possibilities appeared. In these circumstances, theories built on the assumptions of possessive individualism could be, as I have said, substantially scientific within the limits of their vision.

[1] Lionel Robbins: *The Theory of Economic Policy in English Classical Political Economy* (London, 1952).

The limits were there, but were, for the time being, unimportant. Thus, the position that society consisted of free market relations had a real though limited and partial validity: real, because all relations were increasingly being reduced to the market; partial, because the market relation was not a free one but concealed class domination. Similarly, the position that freedom was domination over things had a real though partial validity: real, in that capitalism was enormously increasing man's productive capacity and thereby his freedom from the limits of scarcity; partial, in that each individual was not being made more free from the domination of other men. While there was no alternative system of production or of social relations in view, the limited and partial character of both these positions was not visible; indeed it is anachronistic to call them limited.

About the middle of the nineteenth century, however, the limitations of these assumptions became apparent. The continuing extension of the capitalist market economy had brought more people more completely into dependence on the sale of their one possession (their capacity to labour). The view that social relations were essentially *free* relations of the market, and that individual freedom was domination of things, became untenable, for the market had clearly created a dominant and a subservient class, and freedom for the former was domination over the latter.

What made a change in the classical political theory possible and necessary was not simply that the development of society had made the old assumptions invalid, but that the same development had produced a working class with some class-consciousness, some organization, and some theories of alternatives to capitalist relations (Chartism, Owenism, etc.). Working-class consciousness, we may say, both made the old theory invalid and made it obvious that it was invalid.

We seem to have here a substantial parallel to the position Marx found in political economy in 1848. I think we may say that 'classical' political theory reached, with Bentham and James Mill (somewhat as political economy reached with Ricardo), the limits beyond which it could not pass. Bentham and James Mill drew out the full consequences, for the theory of government, of the 'classical' postulate of possessive individualism. They were the last who could do so scientifically; critiques ranging from Carlyle's to the Christian Socialists', and the practical critiques of Chartism and other working-class movements, made that evident. The threat of mass democratic politics on the Continental model was never entirely absent from the English political mind after 1848.

From about 1848, therefore, it was to be expected that the direction and quality of English political thinking should undergo a marked change. Whether is should be called vulgarization is perhaps a matter of taste, but the subsequent development of theory suggests that the process was of that nature. We need not impute bad faith; to do so would be palpably absurd in the case of the leading figures. But we do, I suggest, everywhere find syncretism—the essence of honest vulgarization—in the form of attempts to abandon possessive individualism while maintaining bourgeois values, or attempts to reconcile bourgeois individualism with social democracy. These attempts increasingly involved the thinkers' concealing from themselves the fundamental nature of the problem.

Thus John Stuart Mill exhausted himself in seeking ways of patching up the contradictions between liberalism and social democracy, though quite explicitly denying a democratic franchise. Bagehot would find disguises for the problem by increasing the apparatus of deference. T. H. Green rejected possessive individualism but, unwilling or unable to see what it was that had made it untenable (i.e. the appearance of the possibility of a class-based social democracy), went to the concept of the Greek city-state for a pattern. The tendency of Idealism as a whole was to disguise from itself, and so divert attention from, the class basis of political problems. The Idealists' concept of the state as a moral idea rather than a Benthamite mechanism appears as the crowning concept of a chain of thought starting from a moral rejection of class conflict and class political action, arguing that the frustration of humanity was due to faulty political concepts, and finding the remedy in instilling into the political structure a more rounded concept of the state, which would recognize and embrace the claims of society as well as of the individual.

Pluralism had (and has) socialist advocates but its influence has not been confined to socialist ranks, and its effect has been to turn social thought away from class by emphasizing the multiplicity and moral value of group life. Finally, what may be called neo-Idealism, which appears now to prevail in English political theory, carries forward the tendencies of both Idealism and Pluralism. The essential problem, it is said, is to get the right relation between the authority of the state and spontaneous (moral) group life. This again neglects or leaves concealed or overshadowed the problem of getting men clear of the class relations of the market.

This neglect in political theory is matched in the 'objective' political science with which so many of us are mainly concerned. In so far as political science does not cut itself entirely away from problems of value, and refuse to go beyond mechanics, it commonly is concerned with the rationale of the liberal-democratic system of government. This is generally presented as a matter of a state whose function is to equate the supply of political goods with the competing demands of the many diverse, shifting, and overlapping groups which between them comprise what is significant in political society. This view of the state appears to be a reflection of neo-Idealism. Or perhaps it is more fitting to say that both are unconsciously a new kind of reflection of the market into political theory, in which associations rather than individuals compete for expression and satisfaction and in which the state, ideally, lets them find their own equilibrium or helps them to find the highest equilibrium. The desire for flexibility and fluidity comes at a time when the economy is becoming more monopolistic and rigid: even the relations of the market seem desirable in retrospect when the old free market has itself disappeared.

This is, of course, only one way of looking at the trend of the last century in political theory, but it has, I suggest, some value in pointing to one characteristic which may be thought fundamental. If the adequacy of a political theory is to be assessed by the penetration of its analysis of human nature, it may be allowed that there has been nothing of classic quality in the liberal tradition since Bentham: narrow as the view of human nature prevailing from Hobbes to Bentham has since appeared to be, it was a penetrating analysis of the human nature which had been produced by the society they knew. A reason why there has been nothing of comparable quality since Bentham now suggests itself: that is, that *pari passu* with the emergence of a conscious and articulate working class which has had to be taken into account, and which has developed unorthodox ideas about human needs and capacities, it has become impossible to make politically meaningful statements about human nature as such, with anything like the previously possible degree of scientific validity. It has become necessary to recognize a class difference in human nature, or at least in concepts of human nature.

But this is just what could not be fully admitted to the minds of liberal thinkers, for it leads to the revolutionary view, common to the eighteenth-century democrats, the utopian socialists, the Marxists, and various agrarian movements, that in order to have democracy human nature must be changed, and changed by 'the people', under a new sort of leadership, taking things in their own hands. This view has been consistently rejected by liberal theory, and (possibly in part because of this) its proponents have become increasingly anti-liberal, so that the gulf between liberal-democratic and mass-democratic concepts and movements has widened. The possibility of recognizing, with any hopefulness, the potentialities of a mass transformation of human nature, recedes. Liberal hope (or despair) puts human nature out of sight or seeks ways to infuse it gradually with higher moral qualities.

Thus what might be called a class differentiation in the understanding of human needs and capacities may be said to have played the same part in the development of political theory as the class differentiation in the view of possible economic relations played in the development of political economy. Abstinence and marginal utility replaced the classical labour theory of value; deference, Pluralism, and Idealism supplanted the classical utilitarian rationalist theory of political obligation.

What then, to come to the title of the paper, is the deceptive task of political theory? A thorough inquiry along the lines sketched here might, I think, show that the task of political theory for something like the last hundred years has been necessarily self-deception. I am suggesting that, setting aside the mere propagandists as outside the range of our central concern here, the solid political theorists in the liberal tradition have been compelled to deceive themselves, to the extent that they have seen beyond the limitations of that possessive individualism which was the core of the liberal tradition in its formative years.

That limitation of vision was fairly constant, and its acceptance was increasing, during the first great developing phase of bourgeois society; from Locke to James Mill the assumption of possessive individualism came to be held and stated more and more consciously. Yet the same extension of capitalist relations which encouraged and for a time rendered scientific the analysis based on this assumption, was producing a new class consciousness. The appearance of this new phenomenon, I have argued, made the assumption less valid, removed the scientific character of analysis made on that assumption, and finally made it intellectually impossible for theorists (while remaining liberal and humane) to stay within the assumption. And the same phenomenon made it almost impossible for them to depart entirely from the assumption, for the class which challenged the assumption denied, by its very existence and aspirations as a conscious class, the validity or superiority of the liberal values. Over the whole span of three hundred years of liberal society and thought, the deceptive task of political theory appears to vary inversely as the limitation of bourgeois vision and directly as the extent of the apprehended threat to liberal values.

PART THREE

Seventeenth-Century Roots of the Twentieth-Century Predicament

ESSAY XII

Servants and Labourers in Seventeenth-Century England

MY assertions that the Levellers, in excluding 'servants' from their franchise proposals, meant to withhold the franchise from all wage-earners, and that the term 'servant' in seventeenth-century England meant anyone who worked for an employer for wages,[1] have been disputed by Mr. Peter Laslett as being contradicted by the evidence of seventeenth-century usage and as being inconsistent with his view of the patriarchal nature of the seventeenth-century English society. I agree that the evidence needs fuller examination. There are certainly contexts in which the term 'servants' was used to mean only one category of wage-earners. But it can be shown that these are irrelevant to the meaning of the term in the context of franchise discussions. And although no one would expect to find consistent precision in the seventeenth century's use of 'servant', any more than in its use of 'yeoman' or 'gentleman', it can also I think be shown that my more sweeping statement—that servants meant wage-earners—remains valid generally, beyond the context of franchise discussions, with only exceptions of a quite specific technical kind.

Laslett has made the following assertions:

(a) The word 'servant' in seventeenth century England simply did not cover all persons receiving wages, as Macpherson insists it did. Ordinarily it meant residents, not always domestic servants but men and women 'included in the persons of their masters', included by virtue of patriarchalism. There are occasions when 'outservants' must have been referred to as well, and they were mostly shepherds or cowmen, people whose functions made it impossible for them to live in the household. In a few scattered contexts, it is true, journeymen out of their time and married are also referred to in this way. It would be surprising if a social description turned out to be quite free of ambiguity, and even the perspicuous Gregory King leaves the status of a certain proportion of wage earners uncertain. But it is completely unjustifiable to argue from these marginal vagaries that when the Levellers excluded 'servants' from the franchise they thereby took the vote away from a substantial body of householders and that they did so in virtue of the wage relationship.[2]

[1] C. B. Macpherson: *The Political Theory of Possessive Individualism: Hobbes to Locke*, p. 107. (Subsequent references to this work use the abbreviation *PTPI*.)

[2] Peter Laslett: 'Market Society and Political Theory', *Historical Journal*, vol. 7, i (1964), p. 152. Cf. Laslett: *The World We Have Lost* (London, 1965), p. 182, note.

(b) The servant in husbandry who married and therefore went to live out ceased to be a 'servant' and became a labourer: 'Day-labourer was now his full description, for he earned what money came his way by contracting for work a day at a time with the husbandmen of his village.'[3]

(c) '"Servants in husbandry" . . . must be sharply distinguished from "labourer", or "agricultural labourer", never called servants under the old order because they did not ordinarily live in.'[4]

Here (I) the evidence about the seventeenth-century usage of the term servants is more fully examined (and some previously unused evidence is presented), and is shown to controvert Laslett's assertions about the generally restricted meaning of the term, and to support my interpretation of its meaning, both in the context of franchise discussions and more generally; and (II) further grounds for the presumption that in the seventeenth century servants generally meant all wage-earners are stated, and the contexts in which the term was used in some narrower sense are shown to be special contexts of enumeration, the schematic requirements of which made it necessary or appropriate to use the generic term for one species.

1. *Seventeenth-Century Usage Re-examined*

Evidence about the seventeenth-century usage of the term 'servants' is not to be found in as many kinds of material as one might expect. Evidence in theoretical and general descriptive writings on society and politics is sparse. Most of those who referred to servants, while making it clear that servants were of no account in society or politics, assumed that their readers would know whom the term included. However, those political writers and actors who had the most lively concern about the position of servants, namely, those who were making broad franchise proposals, did, as we shall see, have explicit or clearly implicit definitions. One other range of sources is relevant: classificatory lists and tabulations of a local or the national population, and classifications of the wage-earners as a whole, made at the time for administrative or statistical purposes. These include: on the national level, Gregory King's justly celebrated *Natural and Political Observations and Conclusions upon the State and Condition of England, 1696*;[5]

[3] Laslett: *The World We Have Lost*, p. 15.

[4] Laslett: 'Clayworth and Cogenhoe', in H. E. Bell and R. L. Ollard (eds.): *Historical Essays 1600–1750 Presented to David Ogg* (London, 1963), p. 169, n. 2.

[5] Subsequent page references to this work are to the version published as an Appendix to George Chalmers' *Estimate of the Comparative Strength of Great Britain* . . . (London, 1804), cited as 'King in Chalmers'.

and, on the county (and city) level, the wage assessments made from time to time for various counties and cities by the Justices of the Peace in Quarter Sessions (as required by the Statute of Artificers), the language of which is, as would be expected from their authorship and their purpose, homespun rather than formally legal. There are also, at the parish level, certain records, including occasional parish censuses called for by the central authorities of the Church, but for a reason that will be apparent (below, p. 222) these afford no evidence on the question that here concerns us.

I shall consider in turn (i) the evidence of King's *Observations*, (ii) the evidence of the Quarter Sessions wage assessments, (iii) the evidence of franchise proponents, and (iv), since the concept of patriarchalism is an integral part of Laslett's case, the evidence of patriarchalism.

(i) Gregory King's *Observations*

These have a bearing on each of Laslett's three assertions.

(a) Laslett's view that the term 'servants' ordinarily meant in-servants and that the term 'outservants' could therefore only have been a marginal vagary is not borne out by King's findings. For by King's account there appear to have been as many men working in husbandry as outservants, so named, as there were working in husbandry as in-servants, even when those he calls in one place labourers are omitted from the count of employees living out.

Before looking at the figures we may take note of the one respect in which King does leave the status of some wage-earners uncertain. We cannot be sure whether, in setting up the category 'labouring people and outservants' in his table 'A Scheme of the Income, and Expence, of the Several Families of England',[6] he was simply combining alternative expressions for the same people (as he apparently was in some of the other categories in that table, e.g. 'merchants and traders by sea', 'artizans and handicrafts'), or whether he thought of them as different, and if so, precisely what the difference was. The only evidence bearing on this is that in another table (Table IX, discussed in the next paragraph) King lists separately 'children of servants in husbandry' and 'children of day labourers'. From this it is clear that he was taking 'servants in husbandry' to exclude day labourers. This does not mean that he was taking 'servants' to exclude 'labourers', since as we shall see (below, p. 222) 'servants in husbandry' was frequently used as a description of one occupational group whereas 'servants' was not.

However, even if we assume that the 'labouring people and out-servants' of his Main Table comprise two separate groups, the number

[6] Reproduced in *PTPI*, pp. 280–1, and in Laslett's *World We Have Lost*, pp. 32–3, and hereafter referred to as King's Main Table.

of outservants is very substantial indeed compared with the number of inservants. The number of inservants is given (in King's Table III)[7] as 560,000 (260,000 male, 300,000 female). 'Labouring people and outservants' are shown (in the Main Table) as amounting to 364,000 'families', which, with some allowance for families (i.e. households) not headed by a male (I have allowed one seventh),[8] amounts to about 312,000 adult male 'labouring people and outservants', substantially more than the 260,000 male inservants of all ages. The relative numbers of labourers and outservants (assuming that King was combining two distinct groups in his joint category) is indicated by the figures in his Table IX,[9] which tabulates the numbers of inhabitants of various kinds excused from the poll tax of 3*d*. William and Mary. This gives separate figures for the numbers of 'children under 16 of day labourers' (260,000) and 'children under 16 of servants in husbandry' (160,000). Clearly there were a lot of men, described as servants in husbandry, who were married, with children, and living outside the employer's household. If we assume that the number of children per couple for each of the two descriptions of parents is 1½ (which is the average for the whole category 'labouring people and outservants' in the Main Table) the number of adult male servants in husbandry married and living out would be 106,500 and of day labourers 173,500. The total, 280,000, is about right in comparison with the number of adult males in the joint category 'labouring people and outservants' of the Main Table (which comes to about 312,000, including outservants in other than husbandry).

A total of some 106,000 adult male outservants in husbandry is about the same as the probable total of adult male inservants in husbandry. Although King gives no figure for the latter, the order of magnitude can be got from the figure for male inservants of all ages and of all occupations, which is 260,000. As this includes boys from the age of ten or so,[10] and does not include married men, it is probable that half this number were not adults, leaving 130,000 adult male inservants of all occupations. If as many as one fifth of these were in occupations other than husbandry (which does not seem an excessive estimate), there would be only 104,000 adult male inservants in husbandry, that is, slightly fewer than the probable number of adult male outservants in husbandry. Whether or not these outservants were, as Laslett suggests, 'mostly shepherds or cowmen, people whose functions made it impossible for them to live in the household'—and

[7] King in Chalmers, p. 39. [8] *PTPI*, p. 285.
[9] King in Chalmers, p. 57.
[10] 'A boy, or a girl, born in a cottage, often, even usually, left home for service at the age of ten, eleven or twelve, though we have found 'servants' only eight or nine years old' (Laslett: *World We Have Lost*, p. 14).

it seems unlikely that they were, since, apart from the fact that their functions did not make it impossible for them to live in (see below, p. 209), it is improbable that of all the men living out there were as many shepherds and cowmen as there were in all the other husbandry occupations together—the number of outservants is too great for them to be dismissed as a marginal group.

(b) King's terminology also controverts Laslett's statement that male servants in husbandry ceased to be called servants and were fully described as day labourers as soon as they married and went to live out. King's Table IX implies, as we have just seen, something of the order of 100,000 male 'servants in husbandry' married and living out.

(c) The same evidence contradicts the reason Laslett gives for the distinction he says must be drawn between 'servants in husbandry' and 'labourers' or 'agricultural labourers'. Since something like half of those adult males who were called servants in husbandry did not live in, it cannot be that the labourers, who also did not live in, 'were never called servants because they did not ordinarily live in.'

(ii) The Quarter Sessions Wage Assessments

The usage of the terms 'servants' and 'labourers' in the wage assessments varies considerably, but an examination of a small sample of the extant assessments indicates that Laslett's assertions are untenable on this evidence as well. In a random sample comprising 13 assessments,[11] I have found that 'servants' was often used to include wage-earners living out as well as in, that outservants were not all day labourers, and that servants in husbandry were not sharply distinguished from labourers.

[11] The sample is random in that, starting from the references given in Roger J. Kelsall: *Wage Regulation under the Statute of Artificers* (London, 1938), assessments were consulted in whatever order they were most conveniently available, in printed collections or as separate documents, in the time available. Forty assessments were seen (including a few from the late sixteenth century). Of the forty, twenty-seven either were so incomplete (e.g. giving rates for maidservants only or for labourers only) as to have no bearing on the question, or merely replicated the wording of a previous year's assessment for the same place. Thus only thirteen different usable assessments were seen. A complete examination of all extant assessments might of course give a different picture, but this sample seems to have enough evidential value to be worth reporting. The thirteen assessments are as follows: Lincoln 1563 (Victoria County Histories, *Lincolnshire*, Vol. II); Cardiganshire 1595 (British Museum, G.6463 (331.B)); Lancaster 1595 (Bodleian Library, Oxford, Arch G.c.6 (350–1)); New Sarum 1595 (Queen's College, Oxford, Sel.b. (331B and C)); Wiltshire 1603 (*Historical Manuscripts Commission, Various*, Vol. I); Lincolnshire 1621 (*Historical Manuscripts Commission, Rutland*, Vol. I); Suffolk 1630 (Cambridge University Library, Add. MSS 22, no. 76, fols 72–3); Somerset 1648 (*Somerset Q. S. Records*, Vol. III, ed. E. B. H. Harbin and McB. Dawes, Somerset Record Society, Vol. 28); Wiltshire 1655 (*Wiltshire County Records of the 17th Century*, ed.

The record is as follows:

(a) That servants 'ordinarily meant' only inservants is controverted by six of the thirteen assessments, which set wages for servants, so named (some in husbandry and some in trades), who are clearly living out.

Thus in three (Herts. 1687, Lincoln 1563, New Sarum 1595) yearly wage rates for several named kinds of 'servants' (in the first case, for eight named kinds of 'servants of husbandry'; in the other two for 'servants' in specified trades) are given both 'with meat and drink' and 'without meat and drink'; it must be assumed that those without meat and drink were not living in the employer's household. In another (Suffolk 1630) 'servants' *sans phrase* are given *daily* rates, with and without meat and drink, as well as yearly rates; and in two others (Lincs. 1621 and Herts. 1678) daily or weekly rates only are given for 'servants' of various descriptions (Lincs. in trades; Herts. in both—weekly rates only for plowmen and horsekeepers, and daily rates only for carpenters, bricklayers, tailors, 'and all other artificers'). Daily and weekly rates are for those living out. And in Herts. 1678, 'servants' includes taskers and shepherds by the week as well as by the year: those by the week must be assumed to be living out.

Nor does the evidence support Laslett's contention that the 'out-servants' sometimes referred to 'were mostly shepherds or cowmen, people whose functions made it impossible for them to live in the household'.[12] The assessments for Cardigan 1595, New Sarum 1595, and Herts. 1687, clearly assume that shepherds etc. will be living in, for they set yearly wages with meat and drink for them; and in Wilts. 1603 and Herts. 1678 they are set yearly wages, which probably were for living in.

(b) That the servant in husbandry, who married and went to live out ceased to be a 'servant' and was fully described as day labourer, is controverted by the three assessments cited in (a) above which describe as servants, not as labourers, men working in husbandry at daily or weekly rates, namely, Suffolk 1630, Herts. 1678 (the taskers and shepherds), and Herts. 1687 (all the servants in husbandry, from bailiffs to shepherds and horsekeepers).

(c) That 'servants in husbandry' must be sharply distinguished from 'labourer' or 'agricultural labourer', never called servants

B. H. Cunningham); North Riding 1658 (*North Riding Q. S. Records 1605–1786*, ed. J. Wake, North Riding Record Society, Old Series, Vol. VI); Hertfordshire 1678 (*Hertford County Records*, Vol. I, ed. W. J. Hardy, Sessions Rolls 1581–1698); Hertfordshire 1687 (*Hertford County, Records*, Vol. VI, ed. W. J. Hardy, Calendar to the Sessions Books etc., 1658–1700); Buckinghamshire 1687 (*Buckinghamshire Sessions Records*, ed. W. le Hardy, Vol. I, 1678–94).

[12] *Historical Journal*, Vol. 7, i, p. 152.

because they did not ordinarily live in, is not borne out by the wage assessments. It is probable that those called labourers did not ordinarily live in. Only one or two of our thirteen assessments assume that they do. Cardigan 1595 specifically provides for labourers who live in: it gives *only* a yearly rate 'with meat and drink' for 'common hindes, threshers, and common labourers'. One other (Herts. 1678) gives only yearly rates for 'labourers at large' (both 'first sort' and 'second sort'), which probably implies that they were living in, though we cannot be certain about this in view of the fact that the Herts. justices nine years later (as cited in (a) above) set *yearly* wage rates *without* as well as with meat and drink for eight kinds of servants in husbandry ranging from bailiffs to horsekeepers. If the Herts. 1678 'labourers' on yearly wages were living out, they are a further contradiction to Laslett's assertion (in (b) above) that all those who married and lived out were day labourers.

But that labourers were never called servants is directly controverted by the three assessments cited in (b) where daily or weekly employees in husbandry are called servants, and is further controverted by the looseness of the usage in some assessments, e.g. Herts. 1678 and Herts. 1687, where 'labourers' are included under the general head 'servants', and Somerset 1648 where 'servants' are included under the general head 'labourers'.

To sum up, the evidence of the Quarter Sessions wage assessments indicates (a) that the term 'servants' was frequently used for wage-earners living out (not surprisingly, since provision was made for their doing the same work as inservants); (b) that servants in husbandry (and in trades) who married and therefore went to live out did not cease to be thought of as servants, and (c) that there was no consistent distinction between servants and labourers. I have not found any evidence for Laslett's statement that, in equating servants with all wage-earners, I was 'demonstrably wrong',[13] nor has he there or subsequently offered any evidence or demonstration.

(iii) Franchise Proponents

As mentioned above, political writers and actors who were making and defending novel franchise proposals sometimes had to make clear their position on servants, and did have explicit or clearly implicit definitions of the term.

The one seventeenth-century political writer who was most explicit in his definition of 'servants' left no doubt that he took the word to include all wage-earners. Harrington defines servants as those who have not 'wherewithal to live of themselves',[14] which in Harrington's terms means those without enough property to live independently of

[13] Ibid.

[14] *Art of Lawgiving*, in *Oceana and other Works*, 1771 ed., p. 409.

employment. This alone, he states, is what distinguishes servants from freemen or citizens. Servants, while such, cannot be freemen or citizens, but 'if they attain to liberty, that is, to live of themselves, they are freemen or citizens'.[15] And he adds that the stipulation that servants cannot have a vote 'needs no proof, in regard of the nature of servitude which is inconsistent with freedom, or participation of government in a commonwealth'. These statements are among the few of Harrington's generalizations to which none of his many critics took exception.

More important, evidentially, than Harrington are the political actors whose arguments about servants in relation to the franchise are recorded in the Army Debates, namely, the Levellers and their opponents. They did not define servants as explicitly as Harrington did, but the reasons they gave, and accepted, for excluding servants from the franchise show what their criterion of servanthood was. It was dependence on the will of other men, dependence on the will of others for getting a living. This was certainly the Leveller view as set out in the Putney debates: 'the reason why we would exclude apprentices, or servants, or those that take alms, is because they depend upon the will of other men and should be afraid to displease (them). For servants and apprentices, they are included in their masters, and so for those that receive alms from door to door...'[16] Servants and beggars have forfeited their birthright freedom.[17] The dependence on the will of others which servants and beggars had in common was dependence on others for a livelihood.

This dependence is as great in the case of employees living out as in the case of employees living in. Indeed, in so far as those living out were on less than annual contract and those living in were on annual contract (which we may presume to be the general rule, although we have seen exceptions to it in the evidence of the wage assessments), those living out were if anything more dependent on the wills of others than were the inservants. For where there is a great deal of unemployment or underemployment (as Laslett acknowledges there was),[18] and hence a buyers' market in labour, those who must come to terms with some employer every week or every day are dependent on the will of other men more frequently than are those on annual contract. We should not make too much of this. The difference in dependence is, as will be seen when the nature of the patriarchal relation is examined (below, pp. 216-17 ff.), not a difference in kind, and not necessarily a

[15] *Oceana*, 1771 ed., p. 77.

[16] A. S. P. Woodhouse: *Puritanism and Liberty* (London, 1938), p. 83.

[17] Leveller *Petition* of January 1648, and Third *Agreement*, as quoted in *PTPI*, pp. 124–5.

[18] Laslett: *World We Have Lost*, p. 31.

difference in degree, but only a difference in form. But at least it is clear that employees living out were *no less* dependent for a livelihood on the will of other men than those living in. Since dependence on others for a livelihood was the criterion of servanthood, the presumption must be that the wage-earners living out were equally regarded as servants.

It is puzzling, therefore, why Laslett has assumed—for it is an assumption, for which no evidence is offered—that the dependence which constituted servanthood was confined to the sort of dependence characteristic of the annual inservant's position. He asserts that servants were ordinarily those who lived in and so were 'included in the persons of their masters', and adds the gloss 'included by virtue of patriarchalism'.[19] This is not supported either by the texts or by an examination of what, on Laslett's own showing, the patriarchal relation amounted to.

As to the texts, the only apparent warrant for taking the essence of servanthood to be a patriarchal 'inclusion in their masters' is the passage quoted above from the Putney Debates. But what Petty, the Leveller spokesman, there says is that servants *and those that take alms from door to door* are included in their masters. It is thus certainly not a patriarchal relation within the household that Petty means by 'included in their masters'. What he does mean by this is indicated in his preceding sentence, where servants and those that take alms are distinguished from freemen by the fact that 'they depend upon the will of other men'.[20] It is their dependence on the will of others in the community, not dependence on a particular person in a household,[21] that leaves them included in their masters and denies them freedom and franchise.

We may sum up the evidence of the franchise proponents by saying that the Levellers, and their opponents in the Army Debates, and Harrington, when talking about 'servants' in the context of the franchise—which is to say, all those who did make stipulations about servants in relation to the franchise—took the criterion of servanthood to be dependence on the will of other men for getting a living, and held that such dependence made the servant ineligible for the franchise, and so, for franchise purposes, left the servant included in the master; and that on this criterion 'servants' meant all wage-earners.

We have still to look at the contention that the patriarchal relation was so important that it distinguished 'servants' from other wage-earners, and did so not merely in the franchise context.

[19] *Historical Journal*, Vol. 7, i, p. 152. Cf. ibid., p. 153, and *World We Have Lost*, p. 20, where the wording is 'caught up, so to speak, [or], "subsumed" . . . into the personalities of their fathers and masters'.

[20] Woodhouse: *Puritanism and Liberty*, p. 83.

[21] Petty's phrase was 'included in their masters', not included in the persons (or subsumed in the personalities) of their masters.

(iv) The Evidence of Patriarchalism

Laslett's view of the meaning of 'servants' rests heavily on his concept of 'patriarchalism' as the dominant master-servant relation in the seventeenth century. The concept will not bear the weight he puts upon it.

We need not dwell on the fact that, by Gregory King's figures, the number of adult male wage-earners who lived in this patriarchal relation, i.e. who were inservants, was substantially less than the number who did not. There were over 300,000 adult male wage-earners living out, and probably only 130,000 living in,[22] so that it was probably less than one third of the adult male wage-earners who were in this patriarchal relation. But although this casts some doubt on Laslett's general thesis of the patriarchal nature of seventeenth-century English society, it is not strictly relevant here. For our concern here is with those who did live in the households of their employers, and who may therefore be said to have been in a patriarchal relation. The question is whether the inservants' patriarchal relation to their employers, and their consequent relation to the community, were so different from the outservants' non-patriarchal relation as to lead to the former being treated by the community as non-persons, included in their masters, and the latter as persons, not included in their masters. When Laslett's concept of the patriarchal relation of the inservant is closely examined it appears not to support this view. We may consider in turn the inservant's relation to his employers and to the community.

As to the inservant's relation to his employers, in one respect, which is the one that has struck Laslett, the inservant appears to be dependent in a more direct way than are other wage-earners. But when the nature of this dependence is examined the difference largely disappears. There are two kinds of dependence involved in the situation of the annually employed inservant. One is his dependence on the rule of the master throughout the whole year, once the year's contract has been made; the other is his dependence on getting employment year after year. As to the first, it need not be doubted that the constant subjection to the discipline of the employer's establishment, from which the inservant could not escape until the year was up, might be grievous. The only thing that would necessarily temper the degree of subjection was the master's knowledge that at the end of the year the servant could leave and go to another master (and Laslett finds that they did so generally after only one or two years).[23] Equally important, the only thing that permitted the subjection was that the servant, having no other resource for a living, had to have employment from someone. The cause of the dependence was the servant's need for employment, not the pattern of

[22] See above, p. 210.

[23] 'Clayworth and Cogenhoe', p. 179.

household discipline. The inservant's dependence on getting employment year after year was more fundamental than his dependence during the year on the particular employer: the former determined the limits of the latter.

The most that can be said is that the inservant's dependence on the master took the form, for one year at a time, of a 'patriarchal' relation within the household. An annual patriarchal relation may seem something of a contradiction in terms. But setting that aside, the point here is that the inservant's dependence, his 'inclusion in his master', was due not to any patriarchal relation but to the market relation: it was due to his having to offer his services in a contractual labour market because he had not the resources to work on his own. In this fundamental respect he was in the same position as the outservant and common labourer: they all had to sell their labour-power to others in order to make a living.

Secondly, we have to look at the inservant's relation to the community. Did the position of the inservant in the household of the employer make his relation to the rest of the community so different from that of the outservants as is implied in Laslett's view that the inservants, and only they, were included in their masters 'by virtue of patriarchalism'? We are asked to believe both that it was *because of* patriarchalism that inservants were never treated by the community as persons in their own right but were included in their masters, and that outservants *were* treated as persons in their own right, and were not included in their masters, because they were not in a patriarchal relation to their employers. This view rests on two assumptions, neither of which is, or I think can be, sustained: (a) that wage-earners were, like anyone else, treated as persons in their own right *unless* there was some special ground for not doing so; and (b) that the patriarchal relation of dependence was a special ground for not doing so.

As to (a), the evidence is the other way: the whole employed labour force tended to be treated in the seventeenth century as a body of persons who were and ought to be subordinate to the purposes of the whole society as determined by their betters.[24] They were means to others' ends, not persons in their own right. True, the community did recognize some minimal obligations to them. They had a right to life and (provided they did not put themselves right out of society by being able-bodied vagrants) to relief from destitution: to that extent they were treated as persons. But nobody thought that this made them full members of the community: they were not full persons. In so far as the wage-earners as a whole were considered not full persons in their own right, no *special* degree of dependence was required to cause any section of them to be so regarded.

[24] *PTPI*, pp. 226–9.

As to (b), in so far as there was any difference between the inservant's relation to his employer and the outservant's relation to his, it is difficult to see how this would lead to the community treating the adult inservant as less of a person than the outservant. The only differences we have seen between the patriarchal wage relation and any other wage relation are that in the former the employee was under closer discipline, and was in enforced contiguity with the employer, for the duration of the contract. And this seems to be all that the patriarchal relation amounted to. The employer did not, so far as we are told, take on any obligation to provide welfare or protection. He was indeed obliged to pay the contracted wage and to provide lodging and food for the year, but beyond that he had no obligation. The servant could be discarded and thrown on the community at any expiry of the contract: there was nothing of the old family retainer about the seventeenth-century inservant. Changing masters every year or two, he was not, as servant, transferred from the responsibility and minimal protection of the community to the responsibility of the household. For the patriarchal household was not, Laslett tells us,[25] the source of welfare: the received view that sickness, unemployment, bereavement, and to a large extent education, were the responsibility of the family is, he says, false. The patriarchal family took no responsibility for its grown children, its in-laws, or its grandchildren. They did not live in the patriarchal household. The inservant did, but since he could (and generally did) move on to another master after a year or two, no master was likely to assume any more responsibility for his servant than for his own kin.

The patriarchal relation, then, did not relieve the community of the minimal obligation for welfare which it had for every member of the community. Inclusion in their masters did not mean, for the inservants, exclusion from the community, any more or any less than it did for the outservants. They were all potentially a charge on the community, and there was therefore no reason for the community to treat them so differently as to acknowledge one kind as persons in their own right and the other not.

Thus, when account is taken of the mobility of inservants and of the limited responsibility of the employers for their welfare, the 'patriarchal' element in their relation to their employers (which was at the same time a contractual market relation) appears rather slight. Neither the inservant's patriarchal relation to his employers, nor his consequent relation to the community, were so different from the outservant's as to lead to the former being treated by the community as non-persons, included in their masters, and the latter as persons, not included in their

[25] *World We Have Lost*, p. 90.

masters. It is more consistent with the evidence to say that the community treated servants as included in their masters not 'by virtue of patriarchalism' but by virtue of their dependence on employment.

What has been said so far may be thought sufficient to show that Laslett's claim that 'servants' ordinarily meant only inservants cannot be sustained, and that in the context of franchise discussions 'servants' meant all those dependent on employment for a living. It may also be taken to show a presumption that as a general rule (beyond the context of franchise discussions) 'servants' meant all wage-earners, for we have noticed how limited the patriarchal element was in the inservant's relation to his employers and the community, and how fundamentally similar in kind and degree his dependence on employers and community was to any other wage-earner's.

It remains to establish this presumption more firmly, and to account for the few types of exception to the general rule.

2. *The General Rule and Special Cases*

(i) The presumption that as a general rule 'servants' meant all wage-earners is strengthened by noticing (a) the lack of any other suitable word to describe all wage-earners, and (b) the historical continuity of the terms master and servant.

(a) Some word was needed to denote those described in our day as wage-earners. That term was not apparently in existence in the seventeenth century. The term 'labourers' was sometimes used to cover all wage-earners, but, for reasons that can easily be seen, it was not a generally suitable term. I have noticed this usage in only two contexts: one, in an economic treatise where wage-earners were being treated as owners of one of the factors of production (i.e. of labour in contradistinction to land and capital), as in Locke's *Considerations of . . . Money*;[26] the other in compilations where the basis of classification was a mixture of social status or rank, and occupation, as in the Quarter Sessions records cited (for all ranks connected with the land) by Mildred Campbell.[27] Laslett's parish censuses, being by households, use 'labourers' only for all wage-earners living out.[28]

But 'labourers' was not a generally satisfactory term to cover all wage-earners, for it sometimes had a status connotation, of a grade below skilled tradesman. This is apparent in Chamberlayne's list o

[26] In two of the three economic arguments there in which he refers to labourers (as cited in *PTPI*, pp. 216–17) he uses the term to cover all wage-earners; in the other he refers to wage-earners as 'the poor labourer or handicraftsman'.

[27] M. Campbell: *The English Yeoman under Elizabeth and the Early Stuarts* (New Haven, Conn., 1942), p. 27.

[28] *World We Have Lost*, pp. 64–7: Goodnestone 'and scores of others like it'; but some of those classified as tradesmen may have been wage-earners.

ranks, where the rank order below gentlemen was yeomen, tradesmen (including merchants, wholesale men, retailers, and mechanics or handicraftsmen), and day labourers.[29] Gregory King's usage sometimes reflects the same status differentiation, as when he puts 'labouring people and outservants' below 'artizans and handicrafts' in his Main Table. Thus where a social (and legal) relation rather than a rank was in question, 'labourers' was not a satisfactory term for all wage-earners.

(b) Where a social and legal relation was to be described, the most natural term to use for the wage-earner was servant. For servant denoted one side of the master-servant relation, and had done so time out of mind, long before that relation had become a contractual wage-relation. This historical continuity of the term, though well attested, seems not to have been appreciated by some modern historians.

Chamberlayne, in his standard description of England,[30] opens his chapter 'Of Servants' by drawing attention to the continuity: 'The Condition of Servants in *England*, is much more favourable than it was in our Ancestors dayes, when it was so bad, that *England* was called the Purgatory of servants . . .'; his reference a few paragraphs later to villeins, who might still be called servants, suggests that it was villeins, whose tenure (or whose tenure and person) was servile, that he had in mind as the servants of the ancestors' days. The continuity was in the use of the term servants; the difference was in the kind and length of their dependence on a master—now, 'Ordinary Servants are hired commonly for one year, at the end whereof they may be free (giving warning 3 Moneths before) and may place themselves with other Masters.'

Similarly Locke:

> *Master* and *Servant* are names as old as History, but given to those of far different condition; for a Free-man makes himself a Servant to another, by selling him for a certain time, the Services he undertakes to do, in exchange for Wages he is to receive: And though this commonly puts him into the Family of his Master, and under the ordinary Discipline thereof; yet it gives the Master but a Temporary Power over him, and no greater, than what is contained in the *Contract* between 'em. But there is another sort of Servants, which by a peculiar Name we call Slaves, who being Captives taken in a just War, are by the Right of Nature subjected to the Absolute Dominion and Arbitrary Power of their Masters.[31]

Here the continuity is between the slave and the contractual wage-earner, both called servants; and again the contrast is in the kind and length of their dependence on masters.

[29] Edward Chamberlayne: *Angliae Notitia: or, the Present State of England* (3rd ed., 1669), pp. 444–5.

[30] Ibid., pp. 461–3.

[31] *Second Treatise of Government*, sect. 85.

Both Chamberlayne and Locke, indeed, have one kind of servant primarily in mind: for Chamberlayne the ordinary servant is 'commonly' one on annual contract, and for Locke the contractual servant is 'commonly' an inservant; but the qualification 'commonly' does not exclude, but implies the inclusion in the term servants of, (respectively) those on less than annual contract and those living out. 'Servant' denoted in the seventeenth century, as it had always done, a relation: it meant a person in a relation of obligation to a master, for as long as he stood in that relation. By the seventeenth century it was a contractual relation, never for more than a year at a time, and often for only a month, a week, or a day. All who stood in that relation, for whatever period, were equally properly described as servants.

We may notice also that in Chamberlayne's treatment of servants, the term never entailed a patriarchal or familial relation in the household. For the term servants, in the feudal use Chamberlayne speaks of, clearly included all the villeins who lived out. It denoted not a patriarchal master-servant relation within the household, but a feudal master-servant relation within the manor or community. The presumption is that it continued to denote a master-servant relation within the community, rather than a patriarchal relation within the household, after the master-servant relation had changed from a servile to a free contractual one.

On these grounds it may be concluded that in the seventeenth century 'servants' as a general rule meant those who stood in the relation of contractual wage-earners, whether on an annual or shorter term, and whether living in or out of the households of their employers.

(ii) We have now to see why, in certain administrative and statistical classifications, the term servants was sometimes used to apply only to some sub-class of wage-earners. This usage is found in only two contexts: (a) lists or tabulations of a village (or larger) population by households, where the description 'servant' is used only for those living in; and (b) some of the administrative sub-classifications of all or part of the whole wage-earning class, where the description 'servant' is used only for those hired by the year (whether living in or out). We may look at these in turn.

(*a*) *Lists and tabulations by households*. In some cases, the nature of the tabulation requires that servants should mean only inservants. Thus, where it is only each person's relation to others in the household that is being recorded, clearly 'servant' cannot be used in any other way than to denote the inservant, as in King's Table III, where the categories are 'husbands and wives, widowers, widows, children, servants, sojourners and single persons'.[32] In other cases, the purpose of the

[32] King in Chalmers, p. 39.

record and the degree of detail in it dictate the same confined usage of 'servants'. Thus, in parish lists by households such as those used by Laslett[33] where both the composition of each household and the occupation of the head of the household are given, 'servants' is used to describe only the inservants, whereas wage-earners living out and being heads of their own households are described by their occupations, as shepherds, thatchers, labourers, etc. The wage-earners living out might have been described simply as 'outservants' or 'labouring people and outservants', as they were in King's Main Table, which was also compiled by households; but the obvious way to describe them in a complete parish listing which gave the occupation of *each* householder (unlike a statistical tabulation of a large population such as King's) was to give the name of each occupation.

In short, whether or not the wage-earners living out were described as (out)servants or as thatchers etc., was simply a matter of the degree of detail or generality that was appropriate to the kind of compilation; and it cannot be inferred from the parish lists, which give the detail, that the wage-earning householders there described by their specific occupations were not also thought of as servants.

(*b*) *Sub-classifications of all or part of the whole wage-earning class.* In some wage assessments (though, as we have seen, not in all) the term servants is used for workers on annual wages (whether living in or out) while the various kinds of workers on daily or weekly wages (all living out) are not described by any generic term but only by their specific occupations. Of the workers on annual wages who are described as servants the most frequent are servants in husbandry, who in most but not all cases lived in. Here, as with the parish records by households just discussed, the most obvious reason for the usage is simply the degree of detail required. The number of different kinds of servants in husbandry for whom different wage rates were set was small, sometimes only two or three, sometimes as many as eight, hence they could conveniently be grouped under that general heading. But there was a far larger number of specific kinds of work done by other wage-earners (in a whole range of clothing, food, implement, and building trades, as well as on the land) for each of which a specific wage rate was to be set. These workers were most frequently on daily or weekly wages, living out. They might have been grouped under a general heading 'outservants' (though in some cases this would not have been an accurate distinction, since some of those called servants who were on annual wages also lived out), but there was no reason why they should be: the important thing was to specify each particular kind of work or each particular occupation and set a rate for it.

[33] 'Clayworth and Cogenhoe'.

In any case the designation, in wage assessments, of many kinds of wage-earners by the specific names of their occupations rather than by the generic term servants does not imply that they were not in a political or social sense thought of as servants.

The above review of the administrative and statistical classes of cases in which the term servant was used to mean only one kind of wage-earner is, I think, sufficient to show that these comprised subordinate uses of the term. In each class of cases there is a simple reason, of logic or convenience, for the narrow usage. In the enumerations of a population by households, the term was only used to mean inservants when that use was logically required or when the degree of detail in the enumeration required a specific occupational designation, rather than a generic description, of all except inservants. Similarly, in those of the wage assessments in which the term servants was used only for wage-earners on annual contract, the degree of detail required to set wage rates for the many kinds of other wage-earners is a sufficient reason for the latter being given specific occupational designations rather than being described generically as servants.

Since there are such fairly evident reasons for the narrower usages in those classes of cases where they are found, it would be reasonable to treat the narrower usages as subordinate or exceptional, rather than as the general rule, even if there were no other grounds for doing so.

But the other grounds for doing so are cumulatively strong. There is the fact that King's figures reveal that about as many (or more) of the men called servants in husbandry lived out as lived in. There is the fact that the wage assessments frequently described as servants wage-earners living out and/or on daily or weekly contract. There is the fact that those who wrote and spoke about servants in relation to franchise proposals defined them in terms of dependence on others for a living, which applies to all wage-earners and not merely those living in or being on annual contract. There are the facts of the annual inservants' mobility and of the employers' limited responsibility for them, which together reduce their supposed difference from all other wage-earners, in the eyes of the community, to rather little. There is the fact that no other term than servants was generally satisfactory to designate all wage-earners. There is the fact that 'servant' has continuously been used to denote one side of any master-servant relation and as such had not been confined to servants living in.

When all these facts are taken together the presumption that as a general rule 'servants' meant all wage-earners, not just those living in, is too strong to be impugned by loose inferences from the supposedly predominantly patriarchal nature of seventeenth-century society.

ESSAY XIII

Natural Rights in Hobbes and Locke

1. *Introduction*

So much has been written about Hobbes and Locke in the last few years that one may wonder whether anything more can usefully be said. But the fact is that all that has recently been written about their ideas, by different interpreters, has not yet resulted in agreement among the interpreters. This suggests that the theories of Hobbes and Locke are, if not inexhaustible, at least not yet exhausted. That they should have such a long life is not surprising. For they have entered deeply into modern individualist and liberal political theory; and as that theory finds itself in need of development to meet changed conditions, it is appropriate that its exponents should look again at its roots, to see if there is anything in them which can show what lines of development of the modern theory may be possible or necessary.

This is particularly appropriate in the context of twentieth-century concepts of the rights of man. The concept of 'Human Rights' has become increasingly important, as well in the old liberal-democratic countries as in the socialist countries and in the new states. Virtually all states now subscribe officially to some doctrine of human rights. And in every state there is, more or less explicitly, a general political theory justifying the kind of society and the political institutions which prevail there. The problem of fitting a doctrine of human rights into the general justificatory theory is different in states with different general theories.

There are many varieties of justificatory theory in the world today, but they all tend to approximate to one of three types: the individualist-liberal theory, whose roots are generally traced back to Locke; the socialist theory, whose roots are essentially in Marx; and the populist general-will theory, whose roots are in Rousseau. In each of these three types of theory there is a problem of fitting the modern notion of human rights into the general lines of the theory. The individualist-liberal theory has no difficulty accommodating the rights of life, liberty, and property, for it was built largely on the assertion of these as the natural rights of the individual; but it finds some difficulty fitting in the modern ideas of economic and social rights. The Marxian and Rousseauian theories find little difficulty with the social and economic rights, but do not find it so easy to accommodate the earlier trilogy of natural rights of life, liberty, and property, which they have tended to mistrust on the ground that these are essentially bourgeois rights.

We may hope that a reconsideration of the natural rights concepts of Hobbes and Locke will throw some light on the possible or necessary relations between those early modern doctrines of natural right and the twentieth-century doctrines of human rights.

2. *Natural Rights in Hobbes*[1]

Hobbes's conclusion in favour of an all-powerful sovereign, against whom the individual has practically no rights, in strikingly different from the conclusions of most natural rights theorists. From the Independents and Levellers of the English civil war, through the American and French revolutions, natural rights doctrines have been doctrines of at least contingent revolution and resistance to constituted authority. Hobbes's doctrine is so different that one may ask whether he should be counted as a natural rights man at all. The question may be answered at three different levels.

First, at the simple technical level, the answer must be yes. For Hobbes's assertion of individual natural rights is an essential part of the logic by which he deduces political obligation. His political obligation depends on his postulate of individual natural rights. It is the transfer of natural rights that produces political obligation.[2]

But at a second level, when one looks at the content of Hobbes's natural right, the answer appears to be in the negative. His natural right is so different from most ideas of natural right that his claim to be a natural rights man might be disallowed by a systematic classifier. A classification which required that the term 'natural rights' must always mean (as it usually does mean) rights which by the nature of things entail an obligation of other men to respect them—such a classification would exclude Hobbes's natural rights. The Right of Nature, says Hobbes,

> is the liberty each man hath, to use his own power, as he will himself, for the preservation of his own nature; that is to say, of his own life; and consequently, of doing any thing, which in his own judgement, and reason, he shall conceive to be the aptest means thereunto . . . And because the [natural] condition of man . . . is a condition of war of every one against every one; . . . and there is nothing he can make use of, that may not be a help unto him, in preserving his

[1] References to the texts of Hobbes's works are given as follows: *Lev.* is *Leviathan*, with pages of the Macpherson edition (Penguin, 1968); *El.* is *Elements of Law Natural and Politic*, Tönnies edition (Cambridge, 1889); *Rud.* is *Philosophical Rudiments concerning Government and Society*, Lamprecht edition (published under the title *De Cive, or The Citizen*, New York, 1949).

[2] *Lev.*, chap. 14, p. 191.

life against his enemies; it followeth, that in such a condition, every man has a right to every thing; even to one another's body.[3]

Since everyone has a natural right to do anything, to take anything, 'to possess, use, and enjoy'[4] anything, to invade any other man, it is clear that nobody has an obligation to respect any other man's natural right. Hobbes makes this point, employing momentarily the more usual concept of right: 'But that right of all men to all things, is in effect no better than if no man had right to any thing. For there is little use and benefit of the right a man hath, when another as strong, or stronger than himself, hath right to the same.'[5] At this second level of analysis, then, one might say that Hobbes's natural rights are no rights at all.

But at a third level of analysis, Hobbes must be accounted a natural rights man, and must indeed be ranked as the originator of modern natural right. For he made the decisive break with the old Natural Law tradition, in which natural rights had been derived from natural law or divine law or sociability, and in which there had been a strong element of hierarchy. He made the break by deducing natural right from the innate compulsion to preserve one's life or motion, and he made this deduction of right from fact by his postulate of *equal* need of continued motion. It is because men are self-moving systems of matter in motion, each of which by the necessity of nature equally seeks to continue its own motion, and is equally fragile, that they must be allowed to have equal rights.[6] The rights are not merely rights to those things necessary to maintain their motion (or preserve their lives): there is an equal right to life itself. Indeed, it is from the right to preserve his life that a man's right to the means of that preservation is deduced: 'It is . . . a right of nature: that every man may preserve his own life and limbs, with all the power he hath. And because where a man hath a right to the end . . . it is consequent that it is . . . right for a man, to use all means and do whatsoever action is necessary for the preservation of his body.'[7] Similarly in the *Rudiments*: 'But because it is in vain for a man to have a right to the end, if the right to the necessary means be denied him; it follows, that since every man hath a right to preserve himself, he must also be allowed a right to use all the means, and do all the actions, without which he cannot preserve himself.'[8] And 'the right of protecting ourselves according to our own wills proceeded from our danger, and our danger from our equality . . .'[9]

[3] *Lev.*, chap. 14, pp. 189–90. Cf. *El.*, I, chap. 14, sects. 6–10; *Rud.*, chap. 1, sects. 7–10.

[4] *El.*, I, chap. 14, sect. 10, and *Rud.*, chap. 1, sect. 10.

[5] *El.*, I, chap. 14, sect. 10.

[6] *El.*, I, chap. 14, sect. 6; *Rud.*, chap. 1, sect. 7.

[7] *El.*, I, chap. 14, sects 6–7.

[8] *Rud.*, chap. 1, sect. 8.

[9] *Rud.*, chap. 1, sect. 14.

Thus in Hobbes the natural right of every man to every thing is deduced from the natural right of every man to preserve his own life, which in turn is deduced from the equal mechanical need each has to continue his own motion, and the equal fragility of each. What places Hobbes at the fountainhead of modern natural rights doctrine is his insistence on mundane (not heavenly or transcendent) equality of right. Even more revolutionary is his assumption that equality of right follows directly from equality of need of continued motion. Instead of inferring from men's observable needs and capacities some purpose or will of Nature or God, and then deducing rights (and obligations) from the purpose or will, as had usually been done (and usually with the result of finding unequal or hierarchical rights and obligations), Hobbes moved directly from observed needs to equal rights.

The equal natural right which he deduced in this way—the right of every man to every thing—was of course unworkable. Since each man's right was infinite, any other man's right (in the more usual sense of right) was zero; therefore every man's right was zero. Reasonable men must give up the right to every thing in order to get effective rights against each other, guaranteed by a sovereign power.

In the last analysis, the reason why Hobbes's natural rights are so different from the traditional ones is that Hobbes was working with a model of society which was essentially contentious, a model in which 'the power of one man resisteth and hindereth the effects of the power of another', so much so, that 'power simply is no more, but the excess of the power of one above that of another'.[10] It was because he started with a model of society in which everyone was always seeking to transfer some of the powers of others to himself, or at least to resist such transfer from himself, that Hobbes was compelled to define natural rights as he did. It is not usually noticed that Hobbes's infinite natural rights depended on his model of society, but this can be readily demonstrated. It is not disputed that his infinite natural right is deduced from the two postulates, (1) an equal right to life, and (2) a universal opposition of individual motions. The second postulate could have been deduced from a prior postulate of innate infinite desire, and if so deduced, no particular model of society would have been required. But Hobbes did not so deduce the universal opposition of individual motions. He did not postulate innate infinite desire for every individual, but asserted repeatedly that not every man naturally desires ever more power or delights.[11] He therefore logically needed (and he did in effect provide) a model of society which would permit and require that every

[10] *El.*, I, chap. 8, sect. 4.

[11] *Lev.*, chap. 8, p. 139; chap. 11, p. 161; chap. 13, pp. 184–5; *El.*, I, chap. 14, sect. 3; *Rud.*, chap. 1, sect. 4.

man constantly should oppose every other man.[12] Breaking away from traditional hierarchical natural law and reciprocal natural rights, he put every man on his own in a market society, and provided a sovereign state strong enough to keep them all in order.

In doing this, Hobbes was, we may say, reflecting the new seventeenth-century demands for bourgeois equality. He does not rest his case on a simple assertion that men are equal, in the sense of being equally in mechanical need of continuous motion and equally liable to destruction, but on the observation that, whether or not men are naturally equal, they think themselves equal. 'If nature therefore have made men equal, that equality is to be acknowledged; or if nature have made men unequal; yet because men that think themselves equal, will not enter into conditions of peace, but upon equal terms, such equality must be admitted.'[13]

3. *Natural Rights in Locke*[14]

Locke's claim as a natural rights man is generally thought to be much clearer than Hobbes's. I shall argue that Locke's claim is, in important ways, less clear than Hobbes's; particularly, in that Locke, after beginning with a beautiful set of natural rights, which are said to be effectively sanctioned (as well as limited) by natural law, then goes on to override one of the most important limits (the limit on infinite appropriation), thus removing the equality of natural rights, and ends by admitting that natural law is a wholly ineffective guarantor of natural rights, which therefore lose the original character he had given them.

The grounds for claiming Locke as a genuine natural rights man are apparently clear: (i) His natural rights are presented as effective rights, rights which others have a natural obligation to respect. (ii) His natural rights, being less wholesale than Hobbes's, are more meaningful and more specific (e.g. the right of private appropriation and the right of inheritance). (iii) Locke uses natural rights to establish a case for limited government, and to set up a right to revolution. In these respects, Locke's natural rights are different from, even opposite to, Hobbes's natural right. All these differences may be said to be based on the

[12] This point is developed more fully in my *The Political Theory of Possessive Individualism*, pp. 40 ff., where I argue further that Hobbes's model of society was essentially the bourgeois market society.

[13] *Lev.*, chap. 15, p. 211. Cf. *El.*, I, chap. 17, sect 1; *Rud.*, chap. 3, sect. 13.

[14] References to Locke's *Two Treatises of Government* are given as follows: 1T is *First Treatise*, 2T is *Second Treatise*; the following number is the section of the treatise, and the line numbers (ll.) are to the numbered lines of the section in the Laslett edition (1960).

logically prior difference that Locke derives his natural rights from natural law: it is 'Reason, which is that Law',[15] that establishes the rights and the corresponding obligations: whereas for Hobbes the rights are logically prior, and the natural law (such as it is) is derived from them. Yet when Locke's natural rights are examined more closely, they have more in common with Hobbes's than is generally allowed. Let us look first at Locke's right to life and liberty, reserving his right to property for later examination.

(i) *The Right to Life*

The first natural right we hear of is the right 'to make use of those things, that were necessary or useful to his Being' or 'serviceable for his Subsistence' and 'means of his *Preservation*'.[16] This right is later called 'the Right a man has to subsist and enjoy the conveniences of Life'.[17] Here, as in the *Second Treatise*,[18] Locke asserts a natural right to preservation of one's life, and hence to the means of subsistence (and even 'conveniences'). And this right to life and the means of life is deduced from the need or 'strong desire' every man has 'of Preserving his Life and Being'.[19] 'The first and strongest desire . . . being that of Self-preservation, that is the Foundation of a right to the [inferior] Creatures, for the particular support and use of each individual Person himself.'[20]

Is this deduction of right from the 'strong desire' of self-preservation at all different from Hobbes's deduction? There is a difference, and it is characteristic of Locke: he deduces the right not directly from the fact of desire but from the intention of the Creator, which intention is deduced from the fact of desire.[21]

A second right is deduced in the same indirect way from observed desire. The natural right of children to inherit the possessions of their parents is deduced from the 'strong desire' men have 'of propagating their Kind, and continuing themselves in their Posterity'.[22] If this desire is to be fulfilled, children must be allowed to have a right to a share of their parents' property. It is the 'strong desire' that 'gives' the right, but apparently only because God planted the desire in men.

(ii) *The Right to Freedom*

The *Second Treatise* opens with an assertion of a natural right to freedom from the arbitary wills of others ('arbitrary' being whatever is not required or permitted by the Law of Nature). It is a right not to be interfered with, except when one has transgressed natural law: a right of '*Freedom* to order their Actions, and dispose of their Possessions and Persons as they think fit, within the bounds of the Law of Nature,

[15] 2T, 6, l. 7. Cf. 2T, 25, l. 1. [16] 1T, 86, ll. 27–8, 14, 15.
[17] 1T, 97, ll. 2–3. [18] e.g., 2T, 25, ll. 2–4. [19] 1T, 86.
[20] 1T, 88, ll. 14–18. [21] 1T, 86. [22] 1T, 88, ll. 18–22.

without asking leave, or depending upon the Will of any other Man'.[23] This is first introduced simply as a freedom, but is later referred to as a right.[24] From this right follows the right[25] to execute the Law of Nature, which includes '*two distinct Rights*, the one of *Punishing* the crime *for restraint* . . . the other of taking *reparation*'.[26] There also follows the right to destroy an aggressor who would take away my liberty.[27]

The basic right to freedom is deduced (a) negatively from the intentions of the Creator and (b) positively from the need for self-preservation. Thus (a), since men are fundamentally members of the same species, and since there is no evidence that some of the species were intended to be subordinate to others, they must be assumed to be equal in jurisdiction, equally free from the will of others.[28] And (b), 'This *Freedom* from Absolute, Arbitrary Power, is so necessary to, and closely joyned with a Man's Preservation, that he cannot part with it, but by what forfeits his Preservation and Life together.'[29]

We may now ask how different is Locke's natural right to freedom from Hobbes's natural right? Both are deduced from the need for self-preservation. And the equality of natural right is in both cases deduced from the species-similarity, i.e. the organic or mechanical sameness of the beings; both writers start from the assumption that men are equal in need and capacity, and deduce natural equal right from that equality.

The great difference, of course, is that whereas Hobbes finds a natural right of every man to every thing, Locke's natural right to freedom is limited by the Law of Nature, which teaches that 'no one ought to harm another in his Life, Health, Liberty, or Possessions'.[30] It is because 'the state of nature has a law of nature to govern it, which obliges every one'[31] that men do not need, and cannot be allowed, the right to every thing.

A further difference, less often noticed, is that Locke's natural right to defend oneself, although based (like Hobbes's) on the need for self-preservation, is not entirely inalienable (as Hobbes's is).[32] The freedom from absolute, arbitrary power, which Locke finds is so necessary to a man's preservation, *can* be forfeited, as can the right to life itself, by the commission of 'some Act that deserves Death'.[33] From this it appears that the source of Locke's natural right is not the need for self-preservation but is the (moral) law of nature which is superior to the right to life.

[23] 2T, 4, ll. 3–6. [24] 2T, 17, l. 9.
[25] First introduced as a 'power' (2T, 7, l. 9), then called a right (2T, 17, l. 15).
[26] 2T, 11, ll. 1–3. [27] 2T, 18. [28] 2T, 4, ll. 7–16.
[29] 2T, 23, ll. 1–4. [30] 2T, 6, ll. 9–10. [31] 2T, 6, ll. 6–7.
[32] *Lev.*, chap. 14, p. 192. [33] 2T, 23, l. 10.

(iii) *The Right to Property*

Let us look finally at Locke's natural right to individual appropriation of the fruits of the earth and the earth itself. For Locke, a property in a thing is a right to exclude others from it, to use, enjoy, consume, or exchange it. The purpose of the chapter on property of the *Second Treatise* is to show that individuals have a natural right to property, a right prior to civil society and government, and not dependent on the consent of others to it.[34]

The right to property is deduced from (a) the right of self-preservation,[35] and (b) the property in, or right to, one's own person—'the *Labour* of his Body, and the *Work* of his Hands, we may say, are properly his'.[36] The right to property is limited, by this derivation, to as much as leaves enough for others, since all have an equal right to subsistence.

I have shown at length elsewhere[37] how Locke turned this limited natural right into an unlimited natural right, and justified the appropriation of all the land by some men, in amounts exceeding the requirements of their comfortable subsistence, leaving others with no land on which to labour for themselves. This extended right is said to be established without express compact. But it does require one kind of consent, i.e. tacit consent to the use of money,[38] which consent Locke assumes men are naturally capable of giving. The extended property right is not, we may say, as pure a natural right as the others, for the others do not require any consent. And it is less pure in another respect: it is established by means of utilitarian argument to productivity. It is the greater productivity of labour on appropriated land that justifies its appropriation beyond the amount which would leave as much and as good for others. Because of the greater productivity, those who are left without any land can get a better subsistence than they would have had if no land were appropriated.[39]

But if the extended property right is less pure than the other rights, because it requires consent, it is none the less natural. It follows from the nature of man, because Locke puts into the nature of man the capacity of making agreements[40] and the desire of having more than he needs.[41] The latter desire, Locke admits, is not present in the most primitive stage of human life: there was a time, 'in the beginning', when this desire was absent.[42] But the desire did arise and flourish in the state of nature: it came with the use of money, which inaugurated the second stage of the state of nature.[43]

[34] 2T, 25, ll. 16–19; 2T, 50, ll. 11–13. [35] 2T, 25, ll. 2–4.
[36] 2T, 27, ll. 2–4. Cf. 2T, 44, l. 3.
[37] *The Political Theory of Possessive Individualism*, pp. 203–20.
[38] 2T, 50, l. 24. [39] 2T, 37. [40] 2T, 14, ll. 11–19.
[41] 2T, 37, l. 2. [42] 2T, 37, l. 1. [43] 2T, 50, ll. 11–14.

It has often been pointed out that Locke's state of nature is a social state, that his natural man is social man. What is more to the point is that his natural man is a man with a socially acquired desire for more wealth than he can use, 'more land than he himself can use the product of',[44] 'to draw *Money* to him by the Sale of the Product'.[45] Locke's natural man is bourgeois man: his rational man is man with a propensity to capital accumulation. He is even an infinite appropriator.[46]

Because Locke's natural men are capable of understanding the law of nature, and because they desire not only to preserve their lives, and not only to maintain their comfortable living, but also to accumulate property beyond the amount required for such living, their natural rights are both less and more than the natural rights of Hobbes's men. Less, in that Locke's men are forbidden by the law of nature to invade the lives, liberties, and properties of other men; more, in that they have a natural right, which others must respect, to unlimited accumulation of wealth.

Locke, then, seems to have reverted to a more traditional notion of natural right, in postulating the social nature of man and hence the existence of a law of nature. It is the law of nature that both limits men's natural rights and, by imposing obligation on others to respect rights, makes the rights more effective than Hobbes's rights. But Locke has not returned to the traditional natural law: he has put into it quite a new content, the right to unlimited accumulation.

And because he has done so, he is forced to admit that men are not naturally as social as he first said they were. He is forced to admit that men are naturally so contentious and invasive that they do not follow the law of nature.[47] If the logical consequences of this admission are allowed, all the effective differences between Locke's natural rights and Hobbes's disappear, for the differences all depended on Locke's assertion that natural law limits do confine men's natural rights and do render them naturally effective. It is perhaps not too much to say that, as soon as Locke had shown how the original natural law limits on private appropriation were made ineffective by men's consent (within the state of nature) to the use of money, he logically destroyed his natural law system. It might be better to say that in thus subordinating natural law to natural consent, he revealed that the natural propensity to unlimited accumulation was inconsistent with his natural law. In spite of this, Locke maintained the reality of his natural law. He had to do so, because it was only from the natural law which gave every man the right not to be harmed by others, that he deduced the limited

[44] 2T, 50, ll. 7–8. [45] 2T, 48, ll. 21–2.
[46] *The Political Theory of Possessive Individualism*, p. 235.
[47] 2T, 123, ll. 6–13.

powers of governments and the right of revolution against arbitrary government. Only if men's rightful natural powers are limited, as Locke limits them by natural law, can it be argued, as Locke argues,[48] that the government's power is limited.

4. *Hobbes, Locke, and Human Rights*

Can either Hobbes's or Locke's concept of natural rights be of any use in formulating a twentieth-century concept of human rights? I think not, except in so far as their concepts of natural rights may show us what to avoid. Neither concept satisfies the minimum requirements of a now acceptable theory of human rights. Moreover, their postulates about the nature of man and society (from which postulates their natural rights are deduced) are such that no generally acceptable scheme of human rights could possibly be deduced from them. These statements can be readily demonstrated.

It is clear that any concept of human rights which would be acceptable in the second half of the twentieth century must meet at least two requirements. First, the rights must be in some effective sense equal. The minimum acceptable equality may be stated as equal access to the means of 'convenient' living (not an equal right to a certain standard of life, but an equal right to attain it by one's energies). Secondly, the rights must be, to use the distinction made by Professor Raphael, rights of recipience as well as rights of action. That is to say, there must be an obligation on others to respect each man's rights.

From our analysis it appears that neither Hobbes's nor Locke's natural rights meet these requirements. Hobbes's natural rights, while absolutely equal, are not rights of recipience; they meet the first requirement but not the second. Locke's natural rights are very unequal and, although stated as rights of recipience, are not really so (because Locke admits that most men do not naturally recognize others' rights). They thus do not meet the first requirement and only appear to meet the second.

The inability of either doctrine to meet our requirements is due to the same basic postulate about the nature of man and society; and it is this postulate which makes it impossible that any extension or reshaping of their concepts of natural rights could produce a now acceptable theory of human rights. Both writers imputed to the nature of society a permanent conflict of interests between individuals. Hobbes's men necessarily sought power over others. Locke's rational men sought unlimited property, which he assumed must be at the expense of

[48] 2T, 135, 137, 149.

others.[49] Both writers thus imputed to the necessary nature of man a predominantly contentious and competitive behaviour. These postulates about the nature of man and society were based ultimately on the assumption of scarcity in relation to the possessiveness or acquisitiveness of some or all men.[50]

Both Hobbes and Locke assumed the natural contentiousness of men because they were drawing their abstractions from a more or less unconscious model of bourgeois man and bourgeois society. Both assumed that the full implementation of the individual's rights of action (rights to seek a 'commodious' or 'convenient' living) required a bourgeois market society. Both saw that this entailed that men are perpetually in competition for unequal power or wealth, all seeking to invade each other. Hobbes made the best of a bad job by urging men to hand over all their power to a sovereign who could impose order on the continuing struggle. Locke, with much ambiguity about the natural contentiousness of men, insisted that they retained an equal right not to be harmed as long as they stayed within the Law of Nature. He then redefined the Law of Nature to make it permit unequal access to the means of labour. By doing so, he effectively denied the equal right he had first asserted. He thus ended by giving full scope to the contentious, competitive nature of his bourgeois man.

Both Hobbes and Locke, then, read back into the nature of man a contentious, competitive behaviour drawn from their model of bourgeois society. Each writer's theory of natural rights was determined by his postulate about the nature of man.

It is easy to see why this postulate was made. It was a necessary postulate for anyone who in the seventeenth (or eighteenth) century was seeking a basis for a freer society (as was Locke), or who was seeking a basis for a stable society consistent with the actual pressure of the bourgeois demand for freedom (as was Hobbes). The postulate of fundamental conflict was unavoidable, because the only alternative postulates could not be entertained by such men at that time. One of the possible alternative postulates—that of a fundamental natural harmony of individual interests—could not be entertained because it led to theories (such as the Thomists' and Burke's) which upheld the old order, against which the natural rights men were revolting. The other

49 'It is impossible for anyone to grow rich except at the expense of someone else.' *Essays on the Law of Nature*, ed. von Leyden (1954), p. 211.

50 Hobbes, who is generally thought to be more extreme in this matter than Locke, was I think really less so. For Hobbes postulated that only some men were by nature infinitely desirous (see note 11 above), whereas Locke's implicit assumption was that all men were naturally so. Locke attributes this infinite desire explicitly only to the second stage of the state of nature, but I think he assumed it also in man's original nature (see *The Political Theory of Possessive Individualism*, pp. 234–5).

possible alternative postulate—that individuals may, by some kind of moral or social transformation, become so changed that there will be a natural harmony—could also not be entertained by the natural rights men. For they saw human nature as essentially bourgeois already, and could not see either the need or the possibility of it being essentially changed.[51]

Only those theorists who rejected the morality of bourgeois society, and rejected the adequacy of the bourgeois model of man, could entertain the postulate of potential harmony of interests. The outstanding theorists who did this were Rousseau (who rejected the bourgeois morality and the bourgeois model of man in favour of petty-bourgeois ones) and Marx (who rejected both bourgeois and petty-bourgeois moralities and models in favour of a vision of a classless society).

In the context of our inquiry, the significant thing is that Rousseau and Marx, and those who have followed in the Rousseauian and Marxian traditions, were not natural rights men. They did not build on natural rights of the individual. For them, the main thing was the social transformation which would restore, or create for the first time, a freedom that would be truly human.

The Marxian and Rousseauian traditions are so strong in the world of the second half of the twentieth century that no doctrine which is inconsistent with them is capable of general acceptance. The natural rights doctrines which we have examined *are* inconsistent with them, because of their postulate of possessive individualism, which makes men's rights either ineffective (Hobbes) or grossly unequal (Locke). Yet neither the Rousseauian nor the Marxian tradition is in itself capable of satisfying all those who now feel the need of a doctrine of human rights. For no one would say that the conditions for the truly human freedom envisaged by either Marx or Rousseau have yet been fully achieved anywhere in the world. And only if they were fully and irreversibly achieved, would there be theoretically no need for a doctrine of human rights of the individual.

We have reached the following position: (1) The natural rights concepts of Hobbes and Locke (and of the subsequent liberal-individualist tradition) are not now generally acceptable, and no extension of them can be made generally acceptable, because of their possessive individualist postulates. Although these natural rights were supposed to express the human essence, and (in the case of Locke and the subsequent liberal tradition) were claimed in the name of human freedom, they

[51] The writers of the French eighteenth-century Enlightenment did assume that men could be changed, but only *to* the bourgeois model (which they thought men had not yet attained), not beyond it. And their theories consequently depended less on natural rights than on a concept of a natural order, or utility.

are not now regarded as a sufficient statement of human essence or freedom, even in the countries where they originated. (2) The rival doctrines of human freedom, embodied in the Rousseauian and Marxian traditions, both of which rejected the natural rights basis, are also presently insufficient. (3) Some doctrine of human rights is still needed, and the need is recognized by virtually all states.

5. *The Near Future of Natural Rights and Human Rights*

The problem we now face is created by the fact that any doctrine of human rights must be in some sense a doctrine of natural rights. Human rights can only be asserted as a species of natural right, in the sense that they must be deduced from the nature (i.e. the needs and capacities) of men as such, whether of men as they now are or of men as they are thought capable of becoming. To say this, is simply to recognize that neither legal rights nor customary rights are a sufficient basis for human rights.

The problem, then, is whether there can be found a doctrine of human rights which is a doctrine of natural rights but which does not contain the factors which have made the early doctrine of natural rights unacceptable. The problem is not insoluble in principle.

Our analysis of the earlier doctrine indicates that the factor which has made it unacceptable is its postulate of the inherent and permanent contentiousness of men. This, we say, rested in turn on the assumption of permanent scarcity in relation to a supposed unlimited desire. These assumptions were intelligible, even unavoidable, in the circumstances of the seventeenth and eighteenth centuries. If they are still intelligible, they are no longer unavoidable.

Unlimited desire (for wealth or power), as a universal characteristic of individuals, can be postulated accurately only of individuals in a bourgeois society.[52] The social transformations of the twentieth century have resulted in two-thirds of the world rejecting the bourgeois order. The basic postulate of the old natural rights doctrine has thus been invalidated to that extent.

But if the social transformations of the twentieth century had done no more than lead two-thirds of the world to a rejection of bourgeois morality and the bourgeois model of man, they would not have opened any very hopeful prospect of solution of our problem of a universally acceptable doctrine of human rights: they would only have increased the difficulty, by increasing and institutionalizing the ideological differences.

There is, however, a contemporaneous social transformation which can offset this. The most economically advanced nations, both capitalist

[52] This is demonstrated in *The Political Theory of Possessive Individualism*, chap. II, section 3, sub-sects. i–iv.

and socialist, are now well within sight of a society of abundance rather than an economy of scarcity. In the measure that abundance replaces scarcity, the postulate of necessary contentiousness becomes increasingly unrealistic and can progressively be discarded. In the measure that it is discarded, the prospect of a generally acceptable doctrine of human rights becomes realistic.

It requires, however, that the replacement of scarcity by abundance be seen as a real possibility in the less advanced nations also. I conclude that the present prospect for a generally acceptable and realistic doctrine of human rights depends chiefly on the generality and rapidity of the transformation from the economy of scarcity to the society of abundance.

ESSAY XIV

Hobbes's Bourgeois Man

HOBBES is as renowned a name in political science as is Adam Smith in economics. Accordingly, prevailing notions of what Hobbes meant to say have varied from time to time. While his materialist utilitarianism has been a strong current since he propounded it, Hobbes's modern reputation dates from the re-emphasis on sovereignty and utilitarian morals by the Benthamists. The reaction against Benthamism led to strong criticism of Hobbes by English idealists such as T. H. Green. Their criticism of his materialist metaphysics and of his behaviourist ethics set the tone of the standard treatment of Hobbes, and seemed to have rendered his political views harmless. As long as Hobbes was regarded as primarily a materialist and his political doctrines were seen as consistent deductions from his materialist position, it was relatively easy to dispose of his unpleasant theory of the state, for materialism has had little standing in English political thinking since the eighteenth century when the historical materialism of Millar, Ferguson, and Robertson enjoyed some prestige.[1]

Hobbes's stature, however, was too great for his political ideas to be tidied away in this fashion. Later generations of scholars set out to detach Hobbes's political theory from his materialism. Croom Robertson in 1886, John Laird in 1934, and Leo Strauss in 1936 have taken the position that Hobbes's political philosophy was not derived from his materialism or decisively influenced by his concept of science.[2] While it is possible to show that Hobbes might have reached his political conclusions from certain moral attitudes and preconceptions unrelated

[1] See Roy Pascal: 'Property and Society, the Scottish Historical School of the Eighteenth Century', *The Modern Quarterly*, Vol. 1, no. 2 (March, 1938). Pascal points out (p. 178) that their emphasis on property relationships as the basis of society took on a different significance in the nineteenth century with the development of an organized proletariat, and so was avoided by bourgeois writers.

[2] G. C. Robertson: *Hobbes* (London, 1910), p. 57; John Laird: *Hobbes* (London, 1934), p. 57; Leo Strauss: *The Political Philosophy of Hobbes, Its Basis and Genesis* (Oxford, 1936), p. xiii, 170. Leslie Stephen in his pleasant volume (*Hobbes*, London, 1904) dismisses the problem as of no importance (p. 73). A. E. Taylor (*Thomas Hobbes*, 1908), while praising Hobbes as a 'consistent philosophical materialist', argues that there is 'no real logical connection between Hobbes's metaphysical materialism and his ethical and political doctrine of human conduct' (pp. 44–5) and concludes that 'the only advantage which Hobbes really derives from his materialism is that it furnishes him with a plausible excuse for his refusal to take theology seriously' (p. 45).

to materialism or science, this position raises other difficulties. In view of the emphasis which Hobbes placed on his materialism and in view of his insistence on the scientific nature of his method it seems unsatisfactory to dismiss these attributes of his thought as merely his share in the current intellectual fashion, especially when the result is to say, as does John Laird,[3] that his thought is medieval, or, as with some current text-book writers, to leave his theory rootless and unexplained except as the reaction of a timid man to the disturbed political conditions of his time.

A clue to a different understanding of these matters is to be found in all three of Hobbes's constructions of his political philosophy.[4] It is the fact, remarked by a few writers,[5] that Hobbes's morality is essentially a bourgeois morality. When this is followed back it can be seen that Hobbes's analysis of human nature, from which his whole political theory is derived, is really an analysis of bourgeois man; that the assumptions, explicit and implicit, upon which his psychological conclusions depend are assumptions peculiarly valid for bourgeois society. Considered from this point of view, his materialism falls into place understandably. It is not necessary either to minimize its place in his thought or to make it the whole explanation. And this approach may afford a new view of the strength and weakness of his political thinking and of its relevance today.

1

Even those who disagree fundamentally with Hobbes's analysis show a remarkable respect for it. We do well to be afraid of Hobbes; he knows too much about us. What more accurate and more displeasing picture of ourselves could we have than that which, Hobbes says, 'they who shall more narrowly look into the causes for which men come together, and delight in each other's company, shall easily find . . .'?

> How, by what advice, men do meet, will be best known by observing those things which they do when they are met. For if they meet for traffic, it is plain every man regards not his fellow, but his business; if to discharge some office, a certain market-friendship is begotten, which hath more of jealousy in

[3] Laird: *Hobbes*, p. 57.

[4] (1) *The Elements of Law Natural and Politic*, circulated in manuscript in 1640, published in 1650 as two treatises (*Human Nature*, and *De Corpore Politico*), edited and published under its original title by F. Tönnies, Cambridge, 1928 (subsequent references are to this edition); (2) *De Cive*, 1642, of which an English version was published in 1651 under the title *Philosophical Rudiments Concerning Government and Society* (subsequent references are to the *Rudiments* as published in Hobbes's *English Works*, ed. Molesworth, Vol. II, cited as *E.W.* II), (3) *Leviathan*, 1651 (subsequent references are to the edition by C. B. Macpherson, Penguin, 1968).

[5] Especially Strauss: *The Political Philosophy of Hobbes*, p. 121.

it than true love, and whence factions sometimes may arise, but good will never; if for pleasure and recreation of mind, every man is wont to please himself most with those things which stir up laughter, whence he may, according to the nature of that which is ridiculous, by comparison of another man's defects and infirmities, pass the more current in his own opinion. And although this be sometimes innocent and without offence, yet it is manifest they are not so much delighted with the society, as their own vain glory. But for the most part, in these kinds of meeting we wound the absent; their whole life, sayings, actions, are examined, judged, condemned. Nay, it is very rare but some present receive a fling as soon as they part; so as his reason was not ill, who was wont always at parting to go out last. And these are indeed the true delights of society, unto which we are carried by nature, that is, by those passions which are incident to all creatures . . .[6]

This passage will serve as well as any to indicate the emphasis which Hobbes puts on pride, or vainglory, as a basic drive of the individual. For Hobbes is here not merely describing the character of men as he found them in contemporary society; he is attributing these characteristics to man's eternal nature. The point he is making is that man is not by nature a social animal. 'We do not . . . by nature seek society for its own sake, but that we may receive some honour or profit from it; those we desire primarily, that secondarily.'[7] Again, 'all free congress ariseth either from mutual poverty, or from vain glory . . .' Men come together for their own good, which relates either to the senses or the mind.

But all the mind's pleasure is either glory, (or to have a good opinion of one's self), or refers to glory in the end; the rest are sensual or conducing to sensuality . . . All society therefore is either for gain or for glory . . . But no society can be great or lasting which begins from vain glory. Because that glory is like honour; if all men have it no man hath it, for they consist in comparison and precellence . . . Though the benefits of this life may be much furthered by mutual help, . . . yet those may be better attained to by dominion than by the society of others.

Dominion therefore, not society, is natural; without *fear* there could be no society but only the struggle of each for power over others. 'We must therefore resolve, that the original of all great and lasting societies consisted not in the mutual good will men had towards each other, but in the mutual fear they had of each other.'[8]

In all his treatments of motivation, as in the passage quoted, Hobbes gives roughly equal prominence to gain and glory, concupiscence and vanity. These he postulates as the basic drives which lie behind that search for power and its obverse, the fear of others, from which Hobbes's political theory directly flows. They deserve further notice.[9]

[6] *E.W.* II, pp. 3–4. [7] Ibid., p. 3. [8] Ibid., pp. 4–6.

[9] The importance of vanity in Hobbes's analysis has not been sufficiently emphasized except by Strauss who argues that it is the most important postulate. Leviathan is the king of the proud.

Vanity or vainglory is no doubt an old trait, yet it is difficult to read Hobbes's various treatments[10] of the theme without seeing in them a generalization of the specifically modern form: the incessant desire for recognition as an individual superior to others. Not only does glory consist in 'comparison and precellence', but the individual search for glory knows no bounds.

For every man looketh that his companion should value him, at the same rate he sets upon himselfe: And upon all signes of contempt, or undervaluing, naturally endeavours, as far as he dares (which amongst them that have no common power to keep them in quiet, is far enough to make them destroy each other), to extort a greater value from his contemners, by dommage; and from others, by the example.[11]

Hobbes is attributing to human nature in the abstract a quality which is largely a product of the social relations set up among members of the upper classes by the Renaissance encroachments of capitalism on the older society.[12] With the development of capitalist relations, with the freeing of more classes of men from the old social bonds, this ambition or striving for vainglory has become a widespread characteristic. So Hobbes's picture may be called an unpleasantly accurate analysis not of man as such, but of man since the rise of bourgeois society.

Look now at Hobbes's other basic postulate. It is, not merely that men seek material gain, but that the competitive search for gain is a constant drive dominating the whole character of the individual. 'The most frequent reason why men desire to hurt each other, ariseth hence, that many men at the same time have an appetite to the same thing; which yet very often they can neither enjoy in common, nor yet divide it; whence it follows that the strongest must have it, and who is strongest is decided by the sword.'[13] Hence again the fear each has of the other where there is no power able to overawe them all, and hence each man's need to be a member of a society which will have that power. The postulate of the dominance of competitive material appetites is crucial to Hobbes's theory of the state. And it is clearly derived from the behaviour of man in bourgeois society. The argument is that men are fundamentally hostile to each other because they have appetites for things which they cannot enjoy in common, and of which there is such scarcity that all who want them cannot have them. It may be said that this scarcity has always existed, but Hobbes's assumption is that men are so conscious of it, and are so determined to avoid it for their part, that

10 *De Cive*, 1, 2–5; *Elements*, I, chaps. 9, 14; *Leviathan*, pp. 125, 163–4, 185.

11 *Leviathan*, p. 185.

12 Cf. Burckhardt's analysis of the desire for personal fame as a product of Renaissance society in *Civilization of the Renaissance in Italy* (London, 1928), part II, chap. 3.

13 *E.W.* II, p. 8; cf. *Elements*, I, 14, sect. 5, and *Leviathan*, p. 184.

their actions are dominated by this consciousness. This is the mark of bourgeois society, in contrast to pre-capitalist societies.[14]

We need not be surprised, then, that to Hobbes, all the relations between men tend to be the relations of the market. 'The *Value*, or WORTH of a man, is as of all other things, his Price; that is to say, so much as would be given for the use of his Power: and therefore is not absolute; but a thing dependant on the need and judgement of another ... And as in other things, so in men, not the seller, but the buyer determines the Price.'[15] And again: 'The manifestation of the Value we set on one another is that which is commonly called Honouring, and Dishonouring. To Value a man at a high rate, is to *Honour* him ... Nor does it alter the case of Honour, whether an action (so it be great and difficult, and consequently a signe of much power,) be just or unjust: for Honour consisteth onely in the opinion of Power.'[16] Thus the relations of power between men are seen in terms of the market. Hobbes is assuming the 'anarchy' of capitalist society.[17]

The anarchy of the market, which tends to be the form (though not the substance) of all social relations in capitalist society, is only possible, as the classical economists from Adam Smith to Marx pointed out, if there is an authority, the state, to maintain the bourgeois freedoms (contract, labour, exchange, and accumulation) against the demands of those who are dispossessed and against other national societies. This was explicitly Hobbes's doctrine.

> It is not enough, for a man to labour for the maintenance of his life; but also to fight, (if need be,) for the securing of his labour. They must either do as the Jewes did after their return from captivity, in re-edifying the Temple, build with one hand, and hold the Sword in the other, or else they must hire others

[14] Tawney in his *Religion and the Rise of Capitalism* has given a classic picture of the contrast, in discussing the assumptions from which the medieval writers could start when building a social doctrine to cope with the effects of the growth of commercial economy within the medieval structure. 'Their fundamental assumptions ... were two: that economic interests are subordinate to the real business of life, which is salvation, and that economic conduct is one aspect of personal conduct, upon which, as on other parts of it, the rules of morality are binding ... At every turn, therefore, there are limits, restrictions, warnings against allowing economic interests to interfere with serious affairs' (pp. 31–2). That such restrictions and warnings were necessary is an indication of the extent to which commerce was disrupting medieval society in the later Middle Ages; that the restrictions could be, with some success until the Reformation, based on the assumption that economic interests are subordinate, is an indication of the basically different medieval attitude.

[15] *Leviathan*, pp. 151–2.

[16] Ibid., pp. 152, 156.

[17] The specifically economic relations of man with man are also reduced to terms of the free market and free contract. 'The value of all things contracted for, is measured by the Appetite of the Contractors; and therefore the just value, is that which they be contented to give' (*Leviathan*, p. 208); and 'a mans Labour also, is a commodity exchangeable for benefit, as well as any other thing' (ibid., p. 295).

to fight for them. For the Impositions that are layd on the People by the Soveraign Power, are nothing else but the Wages, due to them that hold the publique Sword, to defend private men in the exercise of severall Trades, and Callings.[18]

Similarly in the *Rudiments*: 'What is brought by the subjects to public use, is nothing else but the price of their bought peace . . .', and taxes are the payment to 'those who watch in arms for us' without which individual men could not procure their private fortunes.[19]

Consistently with this early bourgeois view of the state, Hobbes argues that taxation should be in proportion to benefits. 'Although all equally enjoy peace, yet the benefits springing from thence are not equal to all; for some get greater possessions, others less; and again, some consume less, others more.'[20] He recommends that taxation be on consumption rather than on income or property, basing his preference on the tendency of consumption taxes to encourage frugality and accumulation, as well as their seeming 'least to trouble the mind of them that pay it'.[21] This view of taxation, and especially the recommendation of taxation of consumption, reflects an entirely different view of society from the functional view which prevailed as late as the Tudor period, whereby the poor were considered to have fulfilled their obligation to the state by working.[22]

There is much other evidence that Hobbes's morality is the morality of the bourgeois world and that his state is the bourgeois state. There is his attitude towards the poor, his view of thrift and extravagance, his insistence that the state should institute private property and provide freedom for individual enrichment, his expectation that the sovereign will provide for equality before the law.[23] And while he was critical of the concentration of wealth by monopolies and of 'the great number of Corporations',[24] he took it for granted that the sovereign state would permit individuals such bourgeois freedoms as 'the Liberty to buy, and sell, and otherwise contract with one another; to choose their own aboad, their own diet, their own trade of life, and institute their children as they themselves think fit; and the like'.[25]

These indications that Hobbes had a fairly clear view of the political needs of the bourgeois society of his time need only be mentioned here; it is of more importance to emphasize that the premisses from which Hobbes deduces his psychology and his view of the state are drawn

[18] *Leviathan*, p. 386. [19] *E.W.* II, pp. 173, 159. [20] *E.W.* II, p. 174.

[21] *Elements*, II, 9, sect. 5; cf. *E.W.* II, p. 174, and *Leviathan*, p. 386.

[22] Cf. M. James: *Social Problems and Policy during the Puritan Revolution* (London, 1930), p. 245.

[23] These and other points are conveniently brought together by Strauss, *The Political Philosophy of Hobbes*, pp. 118–23.

[24] *Leviathan*, pp. 374–5. [25] *Leviathan*, p. 264.

from the picture of man as he has been shaped by the relations of bourgeois society.[26]

The content, in other words, of the basic human drives which Hobbes postulates is peculiarly a bourgeois content. Only because of this does he move to his drastic political conclusions. This might be shown in detail at each stage of his argument but it is enough to summarize here his first steps. The desire of *glory* is the desire to be recognized as a superior individual, not merely to share in the prestige customarily accorded to a superior rank or status. It leads therefore to an unending individual struggle for power. The desire for *gain* is the competitive search to gratify material appetites, necessarily at the expense of others since there is not enough to satisfy all. The novelty of Hobbes's assumption is the novelty of the bourgeois view, that material appetites are boundless and that no moral restraint can or need be placed on them. 'Covetousnesse of great Riches, and ambition of great Honours, are Honourable; as signes of power to obtain them.' 'Riches, are Honourable; for they are Power.'[27]

The desires for glory and gain, when given this peculiar content, lead directly to the famous proposition that the first general inclination of all mankind is 'a perpetuall and restless desire of Power after power, that ceaseth only in Death'.[28] From them too may be deduced the proposition of the universality of fear where there is no power to overawe all men, although Hobbes sometimes presents this as the result of a fixed aversion to violent death. From these two propositions, and from the premiss that man is rational to the extent that he can calculate the consequences of his actions, the whole of Hobbes's political structure is in turn deduced. Even this rationality has a mercantile flavour; it is not the rationality premissed by Aristotle or Grotius whereby men were capable of living in accordance with rules of social conduct; it is not strong enough to withstand the force of competitive appetites, only strong enough to show men that they must submit to a sovereign to avoid worse. Thus the bourgeois assumptions which are found in the premisses of Hobbes's thought lead to the erection of the sovereign state.

[26] Strauss in the work cited, while saying that Hobbes founded 'the ideal of civilization in its modern form, the ideal both of the bourgeois-capitalist development and of the socialist movement' (p. 1), is concerned mainly to argue that Hobbes's fundamental view of human life has its origin in his actual experience of how men behave in daily life, which experience in turn 'must be traced back to a specific moral attitude which compels its holder to experience and see man in Hobbes's particular way' (p. xiv). I am suggesting that the moral attitude itself is to be explained in terms of Hobbes's experience of a society in which bourgeois morals had been making their way since the beginning of the Renaissance.

[27] *Leviathan*, pp. 156, 155. [28] *Leviathan*, p. 161.

2

When Hobbes's thought is seen in this light it is possible to suggest a new view of the place of materialism and science in his political theory. We know that Hobbes wished his political philosophy to be regarded as the final part of a consistent system the first part of which was a mechanical materialist statement of laws of motion. He argued that the sciences of human nature and of politics could be deduced from 'the first part of philosophy, namely, geometry and physics'.[29] He never attempted this task for he discovered a more feasible way. The psychological principles from which a political science could be deduced need not, he said, themselves be deduced from the laws of motion of material but could be obtained directly by self-examination.[30]

This did not mean that his materialist philosophy was cut off from his political thought. Nor does it indicate, as some have suggested, that his materialism was never vitally connected with his theory of human nature and politics. In making a fresh start from observation he did not forget the scientific concepts he had developed in thinking out the outlines of his whole materialist system. For one thing, he remained convinced that by applying his scientific method to politics he could get absolutely demonstrable principles; politics could be reduced 'to the rules and infallibility of reason'.[31] This was to be done by the deductive method of mathematics, of which Hobbes had the highest opinion.[32] Such a method requires self-evident first principles. These Hobbes maintained could be got directly from observation; in the final presentation of his political theory he announced that self-observation was sufficient.[33]

Now it is clear that Hobbes drew his first principles of human nature not entirely from introspection but from observation of the actions of others; his remarks quoted earlier (p. 240) as to 'the true delights of society' are one example of this. It is clear also that his postulates about

29 *E.W.* I, p. 74.

30 Ibid., pp. 73, 74; cf. *Leviathan*, introduction, pp. 82–3.

31 *Elements*, Epistle Dedicatory and chap. 1. Cf. his references in *Behemoth* (Tönnies's edition) to the duties of rulers and subjects as 'a science . . . built upon sure and clear principles' (p. 159), and to 'the infallible rules and the true science of equity and justice' (p. 70). Cf. *Leviathan*, p. 261 and pp. 407–8. Hobbes's classification of science as not absolute but conditional knowledge (*Leviathan*, p. 131) is not inconsistent with his belief in the possibility of reaching principles which are absolute in the mathematical sense: cf. *Leviathan*, p. 147: '*Knowledge of the Consequence of one Affirmation to another* . . . is called *Science;* and is *Conditionall;* as when we know, that, *If the figure showne be a circle, then any straight line through the Center shall divide it into two equall parts.*' Hobbes calls mathematical propositions conditional; I have referred to them as absolute, or absolutely demonstrable, to distinguish them from the propositions of inductive natural science.

32 *Elements*, I, 13, sects. 3, 4.

33 *Leviathan*, introduction, pp. 82–3.

human nature were not directly given by any observation but were the result of his finding a pattern in all the data of observation, a pattern formed by the bourgeois assumptions which we have seen were implicit. It is tempting to conclude from this that Hobbes's conception of the scientific method as the mathematical method had little effect on his political thought except to mislead him as to the method he was actually following and as to the validity of the propositions reached by that method. Such a conclusion must be rejected, though it would be in substantial agreement with the views reached on other grounds by Robertson, Laird, and Strauss as already mentioned. Strauss concludes[34] that Hobbes's mathematical method and materialist metaphysics each contributed to disguise his original view of motivation and thus to undermine his political philosophy. But such a view overlooks important factors which lead to a different interpretation.

Consider first the effect of his mathematical method, which in this context means his almost exclusive use of geometrical deduction from first principles taken as self-evident. Such a method should make the first principles stand out clearly rather than disguise them, yet it may give a false certainty to the first principles. Hobbes's belief in the certainty of his postulates may be due in part to his mathematical approach, but fundamentally their inadequacy is due to the limitations imposed on his vision of man by his observation of a bourgeois society. There is no contradiction here. The predominance of mathematical thinking in the seventeenth century is closely related to the rise of capitalism. Quantitative analysis of the material world, of which mathematics is the purest form, was demanded increasingly from the fifteenth century in the service of capitalist technology and of the nation-state. The bourgeois mind was apt to be a mathematical mind; the mathematical mind was generally a bourgeois mind. The limitations of the one were the limitations of the other. The mathematical method is congruous with the reduction of all men to the equality of the market.

Consider secondly the effect of his materialist metaphysics on his political philosophy. It leads him to define all motives in mechanical terms and to reduce them to a few appetites and aversions, the 'small beginnings of Motion, within the body of Man, before they appear in . . . visible actions'.[35] By stating in this form the generalizations which he made from observation, it may be thought that he complicated his presentation unnecessarily; the main lines of his thought are less clear in *Leviathan* than in the *Rudiments*, from which the mechanistic treatment of human nature is omitted. But Hobbes's materialism, rather than contributing to disguise his original view of human

[34] *Political Philosophy of Hobbes*, p. 170.

[35] *Leviathan*, p. 119.

motivation and so to undermine his political theory, was an integral part of his original view of motivation. The materialism of the seventeenth century was a mechanical materialism which read into the natural world the kind of relations which the materialist philosophers saw in bourgeois society. The relation of material objects to each other could be stated in laws of mechanical force just as the relations of individuals could be seen as the relations of units reduced to equality by the market. The doctrine of final causes could be dropped from the analysis of the physical world by men who saw individuals as directed not by final causes but by the impersonal forces which appear to dominate the lives of individuals in the bourgeois society.

Hobbes's view of human motivation is consistent with and is supported by his materialist philosophy, since both were given by the same fundamental view of the universe. His materialism was so mechanical that it can easily be shown to be untenable, and in this sense it can be said that it weakened his political theory. But this is an anachronistic judgement. With all its crudity his materialism was an advance. It made possible a deeper understanding of the new forces at work in society, as well as helping to destroy the ideological supports of the old order and to provide foundations for the kind of state necessary to contain and support capitalist development.

3

We have seen that Hobbes accepted and regarded as natural a pattern of social relations and human behaviour which we know as one aspect of bourgeois society. To Hobbes the natural relations of men are those in which each is reduced to equality of status and struggles against the others for recognition and material satisfactions. A man's worth is what others will give for his power; society is reduced to the market.

The market in terms of which Hobbes saw society was not the self-regulating market of *laissez-faire*. His society did not manifest an invisible hand. It had nothing of the natural harmony of which some of the eighteenth-century philosophers were assured. Yet both Hobbes and the philosophers of the natural order have consistent pictures of bourgeois society. The difference corresponds to the different stages of development which the economy had reached. The concept of a natural order in society could not become dominant until capitalism had so far broken the restrictions of feudal society that the possibility of a self-regulating market became apparent, or until the usefulness of science to capitalist development had been manifested on such a scale that the philosophy of a scientific order could be automatically accepted by the bourgeois mind.[36]

[36] As it was by the eighteenth century. Cf. Morley's *Diderot and the Encyclopedists*.

The fact that Hobbes's thought does not reflect the self-regulating market economy must not be allowed to obscure the fact that it does reflect the earlier yet specifically capitalist market economy. He sees men as freed from those relations of status and reciprocal aid which had given each of them a relatively secure and understandable place in the world before the rise of capitalism. He sees them, instead, engaged in a naked individual struggle for place and power and a foothold on security. What he did not see as a social force, and what bourgeois thought for the next two centuries generally overlooked,[37] was that the individual in capitalist society is brought under new relations of superiority and subservience, apart from the state, in the measure that the old relations are dissolved. The new relations are largely determined by the individual's relation to capital. Those who control capital have power over those who do not; the latter can only use their labour as a commodity, offering it on the market to those who have capital. This is a relation of social dependence of some individuals on others as real, if not as cohesive, as the feudal relations. But it is not so obvious. The relation between persons in capitalist society, as Marx emphasized in his concept of 'commodity fetishism'[38] is disguised as a relation between commodities. Production is carried on by individuals or groups for exchange; the producers' significant dealings with each other are through the market; in the market the individuals are related only as commodity-owners, whether the commodity is labour-power, capital, land, or a product. As commodity-owners they are free and equal; each sells his commodity for its value, and the return he gets is determined by the apparently impersonal relations of the market. Thus in a developed capitalist economy the relations of dependence between persons have the appearance of impersonal relations between things. The acceptance of this appearance as the reality is one aspect of what Marx called commodity fetishism.

Now commodity fetishism is to be found mainly in those minds which are thinking in terms of the self-regulating market, for it is there that the individuals most clearly seem to be ruled by the relations between their commodities, and that a natural order appears to be imposed by the market itself. But even before the emergence of the concept of the self-regulating market, commodity fetishism appeared in social thinking and had an important effect on Hobbes's thought. In Hobbes it takes the form of seeing individuals as free of all relations of mutual personal dependence, and so constituted that they are not fit for society, but only for the competitive struggle for existence, unless

[37] See the provocative argument of Christopher Caudwell, *Studies in a Dying Culture* (London, 1938).

[38] *Capital* (Kerr edition), Vol. I, chap. 1, sect. 4. Cf. Paul Sweezy: *The Theory of Capitalist Development* (New York, 1942), pp. 34–40.

there is an artificially constructed power sufficient to overawe them all.[39] So a coercive state built from a multitude of isolated wills is necessary. Fear of death and desire for more commodious living drive the individuals to it; their ability to calculate the consequences of continuous atomic competition makes them capable of it; but only a coercive state can prevent them backsliding from it.

The illusion that individuals are naturally free of all social ties and are constituted primarily for struggle is the illusion to which the undeveloped form of commodity fetishism easily leads. The difficulties and contradictions in Hobbes's theory of political obligation which have been pointed out by idealist philosophers might all be traced back to it. In Hobbes, the illusion is so closely related to mechanical materialism that it seems to be the result of it, but both are the result of his appreciation of only one aspect of capitalist social relations. The faults in his political theory which appear to be the result of his rigid mechanical materialism and his one-sided notion of scientific method may better be explained as the result of his imperfect appreciation of the social relations of bourgeois society. The explanations are not inconsistent. For the extent to which his materialism was rigid and mechanical corresponds to the extent of his failure to see society as more than an artificial construction of isolated wills. In his natural as in his social philosophy, his failure was to see only an agglomeration of equal discrete units as the basis of relations.

In spite of this failure, Hobbes understood the essential nature of bourgeois society more thoroughly than most of his contemporaries and many of his successors. The continuing strength and the present pertinence of his political theory are due to this. For it is not entirely an illusion that in a capitalist society men are free from normal social ties except those imposed by the state. There is an obvious sense in which the individual in capitalist society is freer from social ties than the individual in any society based on status. The greater insecurity of men is a measure of their greater freedom. The social ties in capitalist society are real, being largely determined by the individual's relation to capital, but are not as cohesive as the social ties of other societies. The result is that on the whole a stronger state is necessary to maintain a capitalist society than is needed to maintain a society in which the social relations are more obviously personal, or more obviously purposeful, and so more easily understandable. The latter society can be kept going by customary moral codes the strength of which is automatically renewed because the relations are visible and their value is readily perceptible. A capitalist society needs stronger political sanctions. It was

[39] Hobbes sees this as true not only for his fiction, the 'state of nature', from which all social motives are omitted by abstraction, but also for man in society. Cf. *E.W.* II, pp. 3–4, and *Leviathan*, pp. 186–7.

Hobbes's supreme merit to see this and to urge it relentlessly.

If it is the acuteness of Hobbes's analysis of bourgeois man which made him the profoundest political thinker of the seventeenth century, it was the same acuteness that led his political theory to be forgotten in favour of Locke's from the Whig Revolution through the eighteenth century, and that led to the revival of his concept of sovereignty by the Benthamists. The Whig Revolution had secured the political power of the eighteenth-century bourgeoisie and there was no need or desire to raise the fundamental questions of political authority as long as that state was satisfactory. But when the Industrial Revolution brought a new section of industrial capital to the fore and revealed the Whig state to be inadequate to the market relations which the new capitalism required, fundamental questions had again to be raised. They were raised by insisting again on the atomic competitive individual as the basic unit of society. The confusion in the Benthamist theory of society, between the assumption of a natural harmony and the need for the state to create an artificial harmony between conflicting self-interests, comes from the Benthamist failure to resolve into a consistent theory the two views of society, one inherited from Hobbes, the other from the eighteenth-century optimists. The failure is understandable, reflecting a contradiction in the society they were analysing. The idealists' reaction against the crudities of nineteenth-century industrial society and of Benthamist theory drove them to a refutation of Hobbes which neglected the profundity of his analysis of bourgeois society. Hobbes's insight is more relevant in the twentieth century than at any time since he produced *Leviathan*. Modern attempts to go beyond Hobbes in the study of political obligation must still reckon with the basis of his argument.

Index